TENSES OF IMAGINATION

# Ralahine Utopian Studies

**Series editors:**
Raffaella Baccolini (University of Bologna, at Forlì)
Joachim Fischer (University of Limerick)
Tom Moylan (University of Limerick)

**Managing editor:**
Michael J. Griffin (University of Limerick)

Volume 7

PETER LANG
Oxford· Bern· Berlin· Bruxelles· Frankfurt am Main· New York· Wien

Edited by Andrew Milner

# TENSES OF IMAGINATION

RAYMOND WILLIAMS
ON SCIENCE FICTION,
UTOPIA AND DYSTOPIA

PETER LANG
Oxford · Bern · Berlin · Bruxelles · Frankfurt am Main · New York · Wien

Bibliographic information published by Die Deutsche Nationalbibliothek
Die Deutsche Nationalbibliothek lists this publication in the Deutsche
Nationalbibliografie; detailed bibliographic data is available on the
Internet at http://dnb.d-nb.de.

A catalogue record for this book is available from The British Library.

Library of Congress Cataloging-in-Publication Data:

Williams, Raymond.
  Tenses of imagination : Raymond Williams on science fiction, utopia
and dystopia / Andrew Milner.
      p. cm. – (Ralahine utopian studies ; 7)
  Includes bibliographical references and index.
  ISBN 978-3-03911-826-7 (alk. paper)
  1. Science fiction, English–History and criticism. 2. English
fiction–20th century–History and criticism. 3. Utopias in literature.
4. Dystopias in literature. 5. Criticism–Great Britain–History–20th
century. 6. Literature–History and criticism–Theory, etc. I. Milner,
Andrew. II. Title.
  PR830.S35W55 2009
  823'.087609372–dc22
                                                  2009032209

Cover image: photograph of Raymond Williams, courtesy of Ederyn and
Ilona Williams, with thanks to Merryn Williams.

ISSN 1661-5875
ISBN 978-3-03911-826-7

© Peter Lang AG, International Academic Publishers, Bern 2010
Hochfeldstrasse 32, CH-3012 Bern, Switzerland
info@peterlang.com, www.peterlang.com, www.peterlang.net

All rights reserved.
All parts of this publication are protected by copyright.
Any utilisation outside the strict limits of the copyright law, without
the permission of the publisher, is forbidden and liable to prosecution.
This applies in particular to reproductions, translations, microfilming,
and storage and processing in electronic retrieval systems.

Printed in Germany

*For Kathy Wench, my teenage sweetheart and first love,
who grew up to be Kathryn Turnier
and died of cancer on Christmas Day 2007;
and for Marion and Marc,
who must learn to imagine the future without her*

# Ralahine Readers

Utopia has been articulated and theorized for centuries. There is a matrix of commentary, critique, and celebration of utopian thought, writing, and practice that ranges from ancient Greece, into the European middle ages, throughout Asian and indigenous cultures, in Enlightenment thought and Marxist and anarchist theory, and in the socio-political theories and movements (especially racial, gender, ethnic, sexual, and national liberation; and ecology) of the last two centuries. While thoughtful writing on Utopia has long been a part of what Ernst Bloch called our critical cultural heritage, a distinct body of multi- and inter-disciplinary work across the humanities, social sciences, and sciences emerged from the 1960s onward under the name of "utopian studies." In the interest of bringing the best of this scholarship to a wider, and new, public, the editors of Ralahine Utopian Studies are committed to publishing the work of key thinkers who have devoted a lifetime to studying and expressing the nature and history, problems and potential, accomplishments and anticipations of the utopian imagination. Each Ralahine Reader presents a selection of the work of one such thinker, bringing their best work, from early days to most recent, together in one easily accessible volume.

# Contents

Acknowledgements ix

Introduction 1

PART ONE
Space Anthropology, Utopia, and Putropia: Left Culturalism

READING 1    Science Fiction (1956)                              11
READING 2    William Morris (1958)                               21
READING 3    George Orwell (1958)                                33
READING 4    The Future Story as Social Formula Novel (1961)     43
READING 5    Terror (1971)                                       51

PART TWO
Texts in their Contexts: Cultural Materialism

READING 6    *Nineteen Eighty-Four* (1971)                       57
READING 7    The City and the Future (1973)                      73
READING 8    On Orwell: An Interview (1977)                      83
READING 9    On Morris: An Interview (1977)                      87

PART THREE
Learning from Le Guin: (Anti-) Postmodernism

READING 10   Utopia and Science Fiction (1978)                   93
READING 11   The Tenses of Imagination (1978)                   113
READING 12   Beyond Actually Existing Socialism (1980)          125
READING 13   Resources for a Journey of Hope (1983)             149
READING 14   *Nineteen Eighty-Four* in 1984 (1984)              177

PART FOUR
The Future Novels

READING 15  From *The Volunteers* (1978)         205
READING 16  From *The Fight for Manod* (1979)    215

Bibliography                                      231

Index                                             239

# Acknowledgements

I am indebted to friends, colleagues, and students in and around the Centre for Comparative Literature and Cultural Studies and to staff at the Matheson Library, especially the Rare Book Collection, at Monash University, for their encouragement and assistance in preparing the collection. A parallel debt is owed friends and colleagues in the School of English at the University of Liverpool and the staff of the Science Fiction Foundation Collection and the Special Collections Reading Room in the Ernest Jones Library at the University of Liverpool. Further individual debts of gratitude belong to: Andrew Benjamin, Roland Boer, Mark Bould, Ian Buchanan, Verity Burgmann, Sue Cousin, Nikolai Gladanac, David Jack, Darren Jorgensen, Sean Kearns, Andrew Keogh, Michal Kulbicki, David Milner, Richard Milner, Tom Moylan, Joyce Morton, Diane Newsome, Patrick Parrinder, Kate Rigby, Matthew Ryan, Carlo Salzani, Hazel Sanderson, Robert Savage, Andy Sawyer, Simon Sellars, Juliet Trevethick, Dimitris Vardoulakis, Marcus Walsh, Gail Ward, Chris Williams, Merryn Williams, and Stuart Wrathmell. I should also acknowledge the Australian Research Council, which generously funded the research behind this collection.

The editor and publishers are grateful to the following for permission to republish: "Science Fiction," from *The Highway* 48 (December 1956), reproduced with permission of the Workers' Educational Association (WEA) <http://www.wea.org.uk>; "William Morris" and "George Orwell," from *Culture and Society 1780–1950* (1958) by Raymond Williams, published by Chatto and Windus, reprinted by permission of The Random House Group Ltd; "The Future Story as Social Formula Novel," from *The Long Revolution* (1961) by Raymond Williams, published by Chatto and Windus, reprinted by permission of The Random House Group Ltd; "Terror" from *The Listener* (3 June 1971), reproduced with permission of BBC Worldwide; "*Nineteen Eighty-Four*," from *Orwell*, first edition (1971), reprinted by permission of Merryn Williams on behalf of the Raymond

Williams estate; "The City and the Future," from *The Country and the City* (1973) by Raymond Williams, published by Chatto and Windus, reprinted by permission of The Random House Group Ltd and, in the USA, by permission of Oxford University Press Inc.; "On Orwell: An Interview" and "On Morris: An Interview," from *Politics and Letters: Interviews with New Left Review* (1979) by Raymond Williams, reprinted with permission of Verso Editions; "Utopia and Science Fiction," from *Science-Fiction Studies* 5.3 (1978), reprinted by permission of *Science-Fiction Studies*; "The Tenses of Imagination," from *Writing in Society* (1978), reprinted with permission of Verso Editions; "Beyond Actually Existing Socialism," from *New Left Review* 120 (March–April 1980), reprinted with permission of Verso Editions; "Resources for a Journey of Hope" from *Towards 2000* (1983) by Raymond Williams, published by Chatto and Windus, reprinted by permission of The Random House Group Ltd and, in the USA, from *The Year 2000* by Raymond Williams, copyright 1983 by Raymond Williams, used by permission of Pantheon Books, a division of Random House, Inc.; "*Nineteen Eighty-Four* in 1984" from *Orwell*, second edition (1984), reprinted by permission of Merryn Williams on behalf of the Raymond Williams estate; extracts from *The Volunteers* (1978) by Raymond Williams and *The Fight for Manod* (1979) by Raymond Williams, published by Chatto and Windus, reprinted by permission of The Random House Group Ltd.

# Introduction

Raymond Williams was a significant figure in late twentieth-century intellectual life, a pioneer in the early history of what we now know as Cultural Studies and also a central inspiration for the early British New Left. He was variously – and inaccurately – likened to a British Lukács, a British Bloch and even, according to *The Times*, "the British Sartre" (Eagleton, *Criticism and Ideology* 36; Pinkney, "Williams and the 'Two Faces of Modernism'" 28–31). He was a substantial influence on the work of critics as diverse as Terry Eagleton, Stuart Hall, Edward Said, Alan Sinfield, Stephen Greenblatt, and Cornel West (Eagleton, "Introduction"; Hall; Williams and Said; Sinfield 9; Greenblatt 2; West). There are Williamsites in Italy, in Brazil and in Australia (Ferrara; Cevasco; Lawson 33–65). There is also a very substantial secondary literature on Williams. But none of this seems to make much of his enduring interest in science fiction, an oversight the present collection attempts to rectify. I have argued elsewhere that there are three main "phases" in Williams's thought, each explicable in terms of its own differentially negotiated settlement between the kind of literary humanism associated with F.R. Leavis on the one hand and some version or another of Marxism on the other; and each characterizable in relation to a relatively distinct, consecutive moment in the history of the British New Left (Milner, *Re-Imagining Cultural Studies*). Each also gave rise to a relatively distinct understanding on Williams's part of the relationship between science fiction (henceforth sf), utopia, and dystopia.

This periodization provides the organizing framework for the collection. The first and second phases in Williams's work are respectively those associated with the moments of "1956" and "1968," that is, to borrow Peter Sedgwick's terms, the "Old New Left" and the "New New Left." Where the Old New Left had been formed from out of the double political crisis of 1956, occasioned by the suppression of the Hungarian Revolution and the Anglo-French invasion of Egypt, the New New Left was inspired by the May 1968 Events in Paris, the Vietnam Solidarity Campaign, the Prague

Spring, and the revolt on the campuses (Sedgwick). Where the Old New Left had attempted to preserve the particularities of the British national experience from Stalinist internationalism, the New New Left spurned nationalism in general, and the peculiarities of the English especially, in favour of Francophile cosmopolitanism and active political solidarity with the Vietnamese National Liberation Front. Where the Old New Left had situated itself somewhere in the political space between the left wing of the Labour Party and the liberalizing wing of the Communist Party, the New New Left rejected both Labourism and Communism in favour of various "ultraleftisms," Guevarism, Maoism, Trotskyism, and so on. Where the Old New Left had sought to counterpose "experience" and "culture" to Communist dogmatism, the New New Left discovered in various continental European "Western Marxisms" a type of "Theory" which could be counterposed to the empiricism of English bourgeois culture and the pragmatism of the British Labour Party. To this typology we can add a third phase, roughly that from the 1980s to the present, in which a "Postmodern New Left" confronted the developing globalization of corporate capitalism, the emergence of a postmodern radicalism centred on the new social movements and a new theoretical relativism associated with "difference" theory. Each of these three phases registers in a corollary phase in Williams's own thought, which I have termed, respectively, "left culturalism," "cultural materialism," and, a little inelegantly, "(anti-) postmodernism."

Each also registers in Williams's work on sf, utopia, and dystopia. His key texts from the first period were *Culture and Society 1780–1950* and *The Long Revolution*, both of which include discussions of utopia, dystopia, and science fiction, all of which are included in Part I. The primary focus in both books, however, is on a theoretical and practical rejection of the minority culture/mass civilization topos he had found in T.S. Eliot and F.R. Leavis. The distinctiveness of Williams's position was to see utopian sf as essentially exhausted by the mid-twentieth century and dystopian sf as a newly dominant mode, which effectively reproduced the Eliot–Leavis position in generically specific terms. This argument is at its most explicit in the 1956 essay "Science Fiction" which is our first reading. And here, as in neither book, dystopia is specifically defined as the putrefaction of utopia, in Williams's neologism "Putropia," and its positive corollary specifically identified as "Space Anthropology," that is, the fictional encounter with the Other as a way of valorizing Otherness itself. Hence, the title of this first part. Its closing reading, on television sf, written fifteen years after the first, interestingly repeats the argument for a space anthropology focussed on "identity and culture contact."

The second phase of Williams's work, that of the moment of "1968" and the emergence of a second New Left, was characterized above all by his development of a full-blown theory of "cultural materialism." By this, he meant "a theory of culture as a (social and material) productive process and of specific practices, of 'arts,' as social uses of material means of production" ("Base and Superstructure in Marxist Cultural Theory" 243). Here, Williams's engagement with a series of continental European Western Marxisms, and with various forms of Third Worldist political radicalism, clearly ran parallel to that of the younger generation of radical intellectuals associated with the *New Left Review* under the editorship of Perry Anderson. For Williams, the import was a strange double movement by which, on the one hand, his declared politics acquired a more explicitly "leftist" – and presumably "unrealistic" – character; but, on the other, they also became more analytically distinct from his scholarly work, which he increasingly understood as "social-scientific" rather than "literary-critical." Williams sought to substitute a loosely Gramscian theory of "hegemony" for Leavisite notions of "culture" and more orthodox Marxist notions of "ideology." More generally, he also sought to substitute description and explanation for judgement and canonization, as the central purposes of analysis. This is what we have come to call "Cultural Studies," and it is important to note that this move from literary into cultural studies had been occasioned, in part, by an aversion to prescriptive criticism of the Leavisite variety. Hence, Williams's insistence that "we need not criticism but analysis [...] the complex seeing of analysis rather than [...] the abstractions of critical classification" ("A Defence of Realism" 239). The primary methodological implication would thus be an insistence on setting literary texts, sf texts included, in their social contexts: hence the title of the collection's second part.

The key works from this period were *The Country and the City* and *Marxism and Literature*. The latter was "almost wholly theoretical" in form, to borrow his own description and, as such, had nothing to say about sf nor about any other substantive area of inquiry. But, as he insisted, "every position in it was developed from the detailed practical work that I have previously undertaken, and from the consequent interaction with other [...] modes of theoretical assumption and argument" (*Marxism and Literature* 6). And some of this detailed practical work had indeed been concerned with sf. In *The Country and the City*, his primary concern was with the pastoral and the counter-pastoral, but he had found examples of each in the future cities of sf. For our purposes, however, the most important text is the 1971 first edition of *Orwell* – which Williams himself doesn't cite as relevant to *Marxism and Literature* – where he worried away, yet again, at the precise significance of dystopianism in *Nineteen Eighty-Four*. By comparison with the discussion in *Culture and Society*, the extract from *Orwell*, which provides the collection's second part with its first Reading, proposes a much more even-handed treatment of the novel. Here Williams is clearly more responsive to the very real strengths of what is, after all, quite probably the greatest dystopian fiction written in English during the twentieth century. But he remained fixated on Orwell's supposed "anti-socialism," an oddly inappropriate description of a writer whose declared vocation had been to write "*against* totalitarianism and *for* democratic Socialism" (*Collected Essays, Journalism and Letters* Vol. 1 28). Part of the explanation for this animus lies in the more personal, and less analytic, responses to Orwell (and Morris) which Williams volunteered in the extracts from his 1977 interviews with *New Left Review* included in Readings 8 and 9.

The third and final phase of Williams's critical work, that produced mainly during the 1980s, is best characterized by his developing engagement with the globalization of corporate capitalism and with the promise of a postmodern radicalism centred around the new social movements. The key political texts are Williams's deeply sympathetic 1980 review of Rudolf Bahro's *Die Alternative*, included as Reading 12, and the 1983 reworking of the long revolution analysis, *Towards 2000*, a lengthy extract from which is included as Reading 13. Both suggest a greater sympathy for utopianism than hitherto, albeit one cautiously restrained by a strong sense of the realistically possible. Such questions of rational futurological imagination are also broached, however, in his two 1978 discussions of sf:

*Introduction*

"Utopia and Science Fiction," first published in *Science-Fiction Studies* and here included as Reading 10; and "The Tenses of Imagination," originally presented as lectures at the University of Wales, Aberystwyth, and here included as Reading 11. Both suggest how radically impressed Williams had been by Ursula K. Le Guin's *The Dispossessed*, sufficiently so as to lead him toward a more positive evaluation of utopia as a general form and *News from Nowhere* as a particular text – hence the title of Part Three. Le Guin's novel is organized around the contrast between the twin planets (strictly, a moon and a planet) of Anarres and Urras. These represent what Ann Kaplan would later term the "twin faces of postmodernism," the "utopian" and the "commercial" (4). Interestingly, the same twin faces structure both the futurology in *Towards 2000* and the fiction in Williams's own future novels. The collection's third part concludes with the full text of his 1984 essay, "*Nineteen Eighty-Four* in 1984," which was included as an appendix to the second edition of *Orwell* and is clearly by far the most sympathetic of his three discussions of the novel.

The collection's final and fourth part comprises extracts from the opening pages of Williams's two future novels, *The Volunteers*, first published in 1978, and *The Fight for Manod*, begun earlier but not finally published until 1979. Although most secondary accounts of the latter stress its obvious affinity with the earlier volumes in the Welsh trilogy, it is clear from the Readings in Part Three that Williams himself was simultaneously conscious of its affinity, as a future novel, with *The Volunteers*. Both *Manod* and *The Volunteers* exhibit a qualified hope, a realism of purpose in a darkening future: Williams was clear that the future imagined here "is not a desirable one, but it is [...] perfectly possible" (*Politics and Letters* 301). They thus provide the dystopian counterpart to what he had found in Le Guin's ambiguous utopia. In thirty years of writing about sf, Williams had learnt to substitute the complex seeing of analysis for moralistic criticism; and to situate texts in their material and intellectual contexts. He had come to understand the kind of honourable personal motives and socially effective structures of feeling that underpin both utopian and dystopian forms. He had come to realize that neither was inherently antithetical to the space anthropology he had admired in Blish and, later, in Le Guin. But his suspicion of radical dystopia remained largely intact: without resistance, without "realism," without what he termed the "true subjunctive," dystopia would kill hope, as surely as unrealistic utopia will fail to inspire it. Hence, his enduring reservations about *Nineteen Eighty-Four*.

Williams may well be right in this general judgement, but he is mistaken about *Nineteen Eighty-Four*. For he misreads the novel, as many critics have, as if it ends with "it was all right, everything was all right, the struggle was finished. He had won the victory over himself. He loved Big Brother" (Orwell, *Nineteen Eighty-Four* 298). At a superficial level, Orwell invited us to read the novel thus: in the first edition, as in most subsequent, the next words are "The End." But we know he had been deeply impressed by *Nous autres*, the French translation of Yevgeny Zamyatin's *We*, a novel organized into forty chapters, or "Notes," the penultimate of which is entitled "La Fin." *Nous autres* continued for a further six pages after "La Fin" (Zamiatine 227–232), just as the first edition of Orwell's dystopia continues for a further fourteen after "The End" (299–312). *Nineteen Eighty-Four* actually ends at the conclusion to the "Appendix" on Newspeak with: "It was chiefly in order to allow time for the preliminary work of translation that the final adoption of Newspeak had been fixed for so late a date as 2050" (312). In content, these lines add little, but their form is redolent with meaning. For, as Margaret Atwood observes of the whole "Appendix," it "is written in standard English, in the third person, and in the past tense, which can only mean that the regime has fallen, and that language and individuality have survived. For whoever has written the essay on Newspeak, the world of *1984* is over" ("George Orwell" 337).

Atwood herself used a similar device in *The Handmaid's Tale*, which concludes with an extract from the proceedings of a "Symposium on Gileadean Studies," written in some utopian future long after the collapse of the Republic of Gilead (311–324). Moreover, she readily admits that *Nineteen Eighty-Four* provided her with a "direct model" for this ("George Orwell" 337). Both Orwell's "Appendix" and Atwood's "Historical Notes" can thus be read as framing devices, the effect of which is to relativize dystopia by historicizing it. Williams's true subjunctive is, in fact, precisely what occupies the space between "The End" and the "Appendix" on "The Principles of Newspeak." Moreover, it takes a particularly interesting form within the actual text of the "Appendix," that of the subjunctive future perfect. Atwood is right to observe that the "Appendix" is written in the past tense. But there are other tenses at work, notably the subjunctive future perfect. So, in the sentences which provide its chronological frame, Orwell writes that it "was expected that Newspeak would have finally superseded Oldspeak [...] by about the year 2050"; and that "within a couple of generations even the possibility of such a lapse would have vanished [...]. When Oldspeak had been once and for all superseded, the last link with the past would have been severed" (299, 310). This use of the subjunctive functions very much as Williams had observed it in Morris: to mean that these events will not necessarily have eventuated. The subjunctive future perfect is thus the logically informing tense of dystopia. For this is what dystopian future fictions recount, what *would have happened* if their empirical and implied readerships had not been moved to prevent it. That Orwell knew this may well be a part of his lasting significance. That Williams never quite came to appreciate it must remain a source of regret.

The readings collected here were composed over a period of nearly three decades for a very wide variety of publications, each with their own publishing conventions. I have generally regularized these to the conventions now used by Peter Lang for the Ralahine Utopian Studies series. Some standardization seemed necessary, and it might as well be in accord with the series of which the collection will form a part. This means that the references in the texts are only occasionally exactly the same as in the Williams originals. My version almost invariably provides more information than his: mid-late twentieth century footnoting could often be pretty opaque, Williams's own especially so. Unlike Williams himself, I have clearly distinguished book titles, which are given in italics, from essay and short story titles, which are here given in quotation marks. I have also checked and, where necessary, amended his quotations for their accuracy to the original. These are normally only minor matters of capitalization, italicization, variations between American and British spelling, and so on. Williams wrote before accepted usage required that "he or she" be substituted for the gender-specific, "he," and, in this respect, I have kept to the original usage, since these extracts were a product of their time. Wherever I have substantially changed Williams's original – as in the discussion of Morris in Reading 2 – I have indicated this in the reference.

PART ONE

Space Anthropology, Utopia, and Putropia:
Left Culturalism

READING 1

# Science Fiction (1956)

## Editor's Introduction

From the mid-1950s to the mid-1960s, Williams addressed himself very directly to the definition of a third position between Leavisism and Marxism, a peculiarly British "left culturalism" combining Leavisite aesthetics with socialist politics. Williams's intellectual and political reputation was established by *Culture and Society*. As his biographer, Fred Inglis, observed, it became one of the two "sacred texts of" the "new political movement" that was the first British New Left (157). Utopia and dystopia figured prominently in the movement's preoccupations. For the ex-Communist intellectuals associated with *The New Reasoner*, the key theoretical problem was the legacy of Stalinist Marxism, one possible solution to which was a recovery of older utopian socialist traditions. For E.P. Thompson, the historian whose first major work had been a biography of William Morris, this meant a return to Romanticism, to poetry and to *News from Nowhere*. For many of the younger radicals intrigued by the new popular culture and appalled by the Cold War and the threat of nuclear warfare, both George Orwell and his great dystopian novel, *Nineteen Eighty-Four*, seemed to offer a more directly contemporary alternative to Stalinism. As Williams himself would later recall, the "New Left respected Orwell directly, especially in its early years" (*Orwell* 87).

But, at this stage, Williams himself showed little sympathy for either Morris's more explicitly utopian writings or Orwell's more explicitly dystopian. His objections were first aired in a little-known essay Williams published in *The Highway*, the journal of the Workers' Educational Association, in December 1956. The occasion was a critical review of recent sf, entitled simply "Science Fiction." Here, Williams argues that stories of "a secular paradise of the future" had "reached their peak" in Morris, but had thereafter become "almost entirely converted into their opposites: the stories of a future secular hell." Williams prosecutes what might now be termed an "ideological critique" of this recent corruption – literally, the putrefaction – of Morris's earlier utopianism. His immediate targets are three "putropian" novels: Orwell's *Nineteen Eighty-Four*, Aldous Huxley's *Brave New World*, and Ray Bradbury's *Fahrenheit 451*. Williams distinguishes three main types of contemporary literary sf, termed respectively Putropia, Doomsday, and Space Anthropology. By the first, he means dystopian sf of the kind exemplified by Huxley, Orwell, Bradbury, and Yevgeny Zamyatin; by the second, the kind of fictional catastrophe in which human life itself is extinguished, as in A.E. van Vogt's "Dormant," Philip Latham's "The Xi Effect," John Christopher's "The New Wine," and almost, but not quite, John Wyndham's *The Day of the Triffids*; by the third, stories "which consciously use the sf formula to find what are essentially new tribes, and new patterns of living."

While cheerfully confessing to an intense dislike of most examples of the first two, Williams adds that even these are interesting "because they belong, directly, to a contemporary structure of feeling." We should note this early use of a concept that would be distinctive to Williams's work and would be theorized at length in *The Long Revolution* and *Marxism and Literature*. The particular structure of feeling that concerns him here, which underlies both putropian and doomsday fictions, is that of "the isolated intellectual, and of the 'masses' who are at best brutish, at worst brutal" – in short, the myth of the defence of minority culture against barbarism. The reference to T.S. Eliot is made quite explicitly at one point, that to the Leavises clearly implied. These dystopian fictions are often defended as cautionary tales, Williams concedes, but adds that "they are less warnings about the future" than "about the adequacy of certain types of contemporary feeling." "I believe, for my own part," he continues, "that to think, feel, or even speak of people in terms of 'masses' is to make the burning of the books and the destroying of the cities just that much more possible." As he would soon write in the "personal conclusion" to *Culture and Society*: "There are in fact no masses; there are only ways of seeing people as masses" (289).

If utopia and dystopia are the socio-political subgenres of sf, as Darko Suvin famously argued (*Metamorphoses of Science Fiction* 61), then Williams seems to come dangerously close to rejecting a genre in which he had nonetheless shown serious interest. Except that there is still the third sf mode, which inspires his admiration precisely for its capacity to move beyond the then dominant forms of English cultural pessimism. So he found in James Blish's *A Case of Conscience* – a later version of which would win the 1959 Hugo Award – with its "beautifully imagined tribe" of eight-foot tall, reptilian Lithians, "a work of genuine imagination, and real intelligence." Such preferences – for Blish, as against Huxley and Orwell – might seem uncontroversial to contemporary cultural studies, but they were clearly eccentric to the academic literary criticism of the 1950s. Moreover, Williams's preference was for Blish, not only against Orwell, but also against Morris. For if dystopianism as putropia constituted an important part of the problem, utopianism was not thereby part of the solution. It is precisely the less than utopian plausibility of Blish's human voice "far away, among the galaxies," which Williams finds so interesting. For the young Williams, utopia was about perfection, dystopia about radical imperfection – secular heavens and secular hells – and neither allowed for the distinctively "human" voice present in the best space anthropology.

## Science Fiction (1956)

Fiction is a kind of fact, although it takes some people centuries to get used to it. To point out that its substance is imaginary, or fantastic, is no criticism of it, for that is the kind of fact it is: a thing man has thought or imagined, rather than observed or made. In practice we value fiction over a very wide range, from the obviously realistic to the evidently miraculous. When we look, then, at a contemporary phenomenon like sf, we must be careful not to dismiss it because it is fanciful, extravagant, or even impossible, for, on the same limited grounds, we could dismiss *The Odyssey*, *The Tempest*, *Gulliver's Travels*, or *The Pilgrim's Progress*. The facts of sf are fictional, and can only be assessed in literary terms.

Many of us know sf mainly from our children's comics, in which, for example, the inhabitants of the planet Phantos, tall purple bipeds with the heads of cows, led by the Super-Phant Gogol, are invading the planet Cryptos, whose inhabitants are a kind of dun biped sheep. Repulsion guns, aquadetectors, artificial suns, and the suspension of gravity abound. Yet the literary bearings, here, are easy, for the space-gun is just a new kind of tomahawk, and the Super-Phant is our old friend the sheriff of Nottingham. If this were the whole of sf, it would not call for comment.

In fact, in sf written for adults, the Cowboy and Indian, Earthman and Martian type is now quite rare. Wells's *War of the Worlds* keeps being filmed, under various titles, and with varying degrees of acknowledgment, but, in print, the subjects and emphases are now normally different. Sf has been put to service in almost every kind of traditional story. There are the stories of war and banditry, like *War of the Worlds* or Mr E.F. Russell's "A Present from Joe." There are stories of adventure and exploration, beginning perhaps with Poe's story of a flight to the Moon, "The Unparalleled Adventure of one Hans Pfaal," and continuing through nearly all the stories of Jules Verne to a recent example like Mr Arthur Porges's "The Ruum." There is at least one ordinary murder story, Mr John Wyndham's "Dumb Martian," which is also a common kind of love story. Men from flying saucers have been used as a contemporary *deus ex machina* in an otherwise realistic story, such as Mr Henry Kuttner's "Or Else." There are humorous stories, like Mr H. Nearing's "The Cerebrative Psittacoid," and trick stories like Katherine MacLean's interesting "Pictures Don't Lie." Poe wrote a "Thousand-and-Second Tale of Scheherazade" using nineteenth-century scientific and technological wonders as a continuation of Sinbad: Scheherazade is strangled, for although the king believes in a sky-blue cow with 400 horns he will not believe in photography or the steamship. Earlier, Mary Shelley, in *Frankenstein*, had added sf to the Gothic novel, and this horrific strain has been very widely exploited. C.L. Moore's "No Woman

Born" is a recent "Frankenstein" type,[1] and in the general field there is such a profusion of monsters from outer space or the ocean depths as to constitute an entire twentieth-century Bestiary. This element, from the giant octopus to the tiny alien voice at the base of the skull, is commonly present, also, in stories of a different basic type.

The types, and most of the examples, that I have given, belong, ordinarily, to the levels of magazine fiction, and are rarely of much literary interest. Traditional appeals have been exploited with new, or apparently new, material, and the result is neither much better nor much worse than the long line from Horace Walpole through Conan Doyle. The general level compares quite favorably with that of the detective story, and there are the same "literary" exercises in it, in which "style" is put in as a grade-jumping, artificial element: Mr Ray Bradbury doing for sf what Miss Sayers or Mr Michael Innes have done for crime. But these exercises in magazine fiction, whether decorated or not, are not, in my view, the really interesting things in sf. An octopus on Saturn is still an octopus, and a Phant is still a bandit: the interesting new things lie elsewhere.

There are three types of sf which, while varying greatly in the merit of particular examples, are, nevertheless, important to the critic as new modes or norms. These are what I will call, for brevity, Putropia, Doomsday, and Space Anthropology. I dislike, intensely, most of the examples of at least the first two of these modes, but then, in the magazine fiction, intensity of either like or dislike is very rare. These modes are interesting because they belong, directly, to a contemporary structure of feeling, whereas the rest of sf, for the most part, is merely the profitable exercise of a formula. So, I suppose, these modes will in turn become, are already becoming; but the trace of feeling is still on them, and this is determining.

By Putropia I mean the characteristic twentieth-century corruption of the Utopian romances. Stories of a secular paradise of the future reached their peak, perhaps, in Morris's *News from Nowhere*, and since then have been almost entirely converted into their opposites: the stories of a future

---

[1]  RW had "Mr" C.L. Moore, but this is a mistake – Catherine Lucille Moore was a woman.

secular hell. Zamyatin's *We*, Huxley's *Brave New World*, and Orwell's *Nineteen Eighty-Four* are the most famous examples, but there are countless examples among lesser known writers. Mr Bradbury's *Fahrenheit 451* is at once articulate and representative. The title indicates the temperature at which book-paper will burn, and the central character is a member of the Fire Brigade charged with setting fire to all houses in which books are found. The fireman hero starts reading and secreting books, has his own house burned down, kills while resisting arrest, and is chased through the city by an electronic Hound (which Sir Henry Baskerville would have recognized). He gets away to the country, where he meets a band of scholars turned tramps, who preserve literature by committing it to memory. Meanwhile, behind him, the city is bombed.

*Fahrenheit 451* is characteristic of books of this type in that, under the emblem of a story of the future, it presents not so much an observation, but a current form of feeling, related primarily to contemporary society. Here the "myth" is the defense of culture, by a minority, against the new barbarians. In *Nineteen Eighty-Four*, the "myth" is the struggle between clean and unclean intellectuals, who determine the future without reference to the dumb "proles." The form of feeling which dominates this putropian thinking is, basically, that of the isolated intellectual, and of the "masses" who are at best brutish, at worst brutal. The stories are defended as an extension of obvious contemporary tendencies, and it is here that the sf element – telescreen, electronic agent, videophone – most crudely operates. These things, which are properly the extension of existing tendencies, serve as a form of external realism, offering to authenticate and persuade, within which the subtler, and more questionable, version of extension can appear to establish itself. For while atomic war, organized lying, political persecution, and the burning of books exist, as facts, on our side of the worlds of *Nineteen Eighty-Four* and *Fahrenheit 451*, they are distinguished by being human, and social, activities, and are thus subject to a different order of calculation. The tendencies to adulterate or destroy civilization are evident enough, but their extension is subject to a different process from that which will give us the telescreen. The extension of social tendencies is a doubtful process, and any substantial writing of this kind will commonly be rooted in an actual and developed world rather than in the given, unconnected future, the fixed distortion, which the sf convention, confident in its authenticating gadgetry, here so misleadingly allows. I am not disposed to modify this adverse criticism by the fact that the apparent values of such works are liberal and humane. The gentle reader, and the consciousness of the writer, are certainly, by these terms, assuaged. But the tone of all such work that I have read, from Huxley to Mr Bradbury, bears its own, and different, witness. The psychological strains of the isolation from which the myths are endorsed can be seen, very clearly, in much of the actual writing. The preoccupied realization of various extremes of cruelty and disgust is the finally dominant feeling-tone. It is said that these things are warnings; but they are less warnings about the future, or even about television, than about the adequacy of certain types of contemporary feeling which are rapidly becoming orthodox. I believe, for my own part, and against this central myth, that to think, feel, or even speak of people in terms of "masses" is to make the burning of the books and the destroying of the cities just that much more possible.

Putropia, however, stops a little short of Doomsday. Doomsday is the immensely popular genre which, with considerable ingenuity and variety, disposes of life altogether. There are catastrophes which stop just short of this, and move into putropia. Mr John Wyndham's *Day of the Triffids* is an example. Here, the great majority of human beings are struck suddenly blind, and the Triffids – locomotive stinging plants, sources of vegetable oil, developed by Russian scientists – take over. The sighted minority has to decide whether to try to save the blind masses, who, characteristically, have taken to drink and so on, or to abandon them, to regroup the few who can see, and start making a better society. The myth is satisfied, of course, by the choice of the latter alternative, which has an apparent rationality once the sf convention has created the appropriate circumstances.

Doomsday used to have a God; it has none now. The Solar System burns itself out, after an atom bomb has been dropped on a strange rock which is an extra-planetary device of the same kind (Mr van Vogt's "Dormant"). The universe contracts to virtually nothing, and colour, light, and finally life vanish (Mr Philip Latham's "The Xi Effect"). The former, perhaps, is to be rationalized as a warning against combined science and war, though the burning-out is described with brio, and not, I think, without pleasure. The latter is the familiar nightmare of mechanism; nobody does anything wrong, but we are finished all the same. More significant, I think, than either, is Mr John Christopher's "The New Wine," in which the human race is suddenly, by deliberate scientific intention, made fully proficient in telepathy. A hundred years later, life is almost over, for when people can see and know each other as they really are, they prefer to die. Mr Eliot, operating from the same form of feeling, might have been well advised to put *The Cocktail Party* into sf, for the sake of external credibility. With him, however, some at least of the traditional sanctities and renewals are retained, as counter-process. Sf, by its definition of an arbitrary discontinuity, can dispense with these, and, selecting the tendencies that suit its purposes, and extending them, make an end of the human complexity.

Much sf is really anti-sf. An unbearable personal tension, or a particular sterility in social thinking, at once use and make a villain of a large part of man's organized attempt to know and to control. Humanism is discarded in the very affirmation of the familiar contemporary myths of humane concern. Man, in many of these stories, reaches his lowest point; even Faust was eagerly damned. The convention powerfully supports this. Not only catastrophe, but social breakdown, is a donnée. Under new adversity, man and society at once break down (with a few favoured exceptions), but the evidence for this is not from the record; it is, rather, unconsciously from the writer's feelings, consciously from the convention of the thrilling story, which needs trouble; (the central character of an adventure story is usually so criminally careless that he would not survive a day of real danger, but this makes for trouble, and for more story, and so here, with the unacknowledged underlying aim). I conclude myself from this kind of sf (look at the logic of extending tendencies) that we are all still in the caves.

I have left until last my recommendation of Space Anthropology. The old traveller's tale dealt in men with heads in their chests. In deep space, as I have observed, we find beasts and ghoulies and articulate vegetables, but these are the pre-history of the form. There are several moderate stories, and a few good ones, which consciously use the sf formula to find what are essentially new tribes, and new patterns of living. Some tribes are dull, like Mr Ray Bradbury's Martians – passionless blue balls – in "The Fire Balloons." Passionless blue balls we have at home. But the Lithians, in Mr

James Blish's *A Case of Conscience*, are a beautifully imagined tribe, in spite of being erect eight-foot reptiles. Here, for once, among the limitless claims of sf, we find a work of genuine imagination, and real intelligence. Reading all fiction is like that: after the long susurrus, at last a human voice, but here far away, among the galaxies.

READING 2

# William Morris (1958)

## Editor's Introduction

One might expect Williams's *Culture and Society* to echo something of the wider New Left interest in Morris and Orwell. And, to some extent, it did. The book is organized into two main parts, dealing respectively with the years 1790 to 1870 and 1914 to 1950, linked by a less substantial treatment of a turn-of-the-century "Interregnum" which clearly failed to engage Williams. Each of the main parts concludes with a discussion of political writing, the first with Morris, the second with Orwell (Reading 2 and Reading 3, respectively). But neither *News from Nowhere* nor *Nineteen Eighty-Four* excites Williams's interest or sympathy. Rather, the book rehearses much of the critique previously aired in the 1956 essay on sf. Williams sees Morris's significance in the attempt to attach the general values of the "culture and society" tradition to "an actual and growing social force: that of the organized working class." But this is more apparent in the expressly political essays, such as "How We Live, and How We Might Live" or "A Factory as It Might Be," than in the utopian novel, where the weaknesses "are active and disabling." As for Orwell, if the man had been "brave, generous, frank, and good," his dystopia nonetheless fully replicates that very minority culture/mass civilization topos which had propelled Williams away from Eliot and Leavis. "Orwell puts the case in these terms," Williams concludes, "because this is how he really saw present society, and *Nineteen Eighty-Four* is desperate because Orwell recognized that on such a construction the exile could not win, and then there was no hope at all." Hence, the paradox of "a humane man who communicated an extreme of inhuman terror; a man committed to decency who actualized a distinctive squalor."

# William Morris (1958)

The significance of Morris in this tradition, is that he sought to attach its general values to an actual and growing social force: that of the organized working class. This was the most remarkable attempt that had so far been made to break the general deadlock.

Morris's own restrospective account of his development is clear and interesting:

> Before the uprising of *modern* Socialism almost all intelligent people either were, or professed themselves to be, quite contented with the civilization of this century. Again, almost all of these really were thus contented, and saw nothing to do but to perfect the said civilization by getting rid of a few ridiculous survivals of the barbarous ages (*Political Writings* 243).

(This, evidently, is Morris's judgement of the utilitarian liberals.)

> To be short, this was the *Whig* frame of mind, natural to the modern prosperous middle-classmen, who, in fact, as far as mechanical progress is concerned, have nothing to ask for, if only Socialism would leave them alone to enjoy their plentiful style. But besides these contented ones there were others who were not really contented, but had a vague sentiment of repulsion to the triumph of civilization, but were coerced into silence by the measureless power of Whiggery (243).

(*Civilization*, in this last sentence, is used in a Coleridgian sense, as a limited term. In the previous sentence, the limiting function of *mechanical* is also evident. These are the traditional terms.)

> Lastly, there were a few who were in open rebellion against the said Whiggery – a few, say two, Carlyle and Ruskin. The latter, before my days of practical Socialism, was my master towards the ideal (243).

Thus Morris acknowledges both the tradition and his own extension of it. He now restates the grounds of the opposition to "civilization":

> Apart from the desire to produce beautiful things, the leading passion of my life has been and is hatred of modern civilization. [...] What shall I say concerning its

mastery of and its waste of mechanical power, its commonwealth so poor, its enemies of the commonwealth so rich, its stupendous organization – for the misery of life! Its contempt of simple pleasures, which everyone could enjoy but for its folly? Its eyeless vulgarity which has destroyed art, the one certain solace of labour? [...] The struggles of mankind for many ages had produced nothing but this sordid, aimless, ugly confusion; the immediate future seemed to me likely to intensify all the present evils by sweeping away the last survivals of the days before the dull squalor of civilization had settled down on the world. This was a bad look-out indeed, and, if I may mention myself as a personality and not as a mere type, especially so to a man of my disposition, careless of metaphysics and religion, as well as of scientific analysis, but with a deep love of the earth and the life on it, and a passion for the history of the past of mankind. Think of it! Was it all to end in a counting-house on the top of a cinder-heap, with Podsnap's drawing room in the offing, and a Whig committee dealing out champagne to the rich and margarine to the poor in such convenient proportions as would make all men contented together, though the pleasure of the eyes was gone from the world, and the place of Homer was to be taken by Huxley (244).

This kind of opposition is by now very familiar, and we can see in it elements of Carlyle, Ruskin, and Pugin, and of the popularization of these ideas in Dickens. There is also, significantly, the anti-scientific element: the Romantic prejudice that a mechanical civilization had been created by a mechanical science, and that science was attempting to substitute for art. One would have expected Morris to remember, as he elsewhere insisted, that the offered substitute for art was bad art; and that it was not scientific inquiry (however indifferent to it Morris might personally be) but the organization of economic life, which had produced the misery and the vulgarity. Keeping this point aside, we pass to Morris's important new emphasis:

So there I was in for a fine pessimistic end of life, if it had not somehow dawned on me that amidst all this filth of civilization the seeds of a great change, what we others call Social-Revolution, were beginning to germinate. [...] (This) prevented me, luckier than many others of artistic perceptions, from crystallizing into a mere railer against "progress" on the one hand, and on the other from wasting time and energy in any of the numerous schemes by which the quasi-artistic of the middle classes hope to make art grow when it has no longer any root, and thus I became a practical Socialist. [...] Surely anyone who professes to think that the question of art and cultivation must go before that of the knife and fork (and there are some who do propose that) does not understand what art means, or how that its roots must have a soil of a thriving and unanxious life. Yet it must be remembered that civilization has reduced the workman to such a skinny and pitiful existence, that he scarcely knows how to frame a desire for any life much better than that which he now endures perforce. *It is the province of art to set the true ideal of a full and reasonable life before him,* a life to which the perception and creation of beauty, the enjoyment of real pleasure that is, shall be felt to be as necessary to man as his daily bread, and that no man, and no set of men, can be deprived of this except by mere opposition, which should be resisted to the utmost (245–246).[1]

The social revolution, then, was to be the answer to the deadlock of the "railers against progress." The priority of "cultivation" is set aside, in terms that remind one of Cobbett. Yet, unlike Cobbett, Morris uses the idea of culture, in particular in its embodiment in art, as a positive criterion: "the true ideal of a full and reasonable life." Like Cobbett, Morris would have nothing set as a priority over the claims of working men to an improvement in their conditions; but unlike Cobbett, who set his objective in terms of a remembered society, Morris, like Blake or Ruskin, sets his social objective in terms of the fulness of life which art especially reveals.

Morris's principal opponent, in fact, was Arnold. The word "culture", because it was associated in his mind with Arnold's conclusions, is usually roughly handled:

> In the thirty years during which I have known Oxford more damage has been done to art (and therefore to literature) by Oxford "culture" than centuries of professors could repair – for, indeed, it is irreparable. These coarse brutalities of "light and leading" make education stink in the nostrils of thoughtful persons, and [...] are more likely than is Socialism to drive some of us mad [...] I say that to attempt to teach literature with one hand while it destroys history with the other is a bewildering proceeding on the part of "culture" (*The Letters* 262).

The point of this was Morris's opposition to the "modernization" of Oxford:

> I wish to ask if it is too late to appeal to the mercy of the "Dons" to spare the few specimens of ancient town architecture which they have not yet had time to destroy.

---

1   RW's italics.

> [...] Oxford thirty years ago, when I first knew it, was full of these treasures; but Oxford "culture", cynically contemptuous of the knowledge which it does not know, and steeped to the lips in the commercialism of the day, has made a clean sweep of most of them (*The Letters* 242–243).

As so often, a particular argument is here entangled with a much more general judgement. This is very typical of Morris's method, which is often no more than a kind of generalized swearing. Yet the general argument is there, when he troubles to control it. Oxford was for him a test-case, on the issue whether culture could be saved from commercialism by isolating it:

> There are of the English middle class, today [...] men of the highest aspirations towards Art, and of the strongest will; men who are most deeply convinced of the necessity to civilization of surrounding men's lives with beauty; and many lesser men, thousands for what I know, refined and cultivated, follow them and praise their opinions: but both the leaders and the led are incapable of saving so much as half a dozen commons from the grasp of inexorable Commerce: they are as helpless in spite of their culture and their genius as if they were just so many overworked shoemakers: less lucky than King Midas, our green fields and clear waters, nay the very air we breathe, are turned not to gold (which might please some of us for an hour maybe) but to dirt; and to speak plainly we know full well that under the present gospel of Capital not only there is no hope of bettering it, but that things grow worse year by year, day by day (*Political Writings* 116).

For indeed, Morris argues, the commercial habits of the middle class can destroy even those things which many individual members of the middle-class value. It is this commercialism which has destroyed even such a centre of alternative values as Oxford:

> What is it, for instance, that has destroyed the Rouen, the Oxford of my elegant poetic regret? Has it perished for the benefit of the people, either slowly yielding to the growth of intelligent change and new happiness, or has it been, as it were, thunderstricken by the tragedy which mostly accompanies some great new birth? Not so. Neither phalangstere nor dynamite has swept its beauty away, its destroyers have not been either the philanthropist or the Socialist, the cooperator or the anarchist. It has been sold, and at a cheap price indeed: muddled away by the greed and incompetence of fools who do not know what life and pleasure mean, who will neither take them themselves nor let others have them (*Collected Works* XXIII, 92).

To the constant question of this tradition – "can the middle classes regenerate themselves" – Morris returned a decided No. The middle classes cannot or will not *change* the consequences of industrialism; they will only try to escape them, in one of two ways. Either:

> Men get rich now in their struggles not to be poor, and because their riches shield them from suffering from the horrors which are a necessary accompaniment of the existence of rich men; e.g., the sight of slums, the squalor of a factory country, the yells and evil language of drunken and brutalized poor people (*Political Writings* 238).

This way, an energetic entry into commercialism in order to escape its consequences, is a kind of Moral Sinking Fund, which continues to be heavily subscribed. The other way is the way of "minority culture":

> nothing made by man's hand can be indifferent: it must be either beautiful and elevating, or ugly and degrading; and those things that are without art are so aggressively; they wound it by their existence, and they are now so much in the majority that the works of art we are obliged to set ourselves to seek for, whereas the other things are the ordinary companions of our everyday life; so that if those who cultivate art intellectually were inclined never so much to wrap themselves in their special gifts and their high cultivation, and so live happily, apart from other men, and despising them, they could not do so: they are as it were living in an enemy's country; at every turn there is something lying in wait to offend and vex their nicer sense and educated eyes: they must share in the general discomfort – and I am glad of it (*Collected Works* XXII, 56).

The cultivated were indeed "aliens", as Arnold had called them, but they were helpless to prevent further damage, even to themselves. Forty years of publicized revival of the arts had shown, Morris argued, not an improvement in the quality of things seen, but even a deterioration:

> The world is everywhere growing uglier and more commonplace, in spite of the conscious and very strenuous efforts of a small group of people towards the revival of art, which are so obviously out of joint with the tendency of the age, that while the uncultivated have not even heard of them, the mass of the cultivated look upon them as a joke, and even that they are now beginning to get tired of (*Collected Works* XXIII, 86).

Art, Morris argued, in line with his tradition, depends on the quality of the society which produces it. There is no salvation in art for art's sake

> of [...] (which) a school [...] does, in a way, theoretically at least, exist at present [...] its watchword (is) a piece of slang that does not mean the harmless thing it seems to mean [...] an art cultivated professedly by a few, and for a few, who would consider it necessary – a duty, if they could admit duties – to despise the common herd, to hold themselves aloof from all that the world has been struggling for from the first, to guard carefully every approach to their palace of art [...] that art at last will seem too delicate a thing for even the hands of the initiated to touch; and the initiated must at last sit still and do nothing – to the grief of no one (*Collected Works* XXII, 38–39).[2]

The hope for art was not here, but in the belief that

> the cause of Art is the cause of the people [...] One day we shall win back Art, that is to say the pleasure of life; win back Art again to our daily labour (*Political Writings* 122, 121).

This, at the end of the century, is a rejection of the specialization of "Art" which was common at its beginning. But the terms of the rejection are in part a result of the specialization. In particular, Morris profits from Ruskin's thinking about art and labour, as here:

> *Nothing should be made by man's labour which is not worth making; or which must be made by labour degrading to the makers.*
> Simple as that proposition is [...] it is a direct challenge to the death to the present system of labour in civilized countries (*Political Writings* 123).

the aim of art (is) [...] to destroy the curse of labour by making work the pleasurable satisfaction of our impulse towards energy, and giving to that energy hope of producing something worth the exercise (*Collected Works* XXIII, 91).

Art had become a particular quality of labour. Delight in work had been widely destroyed by the machine-system of production, but, Morris

---

2   RW reordered the quotations.

argued, it was the system, rather than the machines as such, which must be blamed.

> If the necessary reasonable work be of a mechanical kind, I must be helped to do it by a machine, not to cheapen my labour, but so that as little time as possible may be spent upon it [...] I know that to some cultivated people, people of the artistic turn of mind, machinery is particularly distasteful [...] (but) it is the allowing machines to be our masters and not our servants that so injures the beauty of life nowadays. In other words, it is the token of the terrible crime we have fallen into of using our control of the powers of Nature for the purpose of enslaving people, we careless meantime of how much happiness we rob their lives of (*Political Writings* 152, 155–156).

That Morris could feel like this is of considerable importance. He was himself a hand-craftsman, and he had a respect born from experience for work of that kind. In his Utopian writings, the removal of machines from the process of work is often emphasized. Yet the reaction "Morris – handicrafts – get rid of the machines" is as misleading as the reaction "Ruskin – Gothic – medievalism." The regressive elements are present in Morris, as they were in Ruskin. These elements seek to compensate for the difficulties in the way of practical realization of certain qualities of life; and because their function is compensatory, they are often sentimental. Yet, although their reference is to the past, their concern is with the present and the future. When we stress, in Morris, the attachment to handicrafts, we are, in part, rationalizing an uneasiness generated by the scale and nature of his social criticism. Morris wanted the end of the capitalist system, and the institution of socialism, so that men could decide for themselves how their work should be arranged, and where machinery was appropriate. It was obviously convenient to many of his readers, and to many of Ruskin's readers, to construe all this as a campaign to end machine-production. Such a campaign could never be more than an affectation, but it is less compromising than Morris's campaign to end capitalism, which lands one directly in the heat and bitterness of political struggle. It is most significant that Morris should have been diluted in this way. The dilution stresses what are really the weaker parts of his work, and neglects what is really strong and alive. For my own part, I would willingly lose *The Dream of John Ball* and the romantic socialist songs and even *News from Nowhere* – in all of which the weaknesses of Morris's general poetry are active and disabling, if to do so were the price of retaining and getting people to read such smaller things as "How We Live, and How We Might Live," "The Aims of Art," "Useful Work versus Useless Toil," and "A Factory as It Might Be." The change of emphasis would involve a change in Morris's status as a writer, but such a change is critically inevitable. There is more life in the lectures, where one feels that the whole man is engaged in the writing, than in any of the prose and verse romances. These seem so clearly the product of a fragmentary consciousness – of that very state of mind which Morris was always trying to analyse. Morris is a fine political writer, in the broadest sense, and it is on that, finally, that his reputation will rest. The other and larger part of his literary work bears witness only to the disorder which he felt so acutely. He was not a Hopkins to make art "when the time seemed unpropitious." The nearest figure to him, in his own century, is Cobbett: with the practice of visual instead of rural arts as the controlling sanity from which the political insights sprang. And as with Cobbett, we come to accept the impatience and the ritual swearing as the price of the vitality, which has its own greatness.

It remains to look briefly at Morris's socialism, since it grew out of the tradition which we have been examining. He is often mentioned by modern members of the Labour Party, but usually in terms that suggest a very limited acquaintance with his actual ideas. He is, for instance, something very different from an orthodox Fabian. Socialism, for him, is not merely

> substituting business-like administration in the interests of the public for the old Whig muddle of *laissez-faire* backed up by coercion (*Political Writings* 227).

This was the socialism the utilitarians had come to, but Morris, always, applied to socialism the modes of judgement which had been developed in opposition to utilitarianism. Thus, for example: Socialism might

> gain higher wages and shorter working hours for the working men themselves: industries may be worked by municipalities for the benefit both of producers and consumers. Working-people's houses may be improved, and their management taken out of the hands of commercial speculators. In all this I freely admit a great gain, and am glad to see schemes tried which would lead to it. But great as the gain would

be, the ultimate good of it [...] would, I think, depend on *how* such reforms were done; in what spirit; or rather what else was being done, while these were going on. [...] (228).

This is a familiar kind of argument, from the tradition, and Morris confirms it in its usual terms:

> The great mass of what most non-socialists at least consider at present to be socialism, seems to me nothing more than a *machinery* of socialism, which I think it probable that socialism *must* use in its militant condition; and which I think it *may* use for some time after it is practically established; but does not seem to me to be of its essence (227).

Yet the result of this point of view is not modification of the Socialist idea, but its emphasis. Morris wonders

> whether, in short, the tremendous organization of civilized commercial society is not playing the cat and mouse game with us socialists. Whether the Society of Inequality might not accept the quasi-socialist machinery above mentioned, and work it for the purpose of upholding that society in a somewhat shorn condition, maybe, but a safe one. [...] The workers better treated, better organized, helping to govern themselves, but with no more pretence to equality with the rich, nor any more hope for it than they have now (230).

This insight into what has been perhaps the actual course of events since his death is a measure of Morris's quality as a political thinker. Yet it is no more than an application, under new circumstances, of the kind of appraisal which the century's thinking about the meanings of culture had made available. The arts defined a quality of living which it was the whole purpose of political change to make possible:

> I hope we know assuredly that the arts we have met together to further are necessary to the life of man, if the progress of civilization is not to be as causeless as the turning of a wheel that makes nothing (*Collected Works* XXII, 31).

Socialist change was the means to a recovery of purpose. The limitation of such change to "machinery" would only be possible

> on the grounds that the working people have ceased to desire real socialism and are contented with some outside show of it joined to an increase in prosperity enough to satisfy the cravings of men who do not know what the pleasures of life might be if they treated their own capacities and the resources of nature reasonably with the intention and expectation of being happy (*Political Writings* 230–231).

The business of a socialist party is not only to organize political and economic change. It is, more vitally, to foster and extend a real socialist consciousness, among working men, so that finally

> they understand themselves to be face to face with false society, themselves the only possible elements of true society (233).

We realize the tradition behind Morris even as, in this remarkable way, he gives a radically new application to its ideas. For Morris is here announcing the extension of the tradition into our own century, and setting the stage for its continuing controversy.

READING 3

# George Orwell (1958)


## George Orwell (1958)

"It is not so much a series of books, it is more like a world" (Orwell, *Collected Essays, Journalism and Letters* Vol. 1, 493). This is Orwell, on Dickens. "It is not so much a series of books, it is more like a case." This, today, is Orwell himself. We have been using him, since his death, as the ground for a general argument, but this is not mainly an argument about ideas, it is an argument about mood. It is not that he was a great artist, whose experience we have slowly to receive and value. It is not that he was an important thinker, whose ideas we have to interpret and examine. His interest lies almost wholly in his frankness. With us, he inherited a great and humane tradition; with us, he sought to apply it to the contemporary world. He went to books, and found in them the detail of virtue and truth. He went to experience, and found in it the practice of loyalty, tolerance, and sympathy. But, in the end,

> it was a bright cold day in April, and the clocks were striking thirteen. Winston Smith, his chin nuzzled into his breast in an effort to escape the vile wind, slipped quickly through the glass doors of Victory Mansions, though not quickly enough to prevent a swirl of gritty dust from entering along with him (Orwell, *Nineteen Eighty-Four* 3).

The dust is part of the case: the caustic dust carried by the vile wind. Democracy, truth, art, equality, culture: all these we carry in our heads, but, in the street, the wind is everywhere. The great and humane tradition is a kind of wry joke; in the books it served, but put them down and look around you. It is not so much a disillusion, it is more like our actual world.

The situation is paradox: this kind of tradition, this kind of dust. We have made Orwell the figure of this paradox: in reacting to him we are reacting to a common situation. England took the first shock of industrialism and its consequences, and from this it followed, on the one hand, that the humane response was early, fine, and deep – the making of a real tradition; on the other hand that the material constitution of what was criticized was built widely into all our lives – a powerful and committed reality. The interaction has been long, slow, and at times desperate. A man who lives it on his own senses is subject to extraordinary pressures. Orwell lived it, and frankly recorded it: this is why we attend to him. At the same time, although the situation is common, Orwell's response was his own, and has to be distinguished. Neither his affiliations, his difficulties, nor his disillusion need be taken as prescriptive. In the end, for any proper understanding, it is not so much a case, it is a series of books.

The total effect of Orwell's work is an effect of paradox. He was a humane man who communicated an extreme of inhuman terror; a man committed to decency who actualized a distinctive squalor. These, perhaps, are elements of the general paradox. But there are other, more particular, paradoxes. He was a socialist, who popularized a severe and damaging criticism of the idea of socialism and of its adherents. He was a believer in equality, and a critic of class, who founded his later work on a deep assumption of inherent inequality, inescapable class difference. These points have been obscured, or are the subject of merely partisan debate. They can only be approached, adequately, through observation of a further paradox. He was a notable critic of abuse of language, who himself practised certain of its major and typical abuses. He was a fine observer of detail, and appealed as an empiricist, while at the same time committing himself to an unusual amount of plausible yet specious generalization. It is on these points, inherent in the very material of his work, that we must first concentrate.

That he was a fine observer of detail I take for granted; it is the great merit of that group of essays of which "The Art of Donald McGill" is typical, and of parts of *The Road to Wigan Pier*. The contrary observation, on his general judgements, is an effect of the total reading of his work, but some examples may here stand as reminders:

*George Orwell (1958)* 35

> In each variant of socialism that appeared from about 1900 onwards the aim of establishing liberty and equality was more and more openly abandoned (*Nineteen Eighty-Four* 211).

## The British Labour Party? Guild Socialism?

> By the fourth decade of the twentieth century all the main currents of political thought were authoritarian. The earthly paradise had been discredited at exactly the moment when it became realizable (213).

## England in 1945?

> The first thing that must strike any outside observer is that Socialism in its developed form is a theory confined entirely to the middle class (*The Road to Wigan Pier* 152).

## A Labour Party conference? Any local party in an industrial constituency? Trade unions?

> All left-wing parties in the highly industrialized countries are at bottom a sham, because they make it their business to fight against something which they do not really wish to destroy (*Collected Essays, Journalism and Letters* Vol. 2, 218).

## On what total evidence?

> The energy that actually shapes the world springs from emotions – racial pride, leader worship, religious belief, love of war – which liberal intellectuals mechanically write off as anachronisms, and which they have usually destroyed so completely in themselves as to have lost all power of action (168).

## But does the shaping energy spring from these emotions alone? Is there no other "power of action"?

> A humanitarian is always a hypocrite (218).

## An irritation masquerading as a judgement?

> Take, for instance, the fact that all sensitive people are revolted by industrialism and its products (*Collected Essays, Journalism and Letters* Vol. 4, 467).

All? By all its products?

I isolate these examples, not only to draw attention to this aspect of Orwell's method, but also to indicate (as all but one of them do) the quality of the disillusion which has, in bulk, been so persuasive. In many of the judgements there is an element of truth, or at least ground for argument, but Orwell's manner is normally to assert, and then to argue within the assertion. As a literary method, the influence of Shaw and Chesterton is clear.

The method has become that of journalism, and is sometimes praised as clear forthright statement. Orwell, in his discussions of language, made many very useful points about the language of propaganda. But just as he used plausible assertion, very often, as a means of generalization, so, when he was expressing a prejudice, often of the same basic kind, he moved very easily into the propagandist's kind of emotive abuse:

> One sometimes gets the impression that the mere words "Socialism" and "Communism" draw towards them with magnetic force every fruit-juice drinker, nudist, sandal-wearer, sex-maniac, Quaker, "Nature Cure" quack, pacifist and feminist in England ... (*The Road to Wigan Pier* 152)
> [...] vegetarians with wilting beards [...] shock-headed Marxists chewing polysyllables [...] birth control fanatics, and Labour Party backstairs crawlers (190).

Or consider his common emotive use of the adjective "little":

> The typical socialist [...] a prim little man with a white-collar job, usually a secret teetotaller and often with vegetarian leanings (152).
> A rather mean little man, with a white face and a bald head, standing on a platform, shooting out slogans (*Coming Up for Air* 145).
> ... the typical little bowler-hatted sneak – Strube's "little man" – the little docile cit who slips home by the six-fifteen to a supper of cottage pie and stewed tinned pears (*Keep the Aspidistra Flying* 53).
> In the highbrow world you "get on", if you "get on" at all, not so much by your literary ability as by being the life and soul of cocktail parties and kissing the bums of verminous little lions (*The Road to Wigan Pier* 144).

Of course, this can be laughed at, and one will only be annoyed if one is a socialist, nudist, feminist, commuter, or so on. But I agree with Orwell that good prose is closely connected with liberty, and with the social possibility of truth. I agree with him also (and so assemble this evidence) that

> modern writing at its worst [...] consists in gumming together long strips of words which have already been set in order by someone else, and making the results presentable by sheer humbug (*Collected Essays, Journalism and Letters* Vol. 4, 163).

To overlook this practice in Orwell himself would be ridiculous and harmful.

Now, in normal circumstances, any writer who at all frequently wrote in the manner of the examples quoted might be simply disregarded. Yet I see this paradox, this permission of such writing by a man who accepted the standards which condemn it, as part of the whole paradox of Orwell, which I wish to describe. He is genuinely baffling until one finds the key to the paradox, which I will call the paradox of the exile. For Orwell was one of a significant number of men who, deprived of a settled way of living, or of a faith, or having rejected those which were inherited, find virtue in a kind of improvised living, and in an assertion of independence. The tradition, in England, is distinguished. It attracts to itself many of the liberal virtues: empiricism, a certain integrity, frankness. It has also, as the normally contingent virtue of exile, certain qualities of perception: in particular, the ability to distinguish inadequacies in the groups which have been rejected. It gives, also, an appearance of strength, although this is largely illusory. The qualities, though salutary, are largely negative; there is an appearance of hardness (the austere criticism of hypocrisy, complacency, self-deceit), but this is usually brittle, and at times hysterical: the substance of community is lacking, and the tension, in men of high quality, is very great. Alongside the tough rejection of compromise, which gives the tradition its virtue, is the felt social impotence, the inability to form extending relationships. D.H. Lawrence, still the most intelligent of these men in our time, knew this condition and described it. Orwell may also have known it; at least he lived the rejections with a thoroughness that holds the attention.

The virtues of Orwell's writing are those we expect, and value, from this tradition as a whole. Yet we need to make a distinction between exile and vagrancy: there is usually a principle in exile, there is always only relaxation in vagrancy. Orwell, in different parts of his career, is both exile and vagrant. The vagrant, in literary terms, is the "reporter", and, where the reporter is good, his work has the merits of novelty and a certain specialized kind of immediacy. The reporter is an observer, an intermediary: it is unlikely that he will understand, in any depth, the life about which he is writing (the vagrant from his own society, or his own class, looking at another, and still inevitably from the outside). But a restless society very easily accepts this kind of achievement: at one level the report on the curious or the exotic; at another level, when the class or society is nearer the reporter's own, the perceptive critique. Most of Orwell's early work is of one of these two kinds (*Down and Out in Paris and London*; *The Road to Wigan Pier*). The early novels, similarly, are a kind of fictionalized report: even the best of them, *Coming up for Air*, has more of the qualities of the virtuoso reporter (putting himself in the place of the abstract, representative figure) than of the intensity of full imaginative realization. We listen to, and go about with, Orwell's Mr Bowling; Orwell, for the most part, is evidently present, offering his report.

Now, it would be absurd to blame Orwell for this "vagrant" experience; he had good reasons for rejecting the ways of life normally open to him. But he saw that the rejection had in the end to be ratified by some principle: this was the condition of vagrancy becoming exile, which, because of his quality, he recognized as finer. The principle he chose was socialism, and *Homage to Catalonia* is still a moving book (quite apart from the political controversy it involves) because it is a record of the most deliberate attempt he ever made to become part of a believing community. Nor can such praise be modified because the attempt, in continuing terms, failed. While we are right to question the assertion of self-sufficiency, by vagrant and exile alike, we have also to recognize the complexity of what is being rejected and of what can be found. Orwell, in exploring this complexity, did work of real value.

But the principle, though affirmed, could not now (Orwell concluded) carry him directly through to actual community. It could, in fact, only be lived in controversy. Orwell's socialism became the exile's principle, which he would at any cost keep inviolate. The cost, in practice, was a partial abandonment of his own standards: he had often to curse, wildly, to keep others away, to avoid being confused with them. He did not so much attack socialism, which was safe in his mind, as socialists, who were there and might involve him. What he did attack, in socialism, was its disciplines, and, on this basis, he came to concentrate his attack on communism. His attacks on the denial of liberty are admirable: we have all, through every loyalty, to defend the basic liberties of association and expression, or we deny man. Yet, when the exile speaks of liberty, he is in a curiously ambiguous position, for while the rights in question may be called individual, the condition of their guarantee is inevitably social. The exile, because of his own personal position, cannot finally believe in any social guarantee: to him, because this is the pattern of his own living, almost all association is suspect. He fears it because he does not want to be compromised (this is often his virtue, because he is so quick to see the perfidy which certain compromises involve). Yet he fears it also because he can see no way of confirming, socially, his own individuality; this, after all, is the psychological condition of the self-exile. Thus in attacking the denial of liberty he is on sure ground; he is wholehearted in rejecting the attempts of society to involve him. When, however, in any positive way, he has to affirm liberty, he is forced to deny its inevitable social basis: all he can fall back on is the notion of an atomistic society, which will leave individuals alone. "Totalitarian" describes a certain kind of repressive social control, but, also, any real society, any adequate community, is necessarily a totality. To belong to a community is to be a part of a whole, and, necessarily, to accept, while helping to define, its disciplines. To the exile, however, society as such is totalitarian; he cannot commit himself, he is bound to stay out.

Yet Orwell was at the same time deeply moved by what he saw of avoidable or remediable suffering and poverty, and he was convinced that the means of remedy are social, involving commitment, involving association, and, to the degree that he was serious, involving himself. In his essay "Writers and Leviathan", which he wrote for a series in *Politics and Letters*, Orwell recognized this kind of deadlock, and his solution was that in such circumstances the writer must divide: one part of himself uncommitted, the other part involved. This indeed is the bankruptcy of exile, yet it was, perhaps, inevitable. He could not believe (it is not a matter of intellectual persuasion; it is a question of one's deepest experience and response) that *any* settled way of living exists in which a man's individuality can be socially confirmed. The writer's problem, we must now realize, is only one aspect of this general problem, which has certainly, in our own time, been acute. But because we have accepted the condition of exile, for a gifted individual, as normal, we have too easily accepted the Orwell kind of analysis as masterly. It is indeed a frank and honest report, and our kind of society has tied this knot again and again; yet what is being recorded, in Orwell, is the experience of a victim: of a man who, while rejecting the consequences of an atomistic society, yet retains deeply, in himself, its characteristic mode of consciousness. At the easy levels this tension is mediated in the depiction of society as a racket; a man may even join in the racket, but he tells himself that he has no illusions about what he is doing – he keeps a secret part of himself inviolate. At the more difficult levels, with men of Orwell's seriousness, this course is impossible, and the tension cannot be discharged. The consequent strain is indeed desperate; this, more than any objective threat, is the nightmare of *Nineteen Eighty-Four*.

A Marxist dismisses Orwell as "petty bourgeois", but this, while one sees what it means, is too shallow. A man cannot be interpreted in terms of some original sin of class; he is where he is, and with the feelings he has; his life has to be lived with his own experience, not with someone else's. The only point about class, where Orwell is concerned, is that he wrote extensively about the English working class, and that this, because it has been influential, has to be revalued. On such matters, Orwell is the reporter again: he is often sharply observant, often again given to plausible generalization. In thinking, from his position, of the working class primarily as a class, he assumed too readily that observation of particular working-class people was an observation of all working-class behaviour. Because, however, he looked at people at all, he is often nearer the truth than more abstract left-wing writers. His principal failure was inevitable: he observed what was evident, the external factors, and only guessed at what was not evident, the inherent patterns of feeling. This failure is most obvious in its consequences: that he did come to think, half against his will, that the working people were really helpless, that they could never finally help themselves.

In *Animal Farm*, the geniality of mood, and the existence of a long tradition of human analogies in animal terms, allow us to overlook the point that the revolution that is described is one of animals against men. The men (the old owners) were bad, but the animals, left to themselves, divide into the pigs (the hypocritical, hating politicians whom Orwell had always attacked) and the others. These others have many virtues – strength, dumb loyalty, kindliness, but there they are: the simple horse, the cynical donkey, the cackling hens, the bleating sheep, the silly cows. It is fairly evident where Orwell's political estimate lies: his sympathies are with the exploited sheep and the other stupid animals, but the issue of government lies between drunkards and pigs, and that is as far as things can go. In *Nineteen Eighty-Four*, the same point is clear, and the terms are now direct. The hated politicians are in charge, while the dumb mass of "proles" goes on in very much its own ways, protected by its very stupidity. The only dissent comes from a rebel intellectual: the exile against the whole system. Orwell puts the case in these terms because this is how he really saw present society, and *Nineteen Eighty-Four* is desperate because Orwell recognized that on such a construction the exile could not win, and then there was no hope at all. Or rather:

> If there was hope, it *must* lie in the proles [...] everywhere stood the same solid unconquerable figure, made monstrous by work and childbearing, toiling from birth to death and still singing. Out of those mighty loins a race of conscious beings must one day come. You were the dead; theirs was the future. But you could share in that future if you kept alive the mind. [...] (*Nineteen Eighty-Four* 72, 230)

This is the conclusion of any Marxist intellectual, in specifically Marxist terms, but with this difference from at any rate some Marxists: that the proles now, like the animals, are "monstrous" and not yet "conscious" – one day they will be so, and meanwhile the exile keeps the truth alive. The only point I would make is that this way of seeing the working people is not from fact and observation, but from the pressures of feeling exiled: other people are seen as an undifferentiated mass beyond one, the "monstrous" figure. Here, again, is the paradox: that the only class in which you can put any hope is written off, in present terms, as hopeless.

I maintain, against others who have criticized Orwell, that as a man he was brave, generous, frank, and good, and that the paradox which is the total effect of his work is not to be understood in solely personal terms, but in terms of the pressures of a whole situation. I would certainly insist that his conclusions have no general validity, but the fact is, in contemporary society, that good men are driven again and again into his kind of paradox, and that denunciation of them – "He [...] runs shrieking into the arms of the capitalist publishers with a couple of horror comics which bring him fame and fortune" (Walsh 35–36) – is arrogant and crass. We have, rather, to try to understand, in the detail of experience, how the instincts of humanity can break down under pressure into an inhuman paradox; how a great and humane tradition can seem at times, to all of us, to disintegrate into a caustic dust.

READING 4

# The Future Story as Social Formula Novel (1961)

## Editor's Introduction

It is tempting to read the young Williams's general aversion to utopia and dystopia as a displaced objection to the content of Morris's particular utopia and Orwell's particular dystopia. Certainly, the latter commanded both his attention and his disagreement. "I would certainly insist that his conclusions have no general validity," Williams wrote in *Culture and Society*. But the argument seems to proceed at a more general level too, where the extremism of the form itself is read as unrealistically anti-human. This is certainly the shape it takes in *The Long Revolution*, where sf is again represented by Huxley, Orwell, and Bradbury, here augmented by two of William Golding's novels, *Lord of the Flies* and *The Inheritors*, and used as a key element in an exercise in literary typology. There were two main types of realist novel in the twentieth century, Williams argues: the "social novel" and the "personal novel," each of which has "documentary" and "formula" sub-types. The "social formula novel" in Williams's schema works by way of the abstraction of a particular pattern from the sum of social experience, accentuating it so as to create a fictional society. The best example of this kind of novel, he continues, is the "future-story," which is virtually coextensive with "serious 'science fiction.'"

This kind of sf is "lively" because "about lively social feelings," but lacks both a "substantial society" and "substantial persons": "For the common life is an abstraction, and the personal lives are defined by their function in the formula." Neither the social nor the personal novel, neither the documentary nor the formula, are at all adequate, Williams concluded. The problem is one of "balance," he wrote, in terms clearly reminiscent of

Leavis – even at one point invoking the "great tradition" – and the effort to create such balance is necessary "if we are to remain creative." An obvious objection to this conclusion is that it illegitimately judges sf according to criteria more appropriate to the realistic "literary" novel and thus ignores the formal conventions of the genre. In the 1965 Pelican edition of *The Long Revolution*, Williams added an endnote explicitly addressing this argument, which insisted to the contrary that: "the form itself, and what 'by definition' it 'cannot do', must submit to be criticized from a general position in experience" (387). The implication is striking: that, if only it would try, sf could indeed create both a substantial society and substantial persons. Which returns us, by implication if not expressly, to space anthropology and James Blish's Lithians.

## The Future Story as Social Formula Novel (1961)

It may [...] be possible to write the history of the modern novel in terms of a polarization of styles, object-realist and subject-impressionist, but the more essential polarization, which has mainly occurred since 1900, is the division of the realist novel, which had created the substance and quality of a way of life in terms of the substance and qualities of persons, into two separate traditions, the "social" novel and the "personal" novel. In the social novel there may be accurate observation and description of the general life, the aggregation; in the personal novel there may be accurate observation and description of persons, the units. But each lacks a dimension, for the way of life is neither aggregation nor unit, but a whole indivisible process.

We now commonly make this distinction between "social" and "personal" novels; indeed in one way we take this distinction of interest for granted. By looking at some examples, the substantial issue may be made clear. There are now two main kinds of "social" novel. There is, first, the descriptive social novel, the documentary. This creates, as priority, a general way of life, a particular social or working community. Within this, of course, are characters, sometimes quite carefully drawn. But what we say about such novels is that if we want to know about life in a mining town, or in a university, or on a merchant ship, or on a patrol in Burma, this is the book. In fact many novels of this kind are valuable; the good documentary is usually interesting. It is right that novels of this kind should go on being written, and with the greatest possible variety of setting. Yet the dimension that we miss is obvious: the characters are miners, dons, soldiers first; illustrations of the way of life. It is not the emphasis I have been trying to describe, in which the persons are of absolute interest in themselves, and are yet seen as parts of a whole way of living. Of all current kinds of novel, this kind, at its best, is *apparently* nearest to what I am calling the realist novel, but the crucial distinction is quite apparent in reading: the social descriptive function is in fact the shaping priority.

A very lively kind of social novel, quite different from this, is now significantly popular. The tenor, here, is not description, but the finding and materialization of a *formula* about society. A particular pattern is abstracted, from the sum of social experience, and a society is created from this pattern. The simplest examples are in the field of the future-story, where the "future" device (usually only a device, for nearly always it is obviously contemporary society that is being written about; indeed this is becoming the main way of writing about social experience) removes the ordinary tension between the selected pattern and normal observation. *Brave New World*, *Nineteen Eighty-Four*, *Fahrenheit 451*, are powerful social fiction, in which a pattern taken from contemporary society is materialized, as a whole, in another time or place. Other examples are Golding's *Lord of the Flies* and *The Inheritors*, and nearly all serious "science fiction." Most of these are written to resemble realistic novels, and operate in the same essential terms. Most of them contain, fundamentally, a conception of the relation between individuals and society; ordinarily a virtuous individual, or small personal group, against a vile society. The action, normally, is a release of tensions in this personal-social complex, but I say release, and not working-out, because ordinarily the device subtly alters the tensions, places them in a preselected light, so that it is not so much that they are explored but indulged. The experience of isolation, of alienation, and of self-exile is an important part of the contemporary structure of feeling, and any contemporary realist novel would have to come to real terms with it.

(It is ironic, incidentally, that it was come to terms with, and worked to a resolution very different from the contemporary formula of "exile versus masses; stalemate", at several points in the realist tradition, notably in *Crime and Punishment* and, through Bezukhov, in *War and Peace*.) Our formula novels are lively, because they are about lively social feelings, but the obvious dimension they lack is that of a substantial society and correspondingly substantial persons. For the common life is an abstraction, and the personal lives are defined by their function in the formula.

The "realist" novel divided into the "social" and the "personal", and the "social novel", in our time, has further divided into social documentary and social formula. It is true that examples of these kinds can be found from earlier periods, but they were never, as now, the modes. The same point holds for the "personal novel", and its corresponding division into documentary and formula. Some of the best novels of our time are those which describe, carefully and subtly, selected personal relationships. These are often very like *parts* of the realist novel as described, and there is a certain continuity of method and substance. Forster's *A Passage to India* is a good example, with traces of the older balance still clearly visible, yet belonging, in a high place, in this divided kind, because of elements in the Indian society of the novel which romanticize the actual society to the needs of certain of the characters. This is quite common in this form: a society, a general way of living, is apparently there, but is in fact often a highly personalized landscape, to clarify or frame an individual portrait, rather than a country within which the individuals are actually contained. Graham Greene's social settings are obvious examples: his Brighton, West Africa, Mexico and Indo-China have major elements in common which relate not to their actual ways of life but to the needs of his characters and of his own emotional pattern. When this is frankly and absolutely done, as in Kafka, there is at least no confusion; but ordinarily, with a surface of realism, there is merely the familiar unbalance. There is a lack of dimension similar to that in the social descriptive novel, but in a different direction. There the characters were aspects of the society; here the society is an aspect of the characters. The balance we remember is that in which both the general way of life and the individual persons are seen as there and absolute.

[...]

I offer this fourfold classification – social description, social formula, personal description, personal formula – as a way of beginning a "general" analysis of the contemporary novel, and of defining, by contrast, the realist tradition which, in various ways, these kinds have replaced. The question now is whether these kinds correspond to some altered reality, leaving the older tradition as really irrelevant as the hansom cab, or whether they are in fact the symptoms of some very deep crisis in experience, which throws up these talented works yet persists, unexplored, and leaves us essentially dissatisfied. I would certainly not say that the abandonment of the realist balance is in some way wilful; that these writers are deliberately turning away from a great tradition, with the perversity that many puzzled readers assign to them. The crisis, as I see it, is too deep for any simple, blaming explanation. But what then is this crisis, in its general nature?

There are certain immediate clarifying factors. The realist novel needs, obviously, a genuine community: a community of persons linked not merely by one kind of relationship – work or friendship or family – but many, interlocking kinds. It is obviously difficult, in the twentieth century, to find a community of this sort. Where *Middlemarch* is a complex of personal, family and working relationships, and draws its whole strength from their interaction in an indivisible process, the links between persons in most contemporary novels are relatively single, temporary, discontinuous. And this was a change in society, at least in that part of society most nearly available to most novelists, before it was a change in literary form. Again, related to this, but affected by other powerful factors, the characteristic experience of our century is that of asserting and preserving an individuality, (again like much eighteenth-century experience) as compared with the characteristic nineteenth-century experience of finding a place and making a settlement. The ordinary Victorian novel ends, as every parodist knows, with a series of settlements, of new engagements and formal relationships, whereas the ordinary twentieth-century novel ends with a man going away on his own, having extricated himself from a dominating situation, and found himself in so doing. Again, this actually happened, before it became a common literary pattern. In a time of great change, this kind of extrication and discovery was a necessary and valuable movement; the recorded individual histories amount to a common history. And while old establishments linger, and new establishments of a dominating kind are continually instituted, the breakaway has continually to be made, the personal assertion given form and substance, even to the point where it threatens to become the whole content of our literature. Since I know the pressures, I admit the responses, but my case is that we are reaching deadlock, and that to explore a new definition of realism may be the way to break out of the deadlock and find a creative direction.

The contemporary novel has both reflected and illuminated the crisis of our society, and of course we could fall back on the argument that only a different society could resolve our literary problems. Yet literature is committed to the detail of known experience, and any valuable social change would be the same kind of practical and responsible discipline. We begin by identifying our actual situation, and the critical point, as I see it, is precisely that separation of the individual and society into absolutes, which we have seen reflected in form. The truly creative effort of our time is the struggle for relationships, of a whole kind, and it is possible to see this as both personal and social: the practical learning of *extending* relationships. Realism, as embodied in its great tradition, is a touchstone in this, for it shows, in detail, that vital interpenetration, idea into feeling, person into community, change into settlement, which we need, as growing points, in our own divided time. In the highest realism, society is seen in fundamentally personal terms, and persons, through relationships, in fundamentally social terms. The integration is controlling, yet of course it is not to be achieved by an act of will. If it comes at all, it is a creative discovery, and can perhaps only be recorded within the structure and substance of the realist novel.

Yet, since it is discovery, and not recovery, since nostalgia and imitation are not only irrelevant but hindering, any new realism will be different from the tradition, and will comprehend the discoveries in personal realism which are the main twentieth-century achievement. The point can be put theoretically, in relation to modern discoveries in perception and communication. The old, naïve realism is in any case dead, for it depended on a theory of natural seeing which is now impossible. When we thought we had only to open our eyes to see a common world, we could suppose that realism was a simple recording process, from which any deviation was voluntary. We know now that we literally create the world we see, and that this human creation – a discovery of how we can live in the material world we inhabit – is necessarily dynamic and active; the old static realism of the passive observer is merely a hardened convention. When it was first discovered that man lives through his perceptual world, which is a human interpretation of the material world outside him, this was thought to be a basis for the rejection of realism; only a personal vision was possible. But art is more than perception; it is a particular kind of active response, and a part of all human communication. Reality, in our terms, is that which human beings make common, by work or language. Thus, in the very acts of perception and communication, this practical interaction of what is personally seen, interpreted and organized and what can be socially recognized, known and formed is richly and subtly manifested. It is very difficult to grasp this fundamental interaction, but here, undoubtedly, is the clue we seek, not only in our thinking about personal vision and social communication, but also in our thinking about the individual and society. The individual inherits an evolved brain, which gives him his common human basis. He learns to see, through this inheritance, and through the forms which his culture teaches. But, since the learning is active, and since the world he is watching is changing and being changed, new acts of perception, interpretation and organization are not only possible, but deeply necessary. This is human growth, in personal terms, but the essential growth is in the interaction which then can occur, in the individual's effort to communicate what he has learned, to match it with known reality and by work and language to make a new reality. Reality is continually established, by common effort, and art is one of the highest forms of this process. Yet the tension can be great, in the necessarily difficult struggle to establish reality, and many kinds of failure and breakdown are possible. It seems to me that in a period of exceptional growth, as ours has been and will continue to be, the tension will be exceptionally high, and certain kinds of failure and breakdown may become characteristic. The recording of creative effort, to explore such breakdowns, is not always easy to distinguish from the simple, often rawly exciting exploitation of breakdown. Or else there is a turning away, into known forms, which remind us of previously learned realities and seek, by this reminder, to establish probability of a kind. Thus the tension can either be lowered, as in the ordinary social novel, or played on, as in the ordinary personal novel. Either result is a departure from realism, in the sense that I am offering. For realism is precisely this living tension, achieved in a communicable form. Whether this is seen as a problem of the individual in society, or as a problem of the offered description and the known description, the creative challenge is similar. The achievement of realism is a continual achievement of balance, and the ordinary absence of balance in the forms of the contemporary novel, can be seen as both a warning and a challenge. It is certain that any effort to achieve a contemporary balance will be complex and difficult, but the effort is necessary, a new realism is necessary, if we are to remain creative.

READING 5

# Terror (1971)

## Editor's Introduction

Williams was an early pioneer of television studies: his 1974 *Television: Technology and Cultural Form* almost single-handedly defined the field. From 1968 until 1972, he wrote a regular column of television reviews for the BBC's *The Listener*. In the column below, taken from mid-1971, he revisits, without naming it, the notion of space anthropology he had aired in 1956. The programme that most concerns him here is *Out of the Unknown*, an anthology series broadcast on BBC 2 over four seasons from 1965 to 1971. By the end of the first it had become the highest rating in-house drama on the BBC. The 1965, 1966–67, and 1969 seasons were each exclusively devoted to sf and mobilized an enormous body of talent in its service: Irene Shubik, who had worked on ABC TV's earlier *Out of this World*, was appointed producer and story editor; stories came from the likes of John Wyndham, Isaac Asimov, Ray Bradbury, J.G. Ballard, Frederick Pohl, C.M. Kornbluth, and E.M. Forster; and television adaptations from the likes of Terry Nation and J.B. Priestley. The 1970–71 fourth and final season veered towards horror rather than sf. Here, Williams argues that, for all the patent inadequacies of television sf, the genre has peculiar "advantages," for the exploration of such essentially anthropological themes as "identity and culture-contact." This notion will persist into his various late 1970s discussions of the work of Ursula K. Le Guin. The two other BBC TV sf shows he mentions are *Doctor Who* and *Doomwatch*. The first needs no introduction: along with *Star Trek*, it is one of the two best-known and longest running sf shows ever broadcast. *Doomwatch* was directed by Terry Nation, the inventor of the Daleks; it ran from 1970 to

1972, and was overwhelmingly concerned with possible Frankensteinian threats posed by science and technology.

## Terror (1971)

Last week I found myself wondering if I had ever been frightened by a television programme. The occasion was paradoxical: half-way through a play in the *Out of the Unknown* series (BBC 2), which the linkman had introduced with some remarks about its being spine-tingling – or was it spine-chilling? It's difficult to remember that this conventional physical vocabulary is supposed to relate to real dramatic effects. There must have been people whose hair stood on end as something dreadful appeared to have happened, just as there must somewhere have been somebody reading a book who found that he couldn't put it down. But it's just as curious to meet people who denounce violence and say how much they enjoy a good crime story – a juicy murder, to revert to the conventional language. So it's interesting to wonder about this wholly respectable terrorization. Some people who talk about a really good thriller aren't at first sight people you would expect to hear talking about thrills in any other capacity. And what is it that produces, in a culture dominated by business and by its versions of common sense and practicality, this persistent taste for the conventionally irrational, with its local repertory and dialect of spooks, creeps and chills? There are traditional arguments about purgation, about discharge or reconciliation, through a play. But they seem rather a long way from the television set. There, the deliberation of the entertaining intention to frighten can come through as chilling in quite another sense.

*Out of the Unknown* used to be mainly what is called science fiction. In the current series the operative word seems to be "psychological." "Welcome Home", which provoked these reflections, used an internal dramatic viewpoint to persuade us that the man coming home after an accident was the husband and doctor he believed himself to be and that the husband and doctor he found there, with the same – his own? – name, was some kind of impostor (Farhi). Every convention was then spoken about: invasion by an alien species or a hostile foreign power; the fingerprints of a man who had died two years before in the West Indies (voodoo!); sinister mind-bending drugs. Or it could, take your pick, be paranoia, as everyone including his supposed friends seemed to be part of the conspiracy, though since we had seen the other man apparently committing a murder, with local dramatic effects suggesting furtiveness, we were still inclined to take the conspiracy as objective. As in the end, rather hurriedly and in a different way, it was: the field-trial of a new suggestibility drug, to give the man an identity that would be preferable to his past. Though why the alternative identity should be that of one of the doctors treating him wasn't exactly clear. Unless – but of course: the irresponsibility of science. A clear case for *Doomwatch*.

What would it be, I wondered, that could come anywhere near fulfilling the conventional promise of desirable frightening effects? I'd better say, as a check, that I've been startled often enough by footsteps in empty houses, strange figures at windows, shadows, knives, abysses, mirrors, wrong faces above the pram. Mostly in print or the cinema: I can't remember an instance on the box. When the figure at the window turned up in "Welcome Home" I found that I was looking at almond leaves through our own blue venetian blind. Perhaps the frame is too small to enclose us dramatically; the world around the frame too insistently present and domestic. I've often noticed in the cinema those moments when one comes back from enclosure in the frame; when through the half-dark one sees the clock again, and the red light for Exit, and the signs for Ladies and Gentlemen. Usually the film is still going on, but for a time not easily measured – and when measured still qualitatively different – there has been no conscious space between the absorbed eyes and the moving sequence of images. I don't know how many people ever find this happening on television. For me it is less frequent but not unknown. Yet the dominance of the images – for it is also that – never seems to occur when it would be useful to people trying to entertain us out of our wits. Horror and terror still run in the cinema, with old images of vampires, bats, pterodactyls, mad scientists, automata and the walking dead. Television by contrast is silvery and cool.

Is it different in televized "science fiction"? The difficulty there is the wide variation that description now covers. A sharply written play a week earlier in *Out of the Unknown* – Edward Boyd's "The Sons and Daughters of Tomorrow" – had us assuming some murderous coven, with strong smells of traditional witchcraft, and then revealed a community of telepaths and energy-throwers. Mutants, an alien outpost, a Tarot seminary? One wasn't encouraged to make any final identification. But this is a world away from, say, the adventures of *Doctor Who*, where odd things regularly happen and there have been some memorable monsters, but where there is also Brigadier Lethbridge Stewart and some familiar office politics and a general air of suffused charm. Not much of the best science fiction has yet got to the screen. Its critical themes are identity and culture contact, and in many ways it has advantages for the exploration of these, not only over realism but over the medieval and romantic repertories. Visual realization, however, is a complicated matter. Watching *Yesterday's Witness* (BBC 2) on how the talkies came to Britain, I was interested to see how the sound-effects man used to suggest dripping blood by tapping the back of his hand, but something else was also happening which was much more dramatic. There were some conventional dissolves from the faces of the men talking to their younger faces, and then back again. And this was strangely powerful, in ways that pushed past the abstractions – time, change, identity. I could hardly listen to what was being said as these dissolving images recurred. Nothing to do with the spine or the hair but an arrest, a disturbance: something out of the known.

PART TWO
# Texts in their Contexts: Cultural Materialism

READING 6

# *Nineteen Eighty-Four* (1971)

## Editor's Introduction

Williams's 1971 study of Orwell developed an apparently more even-handed account of *Nineteen Eighty-Four* than that in *Culture and Society*, weighing the novel's strengths against its weaknesses, rather than the author against his text. For Williams, the convincing elements were twofold: the treatment of language on the one hand and of international power politics on the other. Against this, the identification of totalitarianism with socialism and the pessimism about human capacity, evident in Winston's loveless relationship with Julia and in the reduction of the people to passive "proles," amount to a failure of experience. Here, as in *Culture and Society*, Williams concluded that "the question about *Nineteen Eighty-Four*" is why Orwell should have "created situations and people that, in comparison with his own written observations, are one-dimensional and determined." But here the answer is essentially sociological in character, "not in the personal contradictions but in the much deeper structures of a society and its literature." Hence, the book's final conclusion that the only "useful" thing, now, "is to understand how it happened."

The aspiration to understand is betrayed, nonetheless, by Williams's aversion to Orwell's "anti-socialism," which falls far short of the "complex seeing of analysis." At one point, Williams chides Orwell that "he had the best of reasons" to know that political police "were not a socialist or communist invention," that his analysis is "cut short" by "assigning all modern forms of repression and authoritarian control to a single political tendency." But, in the immediately preceding paragraph, Williams quotes from Orwell's 1949 letter to the American United Auto Workers Union, to the effect that *Nineteen Eighty-Four* had been intended not as an attack on socialism, but on perversions "partly realized in Communism and Fascism." In short, Orwell intended neither to represent political police as a "socialist invention" nor to assign authoritarian control to a "single political tendency," but had rather assigned it quite expressly to both communism and fascism, totalitarianisms respectively of the left and the right. Williams quotes from this letter with scrupulous accuracy, but nonetheless appears not to hear what it says.

## *Nineteen Eighty-Four* (1971)

*Nineteen Eighty-Four* is obviously very different. The curve of isolated feelings, of a ragged and breathless exposure, has returned and is decisive. Yet there are still many elements of the novel which belong to a more liberating consciousness. The appendix, "The Principles of Newspeak", was never fully incorporated in the imaginative world, but its central perception of a relation between linguistic and social forms is powerful: "the special function of certain Newspeak words, of which *oldthink* was one, was not so much to express meanings as to destroy them" (*Nineteen Eighty-Four* 318). Some Newspeak words – *prolefeed, speedwise, sexcrime* – have already, a generation later, an ominously familiar sound. So too have the names of new government departments: in Newspeak, Minitrue, Minipax, Miniluv, and Miniplenty. I would expect that the copywriters of Mintech were admirers of Orwell, but if they had read him they had certainly not understood him. Much of the jargon of "modernization" – that extraordinary substitute for social democracy which the British Labour Government adopted and propagated in the sixties – is almost wholly Newspeak. Some of the techniques of news management sound similarly familiar. The Fiction Department, as an institution, would now hardly even be noticed. And when Winston Smith describes a typical film show – "*the helicopter planted a 20 kilo bomb in among them terrific flash and the boat went all to matchwood. then there was a wonderful shot of a child's arm going up up up right up into the air a helicopter with a camera in its nose must have followed it up*" (10–11) – it is as if he had seen the television newsreels from Vietnam; only the weight of the bomb is an absurd underestimate.

Again, in a rather different way, "Big Brother Is Watching You" has also made its way into ordinary language, as the motto of a sceptical resistance. In these very simple and powerful ways Orwell succeeded in articulating certain quite evident elements of our prolonged social crisis. As an intransigent enemy of every kind of *thoughtcrime* and *doublethink*, Orwell is still very close and alive. His vision of power politics is also close and convincing. The transposition of official "allies" and "enemies" has happened, almost openly, in the generation since he wrote. His idea of a world divided into three blocs – Oceania, Eurasia, and Eastasia, of which two are always at war with the third though the alliances change, is again too close for comfort. And there are times when one can believe that what "had been called England or Britain" has become simply Airstrip One.

With these elements of the projection so recognizable, at least in their general outlines, it is necessary to ask why so much else is so wrong. It is significant that Orwell took his model of a controlled and military society from Soviet communism, even including detailed elements of its past such as the conflict between Stalin and Trotsky (Big Brother and Goldstein). The ideology of Airstrip One is Ingsoc – English socialism – and when the book became a success in the United States he had to issue a denial that this related to the postwar Labour Government:

> My recent novel is NOT intended as an attack on Socialism or on the British Labour Party (of which I am a supporter) but as a show-up of the perversions to which a centralized economy is liable and which have already been partly realized in Communism and Fascism (*Collected Essays, Journalism and Letters* Vol. 4, 564).

Ingsoc, it might then be said, is no more English Socialism than Minitrue is the Ministry of Truth. But the identification was in effect made, and has been profoundly damaging. Not in what it says about Soviet society – Orwell's position there was clear and consistent – but in what it implied generally about socialism and a "centralized economy." This connects with the most evident error in Orwell's projection: that the permanent and controlled war economy is shabby and under-supplied. The structural relations, that we can now see, between a militarist economy and a controlled consumer affluence amount to more than a historical development which Orwell did not foresee. They indicate some of the social facts which, in what became an obsession with ideology, he did not take account of. There are good reasons why Orwell might not have foreseen an affluent and militarist capitalism, or a world of international corporations which function, internally and externally, very much like his projected Party. But he had the best of reasons – in direct experience – for knowing that political police, for example, were not a socialist or communist invention; or propaganda, or censorship, or *agents provocateurs*. By assigning all modern forms of repression and authoritarian control to a single political tendency, he not only misrepresented it, but cut short the kind of analysis that would recognize these inhuman and destructive forces wherever they appeared, under whatever names and masked by whatever ideology. For it would certainly, now, be *doublethink* to suppose that the only source of these elements is a form of socialism, just as it is only *thoughtcrime* that could prevent us from seeing a propaganda phrase like "the free world" as a very clear example of Newspeak. In projecting a world that is all too recognizable, Orwell confused us about its structures, its ideologies, and the possibilities of resisting it.

This point about resistance has a further importance, when we remember Orwell's earlier work. At the most general level, his projection has undoubtedly been falsified. Under controls as pervasive and as cruel, many men and women have kept faith with each other, have kept their courage, and in several cases against heavy odds have risen to try to destroy the system or to change it. We can write Berlin, Budapest, Algiers, Aden, Wattsville, Prague in the margins of Orwell's passivity. He himself could have written St Petersburg, Kronstadt, Barcelona, Warsaw. It would be right to acknowledge that many of the risings were defeats, but Orwell goes further, cutting out the spring of hope. He projects an enormous apathy on all the oppressed: a created mood, if ever there was one. Eighty-five per cent of the population are seen as an apathetic mass, and *proles*, as a description of them, seems more than Party jargon. The Party sees them as "natural inferiors [...] like animals", but how does Orwell see them? As a shouting, stupid crowd in the streets; drinking and gambling; "like the ant, which can see small objects but not large ones"; "people who have never learned to think." It is the world of working people, before 1914, as seen by the prep-school boy: "To me in my early boyhood, to nearly all children of families like mine, 'common' people seemed almost sub-human" (*The Road to Wigan Pier* 110). But, as in another earlier experience, this "almost sub-human" world can be seen, in a moment of revulsion from his own class, as the hope of the future, redeemers to be looked at with "mystical reverence": "people who had never learned to think but who were storing up in their hearts and bellies and muscles the power that would one day overturn the world" (*Nineteen Eighty-Four* 229). "Out of those mighty loins a race of conscious beings must one day come" (230).

This stale revolutionary romanticism is as insulting as the original observation. It is the rising of the animals, as in the fable. "When you put it in words it sounded reasonable; it was when you looked at the human beings passing you on the pavement that it became an act of faith" (89). It needs to be said, however bitterly, that if the tyranny of 1984 ever finally comes, one of the major elements of the ideological preparation will have been just this way of seeing "the masses", "the human beings passing you on the pavement", the eighty-five per cent who are *proles*. And nobody who belongs to this majority or who knows them as people will give a damn whether the figure on the other side of the street sees them as animals to be subjected or as unthinking creatures out of whose mighty loins the future will come. The incomplete humanity will be too clearly visible in the gesticulating observer himself.

That is how it goes, politically, throughout. Orwell had seen clearly the world of the power blocs, but the "hundreds of millions of ill-paid and hard-working coolies", inhabiting "a rough quadrilateral with its corners at Tangier, Brazzaville, Darwin and Hong Kong" (195) are also passive: "if they did not exist, the structure of world society, and the process by which it maintains itself, would not be essentially different" (196). It is a dreadful underestimate, not only of those people but of the structures of exploitation through which the metropolitan states are sustained. By viewing the struggle as one between only a few people over the heads of an apathetic mass, Orwell created the conditions for defeat and despair.

He continues his underestimate. He had seen people go back into Spain, under the threat of arrest, because of general and particular loyalties. He had seen hundreds of cases of fidelity under pressure. His wife had stayed in Barcelona, even lying in bed while the police searched her room, to be near him and to help him. But still

> *Under the spreading chestnut tree*
> *I sold you and you sold me* [...] (80)

He can describe this accurately as "a peculiar, cracked, braying, jeering note [...] a yellow note" (80), but still it is what he makes happen. The cynical jingle of the rat-race, which in similar forms we have been hearing ever since from the agency offices and parties, leads straight to the nightmare of the rat in Room 101. Of course people break down under torture, but not all people break down. And in a filthy and repressive world there are deeper forms of personal resistance – as Orwell had reason to know – than the temporary affair between Winston and Julia.

The Party campaign against sex is one of the stranger elements of the projection (that it seems to have been taken from Zamyatin's *We* is relevant but secondary). The object of the campaign is to prevent uncontrollable loyalties but even more to "remove all pleasure from the sexual act." There have been such campaigns, though in some exploiting systems the first purpose can be achieved by a kind of abstract reversal of the second: pleasure without loyalty is even a marketable and institutional commodity. It is strange that Orwell could oppose the controls and the perversions with nothing better than the casual affair between Winston and Julia. This begins like the lovemaking trip to the country in *Keep the Aspidistra Flying*, but then it moves right away from any mutually recognizing personal experience:

> His heart leapt. Scores of times she had done it: he wished it had been hundreds – thousands. Anything that hinted at corruption always filled him with a wild hope (131).

It is not the ordinary and continuing love of men and women, in friendship and in marriage, but a willed corruption or indifference – "the simple undifferentiated desire" – that is presented as opposed to (though it is usually part of) that joyless world. Winston's marriage is a cold and miserable routine; only with the hint of corruption can the pleasure come.

Of the many failures in *Nineteen Eighty-Four* this is perhaps the deepest. All the ordinary resources of personal life are written off as summarily as the *proles*. The lonely fantasy of "mighty loins" of the future is joined by the lonely confusion of the adolescent – so guilty about lovemaking that corruption of the object is a necessary element of its pleasure. Winston Smith is not like a man at all – in consciousness, in relationships, in the capacity for love and protection and endurance and loyalty. He is the last of the cut-down figures – less experienced, less intelligent, less loyal, less courageous than his creator – through whom rejection and defeat can be mediated.

The question about the view of the future in *Nineteen Eighty-Four* is not an abstract one concerning a change from the optimism of Mercier or Wells to the pessimism of Huxley or Orwell. Abstract optimism and pessimism are almost equally beside the point, and there are plausible grounds for seeing a generalized future that is either dark or bright. What matters much more than the imposed general mood is the amount of experience that is drawn on. Promises or warnings that limit experience have limited relevance. So the question about *Nineteen Eighty-Four*, as about Orwell's earlier novels, is why he created situations and people that, in comparison with his own written observations, are one-dimensional and determined. This is not primarily a matter of politics, but of a more extended experience of self and society. Under the strength and sense of his only successful character, "Orwell" – a man physically and intellectually alive and conscious and tough and persistent – moved these feebler and less conscious figures in an undifferentiated theatrical landscape. The central significance is not in the personal contradictions but in the much deeper structures of a society and its literature. In making his projections, Orwell expressed much more than himself.

[...]

Soon after his death Orwell became, in effect, a symbolic figure. He was one of those men whose life and writing were in practice inseparable, and who seemed to offer a style in which others could live and write. It would be easy to say that this was because he was a disillusioned, decent, and plain-living anti-communist: a figure the age needed. Of course the promotion of this image took place, but most people who had read him saw past it. It is significant that he was not respected only by people who had given up their commitment to radical social change and who were using Orwell's disillusion as a cover. There were plenty of these, and others who didn't even have to live the process through, who could take Orwell's disillusion neat. But there were just as many who began their political commitment from the point where Orwell left off, who agreed with him about Stalinism and about imperialism and about the English establishment, and who made a new socialist politics out of his sense of a failure.

There is a clear line, certainly, from Orwell's "Inside the Whale" and *Nineteen Eighty-Four* to an orthodox North Atlantic mood in which all humane and positive beliefs, and especially a belief in radical change, can be recognized in advance as either a projection of some personal or social maladjustment, or as an inexperienced, naïve, adolescent idealism, which despite the will and vision of its bearers leads in practice straight to the authoritarianism which more sinister figures are all the time preparing, behind this apparently innocent front. These explanations and warnings are still being confidently offered, sometimes with Orwell's name attached, as to the student movements of the past few years. Again, in some relation to this, there is certainly a clear line from Orwell's social thinking in "The Lion and the Unicorn" and similar essays to the British Labour Party revisionists of the fifties and sixties. Their definition of socialism as the pursuit of equality had a traditional sound but a more precise contemporary significance: what had been understood as a socialist economy was (they argued) outdated by the development of an affluent industrial society; a new classlessness was emerging of its own accord and would be confirmed by measures of pragmatic social reform. Or, in Orwell's terms, the "wrong members of the family", the old "feudal" or "aristocratic" elements, would be displaced by the new men, the "new Britain", and then the nation would become more civilized, more humane, more generally and equitably prosperous – just what Orwell had wanted as far back as *The Road to Wigan Pier*. This relates to the feeling held by radicals who were not directly involved in the political arguments that Orwell, unlike other socialist writers, understood English life – its pace, its tolerance, its distrust of abstractions and of any theory pushed to extremes: a sensible, moderate, decent kind of life, which any hurried or drastic changes would disturb or put at risk, but which was still the basis for a steady extension of humane and responsible living.

We could call these views and moods Orwell's inheritance. But it is then all the more remarkable that the generation for whom Suez, Hungary, and the Bomb were signals for the renewal of political action looked to him with respect; a generation that believed not only in a new socialist movement, but one based on disturbance: on demonstrations, on direct action, on the politics of the streets and the localities. This New Left respected Orwell directly, especially in its early years. The invasion of Suez was an open exercise of the British Imperialism he had so consistently attacked. The Hungarian revolution, a popular and socialist rising against a bureaucratic and authoritarian communism, was at once a confirmation of what he had said about Stalinism and a demonstration of the authentic movement to which he had paid homage in Catalonia. The danger of the Bomb – "either we renounce it or it destroys us" – was as he had seen it: not only the weapon which could destroy civilization, but the shadow under which a new authoritarian war economy would grow and extend. And then, closely involved with these political positions, there was the Orwell who had written about work, about poverty, about popular culture, the Orwell who had tried to live and feel where the majority of English people were living and feeling: reporting, understanding, respecting, beyond the range of an Establishment culture. These discernible elements of the New Left in Britain are, equally clearly, Orwell's effective inheritance.

What kind of phenomenon is this, then, when the same man, the same writer, symbolizes such different tendencies, is appealed to and respected by opposing groups? It would be easy but pointless to start a quarrel over Orwell's inheritance: body-snatching or mantle-snatching; a figure or a style to dignify his reputed successors. No useful analysis can go in for that. There has been too much of it already, in everything from anecdote to impersonation. "Father Knew George Orwell" is a cracked old song.

Nor is it very useful to attempt some reductive analysis. It would be easy to say that these different tendencies can be explained chronologically: the thirties Orwell is the socialist, the forties Orwell the reactionary, the radical somewhere in between. But I have looked carefully through his writings, considering this explanation, and I am sure it doesn't work. Evidence for each of the positions can be drawn from each of the periods, though of course with differences of emphasis. There is the anti-imperialist of the early thirties, the revolutionary socialist of the late thirties, the radical essayist of the late thirties and forties. Yet in the same periods there are the patterns of defeat, the figure of the isolated honest man who has seen beyond the socialist talk, and the propagation of the myths of England. Or there is the disillusioned and embittered prophet of the forties, seeing progress as a swindle and revolution as self-defeating, but this man is also the radical essayist of the *Tribune* articles, active not only in defence of the victims of Stalinism but also in defence of "the civil liberties of any citizens of the British Empire", even including, past his doubts and reservations, a man convicted for passing atomic secrets to the USSR (*Collected Essays, Journalism and Letters* Vol. 4, 232–233, 431). That there are phases of Orwell's development is clear enough, but within each period there are some of the same contradictions.

A reductive analysis by forms of writing may again seem plausible but does not really work. Most radicals, I have noticed, prefer his essays, as if "The Art of Donald McGill" or "Dickens" or "How the Poor Die" or "Raffles and Miss Blandish" were somehow his major works. I admire these and many of the other essays, but I don't believe they can be isolated from his other work, and an Orwell restricted to them would be a very much smaller figure. Or take the novels, up to *Coming Up for Air*. They have been much more influential than has been commonly noticed; indeed one could say they created the style of the drifting anti-hero English novel of the fifties, though themselves based on such diverse sources as Wells and Joyce, Gissing and Somerset Maugham. But the point is that all the contradictory tendencies are in the novels: the colloquial style and the seeking-out of ordinary life, but also the patterns of defeat, self-hatred, and that generalized swearing which covers reabsorption. In the journals and reporting there is usually a stronger and more consistent position, but some of the basic ambiguities are evident in almost everything but *Homage to Catalonia*. The creation of "Orwell" – the honest observer – is more successful than the creation of the fictional characters, but we still have to explain the contradictions in that central consciousness.

Indeed the contradictions, the paradox of Orwell, must be seen as paramount. Instead of flattening out the contradictions by choosing this or that tendency as the "real" Orwell, or fragmenting them by separating this or that period or this or that genre, we ought to say that it is the paradoxes which are finally significant. No simple explanation of them will do justice to so complex a man (the more complex because he appears, on the surface, so plain). Some of the concepts we need for any full explanation may be beyond our reach just because of what we share with Orwell: a particular kind of historical pressure, a particular structure of responses and failures to respond. But two points can be suggested.

First, the key to Orwell as an individual is the problem of identity. Educated as he was to a particular consciousness, the key to his whole development is that he renounced it, or attempted to renounce it, and that he made a whole series of attempts to find a new social identity. Because of this process, we have a writer who was successively many things that would be unlikely in a normal trajectory: an imperial police officer, a resident of a casual ward, a revolutionary militiaman, a declassed intellectual, a middle-class English writer. And the strength of his work is that in the energy of his renunciation he was exceptionally open to each new experience as it came. Different kinds of life flowed through him with only a minimal check from a more established identity, and the style he evolved – a studied simplicity, "letting the meaning choose the word" – shows that while always travelling seriously, he was always travelling light. This quality can be related to his willingness to renounce his earlier attitudes and experiences and to write about them – or about others now in them – with contempt or anger, as if they were some other, quite separated thing. Yet in a period of exceptional mobility, this has positive as well as negative elements. Orwell could connect as closely and with as many different kinds of people as he did, precisely because of his continual mobility, his successive and serious assumption of roles. When he is in a situation, he is so dissolved into it that he is exceptionally convincing, and his kind of writing makes it easy for the reader to believe that this is also happening to himself. The absence of roots is also the absence of barriers.

It would be possible to say that this is the writer's "negative capability" of which Keats wrote. But there is no permanent psychology of "the writer." This is the social psychology of a particular kind of writer in a particular epoch. It is even, in Orwell's period, a class psychology: Aldous Huxley, W.H. Auden, Graham Greene, Christopher Isherwood, for all their differences, share with Orwell important elements of this position: travelling light and often, which is their overt social history; realizing others – other lives but especially other beliefs, other attitudes, other moods – through their own shifting negations. This structure of feeling is not what Keats meant by "negative capability"; it is at once sharper and smaller. The clarity and memorability of the successive realizations are an undoubted achievement, but there is also a characteristic coldness, an inability to realize the full life of another, seeing the other instead as a figure in an unrolling private landscape. In the case of Orwell, this coldness is most evident in his novels, where the presence of another as someone more than a stranger met or seen on a journey is expected and does not come. Relationships are characteristically meagre, ephemeral, reluctant, disillusioning, even betraying, and this is very remarkable in the work of so generous a man. But one is reminded, very sharply, that in this at least Orwell was writing with the grain of his time. The relationships in his novels are characteristic relationships in the fiction of a period – a period marked by the certainty, even dogma, that this, now, is what all relationships are like. This is what I meant in saying that to describe the paradox of Orwell we would need concepts beyond the consciousness and the social structures of his period. All we can now propose is experience: that there are other, fuller, more continuing relationships; that there are ways beyond even this alienation.

Yet Orwell tried again and again to affirm, putting his life on the line. That is what makes him much more than a passive figure in this dominant structure of feeling. He shared it, but he tried to transcend it. As clearly as anyone in his generation, he sensed that this was, after all, a historical crisis, not a human condition or a metaphysical fact. His mobility, then, had a clear social intention. He was travelling light, but it was sureness of instinct, not chance, that took him to all the critical places and experiences of his epoch; and he was not only a visitor, either, but a man wanting and hoping to join in. He made a single life contain, at first hand, the experiences of imperialism, of revolution, of poverty. He had no theory to explain them and no rooted positive beliefs extending beyond his own role. But with great stubbornness and persistence and courage he went to the centres of the history that was determining him, so that it might be experienced and differently determined. This, above everything, was his individual achievement. He was the writer who put himself out, who kept going and taking part, and who learned to write as a function of this very precise exploration.

But it is therefore more than an individual history. Nobody who shared or overlapped with his epoch can, in good faith, reduce his crisis to a personal development. There were important personal factors in his successes and in his failures, but some of the deepest contradictions are part of a shared history, and we cannot set ourselves above it, as if he were an abstract critical problem.

The second key to an understanding is, then, the nature of capitalist democracy in an epoch of socialist revolutions, of imperialism, of fascism, and of war. In the thirties it was not difficult to see capitalist democracy in the context of political imperialism and economic depression. Its complicity with fascism, or at best its willingness to deal with fascism in a common opposition to socialism, could be seen not only in its dealings with the Soviet Union but in Spain. Reservations could be made about the nature of Soviet communism, or the internal politics of the Spanish Republic, yet a set of bearings held, or for many years seemed to hold. Capitalist democracy would not fight fascism, any more than it would liberate the colonial peoples or end the poverty which disfigured it in its own societies. Socialism had its profound internal differences and its own deep distortions, but it was the name, everywhere, for opposition to that dangerous and exploiting alliance.

Under massive historical pressures, in a very intricate process of cause and effect, this world view was profoundly modified. The development of revolution in the Soviet Union and in Spain was itself deeply and bitterly affected by the character of the alliance against it and by its own desperate need for survival. Within a few years, what had seemed impossible became inescapable history: not only the further degeneration of Soviet communism in the Stalin trials, and the betrayal of Spain, which were bitter enough, but the world-altering events of 1939: the pact between Stalin and Hitler and the beginning of war between fascism and the capitalist democracies. It may be easier, now, to gain some perspective on this process: to see the shadow of the incredible in the long earlier history of betrayal and default, the submerged contradictions coming at last into the open.

But it is not only the shock of those years that is important. The most important effect, for anyone in Orwell's position, was the consequent response to capitalist democracy, for it was here that, beyond the old contradictions and illusions, new contradictions and illusions were being laid down almost unnoticed. For Orwell the physical inevitability of the war against fascism combined first, as we have seen, with a traditional attachment to his country: Orwell's mature myth of England was written at just this point. But it was not just England that was in question, but the nature of capitalist democracy. In adjusting to England, and to the war against fascism, it was easy to over-adjust. "Capitalist", as a qualification of "democracy", could in effect be omitted or its reality underestimated, as it was in the illusion that the war against Germany could be turned into a revolutionary war, or as in the deeper, much more persistent illusion that it would be possible, quite quickly and without major disturbance, to bring the real England – democratic England – to the surface, breaking through the thin upper crust of an exhausted and archaic system. To the extent that "democracy" could be isolated, as in the alliance against fascism seemed plausible, it could be made the basis of an unanswerable criticism of a socialist order which under long historical pressures had become authoritarian. This would not have made so much sense if the experience of democracy had not been real: both in the inheritance of a liberal capitalism, and in the bitterly fought-for freedoms of what was in effect a popular and anti-capitalist culture. Physically it was there, its radically diverse elements confused and apparently inextricable. But in isolating the contrast between democratic and authoritarian regimes, abstracting them from the developing and contradictory character of their real social systems, a new set of illusions, a new and historically fragile world-view, was in fact prepared. This was, indeed, similar, in structure and effect, to the earlier isolation and abstraction of "socialism."

In other West European countries, where elements of the old order collaborated with fascism and new alliances had to be made in the necessary resistance, other choices were possible. But in England capitalist democracy survived with its main contradictions intact, and then the pretence or hope that it was social democracy, or was about to become so, lasted longer than was good for anybody's reason. Even after the profound disillusions of 1945–51 and 1964–70, the pretence or hope survived. Yet no such illusion is static. If the only effective social contrast was between "democracy" and "communism", then some sort of accommodation with capitalism – that capitalism which was "on the point of" becoming a social democracy – was at first temporarily and then habitually conceivable. Having made this accommodation, and the corresponding identification of "communism" as the sole threat, it became harder to see and to admit what capitalist imperialism was still capable of doing: what, in the years since Orwell died, it has done again and again, in repression and in war.

This is the knot that was tied in the middle 1940s. And Orwell, indeed, helped to tie it. Then in his last fiction he discarded the apparently positive element of the illusion – the belief in the imminence of social democracy and was left with only its negative effects. He could see only authoritarian communism in the future, with no alternative or countervailing social forces. The first proposed title for what became *Nineteen Eighty-Four* was *The Last Man in Europe*, and that is clearly how it felt. It has a certain bleak honesty, but it reveals a point at which the political contradictions, and the isolation and abstraction involved in them, combined with the lack of any independent social identity to produce a genuine terror.

This would not have got through to so many people if the contradictions had not been so general. But what in Orwell was a last desperate throw became for many others, absurdly, a way of life. His radical pessimism was combined with an accommodation to capitalism and with an illusion of the imminence of social democracy. What in Orwell broke down in terror became a comfortable and persistent world view (in an older generation even lasting beyond Vietnam).

The only useful thing, now, is to understand how it happened. In a confused and mobile history, his kind of loss of identity has continued to occur. The affiliation he tried to make, that he was ready to die for, was prevented by the political contradictions of those years and was lost, finally, in illusion and terror. The writer had to split from the political militant. Faith in the people had to be projected to an evolutionary distance: much farther than would ever have been necessary if his original class idea of unthinking sub-humans had not translated so easily into a disillusioned view of the apathetic and tolerant mass. Beyond and past him, in and through many of the contradictions he experienced, real popular forces have continued to move, and the fight he joined and then despaired of has been renewed, has extended, and has gained important new ground.

We are never likely to reach a time when we can do without his frankness, his energy, his willingness to join in. These are the qualities we shall go on respecting in him, whatever other conclusions we may come to. But they are real qualities only if they are independent and active. The thing to do with his work, his history, is to read it, not imitate it. He is still there, tangibly, with the wound in his throat, the sad strong face, the plain words written in hardship and exposure. But then as we reach out to touch him we catch something of his hardness, a necessary hardness. We are acknowledging a presence and a distance: other names, other years; a history to respect, to remember, to move on from.

READING 7

# The City and the Future (1973)

## Editor's Introduction

In *The Country and the City*, Williams's primary concern was with the pastoral and the counter-pastoral, but he found examples of each in the future cities of sf. The essential novelty of his procedure here was to compare literary representations with "questions of historical fact," so as to test literary texts for the extent to which they misrepresented their contexts (12). In his treatment of sf, Williams stresses the importance of the city as a site of utopian and dystopian imaginings, emphasizing the historical recency of the social experience of the megalopolis. The science-fictional "experience of the future" came out of an "experience of the cities," he wrote. He traced this "deep transformation" in the first instance to late nineteenth-century London, citing as key examples Morris's *News from Nowhere* and H.G. Wells's "A Story of the Days to Come." But he is clear that the central dynamic extends into the twentieth century, into cities elsewhere, and into film as well as the novel, tracing a line of descent from Wells to Fritz Lang's *Metropolis*. Williams follows the history of the sf city through Huxley and Orwell, James Thomson, Brian Aldiss and Arthur C. Clarke, J.G. Ballard and Walter M. Miller, Don A. Stuart, Henry Kuttner, E.M. Forster, Robert Abertheney, and, once again, James Blish. Interestingly, he still seems to prefer Blish to Orwell, specifically the flying cities of *Earthman, Come Home* to the "shabby, ugly, exposed and lonely city" of *Nineteen Eighty-Four*. The comparison is much less pointed, however, than in earlier formulations. For the intent of the analysis is now not so much to take sides – or at least not immediately so – as to chart and explain the more general movement. "In a sense," Williams concludes, "everything about the city – from the magnificent to the apocalyptic – can be believed at once." One source of this unevenness is in complexity, but another, he continues, is "the abstraction of the city, as a huge isolated problem," which contemporary culture inherits from more traditional images of the country and the city.

## The City and The Future (1973)[1]

Out of an experience of the cities came an experience of the future. At a crisis of metropolitan experience, stories of the future went through a qualitative change. There were traditional models for this kind of projection. In all recorded literature there had been the land after death: a paradise or a hell. In the centuries of exploration and voyaging, new societies were discovered, for promise or for warning, in new lands: often islands: often the happy island, itself a shaping element in the myth. But within metropolitan experience these models, though widely drawn on, were eventually transformed. Man did not go to his destiny, or discover his fortunate place; he saw, in pride or error, his own capacity for collective transformation of himself and of his world.

As early as the eighteenth century, Louis Sébastien Mercier wrote both a contemporary topographical *Tableau de Paris* (1782–89) and a story of the secular future, *L'An 2440* (1770). But it was in the late nineteenth century, and significantly in London, that the deep transformation occurred. We can see it in writers as different as William Morris and H.G. Wells. Each, in his own way, draws on the transforming experience of contemporary London, then at the centre of social and literary attention. Each, again in his own way, draws on the new collective consciousness which is the social product of the urban experience even where its impulse is its criticism and

---

[1] From *The Country and the City* by R. Williams (1973), pp. 272–278, by permission of Oxford University Press Inc., USA.

rejection. Morris in *News from Nowhere* (1890) has his observer wake, during a restless night after a political argument, and find himself in the London of the twenty-first century. Two features are then significant: the kind of London Morris foresaw, which is a qualitative break; and the social ideas and feelings that created it, which are continuous with the socialist movement of his own day. If we look only at that imagined London, we find the dreaming and often backward-looking Morris:

> The soap-works with their smoke-vomiting chimneys were gone; the engineer's works gone; the leadworks gone; and no sound of riveting and hammering came down the west wind from Thorneycroft's. Then the bridge? I had perhaps dreamed of such a bridge, but never seen such an one out of an illustrated manuscript. [...]
> [...] I opened my eyes to the sunlight again and looked round me, and cried out among the whispering trees and odorous blossoms, "Trafalgar Square!" (*News from Nowhere* 186–187, 222)

London has been decentralized, keeping some of the best older parts but restoring some of the slum areas to separate small towns and villages. The industrial manufacturing cities have "like the brick and mortar desert of London, disappeared." Most of the smaller towns have survived, with their centres cleared; the suburbs "have melted away into the general country." This is a combination of what is essentially restoration, turning back history and drawing on medieval and rural patterns, and what was to express itself, formally, as town-planning, the creation of urban order and control. It is an imagined old London, before industrialism and the metropolitan expansion, and a projected new London, in the contemporary sense of the garden city. These contradictory impulses are never wholly resolved, and indeed cannot be resolved without considering what is offered, throughout, as the directing spirit; the new social idea. For it is from the struggling misery of nineteenth-century London, and from the socialist movement that emerged as a response to it, that the energies of change are seen as being generated: energies of angry rejection; energies of new cooperation and trust. The new social movement, once only a vision, becomes hardened in struggle, as in the experience of Bloody Sunday in Trafalgar Square, and it then finds organizers who can take it through the necessary civil war to the new and peaceful society.

We have only to compare this with, say, Thomson's *Doom of a City* and *City of Dreadful Night* to see the essential change. The judgements are similar, as is the narrative convention. But what has entered and altered the experience is just this historical sense of the growth of a movement. Thomson's social criticism is as harsh, but his observer remains isolated. In Morris the negative energy has found a positive cause.

Wells's vision is harsher. He has added not only an historical but an evolutionary dimension. As he said of *When the Sleeper Awakes*, 1899 (which had developed the formal narrative mode of Thomson or Morris, but taken it, following Edward Bellamy, into a further emphasis of historical movement), it is

> essentially an exaggeration of contemporary tendencies: higher buildings, bigger towns, wickeder capitalists and labour more downtrodden than ever and more desperate (*Experiment in Autobiography* 645).

But more specifically, as in "A Story of the Days to Come" (1899), there is a direct extension of an older vision of the city:

> a vast lunatic growth, producing a deepening torrent of savagery below, and above ever more flimsy gentility and silly wastefulness (384).

This is the vision that had been given an evolutionary dimension in *The Time Machine* (1899), when the "savagery below", of the working poor, has evolved into the blind and brutal Morlocks, and the flimsy silliness of the rich has evolved into the doll-like Eloi, the lay things who are also the Morlocks' food. This image often recurs in different forms: the "nether world" of Gissing has become the underground area of the enslaved workers. The sombre vision of man divided into brute labour and trivial consumption, and then of the city shaped physically to embody these worlds, is expressed again and again. This way of seeing was to have a great influence. One of its most remarkable successors is Lang's film *Metropolis*, in the 1920s.

Wells's sombre vision is then the counterpart of Morris's gentler and more idyllic vision. But just as Morris's ideal cannot be separated from his sense of a new social movement, so Wells's apocalypse cannot be separated from his sense of a new social idea. Each, in its varying forms, has come from the city experience. In Wells the solution is only in part technology, though it is emphatically that: new means of communication and transport will dissolve the hideous concentration of nineteenth-century industrial and metropolitan development; new physical and social settlements will then become practically available. But this depends fundamentally on a new sense of society – what Wells calls "human ecology": a new collective consciousness, scientific and social, which is capable of taking control of an environment in a total way and directing it to human achievement. This dimension of thought is new, and it is provoked by observation of what has been done to men and animals, to the country and the city, by unplanned and ignorant and aggressive development. The new city, when it comes, will be a new world, directed by the new kind of science.

It is important to see these responses of Morris and Wells in this context of the crisis of metropolitan and industrial civilization. Their views have often been described as if they were idle dreaming or voluntary and arrogant projection. Yet they were nearer a real crisis which has both continued and deepened than some subsequent writers who merely reacted against them.

Huxley's *Brave New World* (1931) and Orwell's *Nineteen Eighty-Four* (1949) are still often seen as necessary correctives of the Wellsian response. But they are also "correctives" of the Morris response, and indeed of that whole positive movement of social change. Huxley shows a world which has reached a Morris kind of ease by Wellsian means (scientific breeding, improved production and transport, drugs, a scientific social order). He diagnoses its emptiness and contrasts it with a primitive vision: a new version, owing something to Lawrence, of a simple rural vitality, not innocent now but savage; the rhythms of the blood. Orwell cuts the vision to pieces by showing the socialist movement reaching its climax in Ingsoc, with its totalitarian system of lying, torture and thought police, and with the city in which it is established dirty, half-broken, reduced to perpetual wars. There have been many grounds for these reactions, in the twentieth century, but it is significant that the central crisis, to which Morris and Wells so powerfully responded, is then to an important extent overlooked. The movements of change, rather than the conditions that provoked them, have become the centres of critical interest. In the satisfactions of an often justified criticism, the crisis itself can come to seem secondary. Orwell, as it happens, had in many ways followed Gissing: in his deliberate explorations of urban squalor, to which he responded with some of the same anxious distaste but in the end with a much finer and more generous humanity: a resolution that reached its climax in his celebration of Barcelona, the revolutionary city. In his deep disillusion with the development of socialism, he returned, in his later work, as in *Coming up for Air* (1939) to a vision of the country, the old unspoiled country, as a place of human retreat and rest, an innocence which the new civilization, capitalist or socialist, was aggressively destroying. The shabby, ugly, exposed and lonely city of *Nineteen Eighty-Four* is the result of a perversion of the collective idea.

These were important shifts within a movement of ideas. Yet all the time the crisis itself was becoming more acute and more widespread. What has been, in the early nineteenth century, a primarily English phenomenon, was becoming international and in a sense universal, extending to industrialized Western Europe and North America in the late nineteenth and early twentieth centuries, and in the first half of the twentieth century extending to Asia and Latin America. In the United States, often now seen as a model of metropolitan civilization, the rural population still exceeded the urban as late as 1910, and was only surpassed by it between the wars. In the world as a whole, the population living in towns (over five thousand inhabitants) rose between 1850 and 1950 from seven to almost thirty per cent. More significantly, in the first half of the twentieth century the population living in cities (over a hundred thousand inhabitants) rose at the rate of two hundred and fifty per cent. In many parts of the world, older cities moved into the metropolitan phase, during a period of rapid increase in total population. It was not only a fundamental transformation in the pattern of human settlement. It was also a new kind of exposure: to problems of the relations between population and food; to problems of land-use and pollution; and, deeply affecting the imagination, to kinds of physical mass attack, as in the obliteration bombing of the Second World War and, at its peak, the destruction of cities by atomic bombs. James Thomson had imagined a natural storm which destroyed the city of the stone people. Wells had imagined a Martian attack on London, with the "Black Smoke" and the "Heat Ray": the paralysed inhabitants of the city exposed to this crushing destruction are saved only by the accident of differential bacterial infection. In an epoch of wars, rising populations and international social crisis the image of the city then went through a further rapid development.

This is most evident in what we now call science fiction: the linear descendant of Wells's response to the city. And there was an added element, also developed from Wells: the alternative civilizations of other planets and solar systems. James Thomson, looking from the city to the stars, had written:

> If we could near them with the flight unflown,
> We should but find them worlds as sad as this,
> Or suns all self-consuming like our own
> Enringed by planet worlds as much amiss [...]
>     (*The City of Dreadful Night* 43)[2]

In explicit scientific romance, the opposite feeling – the stars as the new frontier, for the expansion and progress of man – has been an evident element. Glittering cities have been imagined, on a thousand planets, with every kind of technical wonder. (A representative example, drawing directly on Wellsian ideas, is Brian Aldiss's "The Underprivileged"; there is also Arthur C. Clarke's *The City and the Stars*.) There has been also a significant imagining of civilizations which have evolved beyond their urban and technical phases: people living in what one can recognize as the old pastoral places – open country, small villages – but possessing great power because they have internalized the communication and productive capacities of the urban-scientific-industrial phase (Don A. Stuart's "Forgetfulness" is one of many possible examples). Every element of the long history, between country and city, has been projected in these ways.

Yet it is important to notice also a deeply pessimistic projection of the city itself. It is by now a convention. An anthology of future stories, edited by Damon Knight under the conventional title *Cities of Wonder*, contains several examples which are in effect linear descendants of the urban fiction

---

2    RW misquoted slightly.

of the nineteenth century and its transmutation through Wells. There is J.G. Ballard's "Billennium", for example, in which

> ninety-five per cent of the population was permanently trapped in vast urban conurbations. [...] The countryside, as such, no longer existed. Every single square foot of ground sprouted a crop of one type or another. The one-time fields and meadows of the world were now, in effect, factory floors (92).

Or there is the city largely destroyed by bombing and radiation, in Walter M. Miller's "Dumb Waiter": still functioning physically by electronic control from the Central Service Co-ordinator but a dangerous place for men to re-enter and try to salvage. There is the city which to solve its own internal problems of water, food, power and waste-disposal has become, in Henry Kuttner's "Jesting Pilot", "so artificial that [...] nobody could use it" (60),[3] and the survival of its inhabitants is ensured only by collective hypnosis. Such self-enclosed automatic cities, in which the inhabitants cannot believe in a world outside the walls, have been imagined again and again, often with the theme of an attempt to break out into the wild country beyond. An early example is E. M. Forster's "The Machine Stops", which ends with "the whole city [...] broken like a honeycomb" by a crashing airship, while outside "in the mist and the fens" other people, the Homeless, wait to take over, but not to rebuild the destructive machine (140). Or there is the city which has become an organism, as in Robert Abernethy's "Single Combat":

> For three hundred years the city had been growing [...] Like a cancer budding from a few wild cells. [...] As it grew it drew nourishment from a hundred, a thousand miles of hinterland; for the land yielded up its fatness and the forests were mown like grain, and men and animals lived also to feed its ever-increasing hunger [...] as it fed it voided its wastes into the sea and breathed its poisons into the air, and grew fouler as it grew more mighty.
> 
> It developed by degrees a central nervous system of strung wires and buried cables. [...] It evolved from an invertebrate enormity of wild growth to a higher creature having tangible attributes that go with the subjective concepts of *will* and *purpose* and *consciousness* (7–8).

3   RW had Ruttner, but this is a mistake.

Finally, on voyages to Utopia and elsewhere in the galaxy, there are the flying cities of James Blish's *Earthman, Come Home*, moving out into new worlds but recapitulating within their total environments every phase of human history.

These fictions of cities of the future interact, in the mind, with the long fictions of pastoral. But whereas, in the development of pastoral, there was a movement away from the realities of country life, in this city fiction there is an evident overlap with quite different work: in urban sociology and planning; in studies of the government of cities; in work on the physical environment of an industrial and metropolitan civilization: in all of which, though with variations of emphasis, the problems of the city – from traffic to pollution, from social to psychological effects – are often seen as overwhelming and as, in some views, insoluble.

It is a strange situation, because this coexists not only with a still rapid and often unplanned metropolitan growth, but with specific planning on an ever larger scale: linear cities of up to a hundred miles; new cities conceived and built with an established confidence of mapping and projection. There is an evident unevenness in the dominant consciousness. In a sense, it seems, everything about the city – from the magnificent to the apocalyptic – can be believed at once. One source of this unevenness is the complexity of the pressures and the problems. But another source, less easily traced, is the abstraction of the city, as a huge isolated problem, and the traditional images have done much to support this. For what we need to notice, as we look at the facts and the images of the city, is that both have been developed within a wider world history, in which, in a surprising new dimension, both the city and the country have been given new and at first scarcely recognized definitions.

READING 8

# On Orwell: An Interview (1977)

## Editor's Introduction

During June–November 1977 and again in September 1978, Williams was interviewed at length by Perry Anderson, Anthony Barnett, and Francis Mulhern, three members of the editorial committee of the *New Left Review*. The edited transcript of these interviews was published in book form in 1979. Their discussions of Orwell cast light on Williams's own misreadings, which I noted in Reading 6. It is clear here that Williams's private judgements were far more hostile to Orwell and *Nineteen Eighty-Four* than those actually published in his 1971 book. Witness the astonishing admission that "I am bound to say, I cannot read him now." Fortunately, this would not be Williams's last word on the subject.

## On Orwell: An Interview (1977)

NLR: In the case of Orwell, what his writing seems to suggest is an active predisposition from the start to see – not specifically about socialism in the first instance – the dark side of his subject. That was to bring him a certain kind of truth, when he was later writing about the English left or about Soviet Russia. But what is striking is that Orwell seems to have been temperamentally in his element when he was vituperating causes which in another part of himself he hoped to advance. His very tense and ambiguous relationship to socialism is the most obvious, but not the only example of this strain. It pre-existed the political demand, to which Orwell himself never voluntarily accommodated, for parables of the Cold War.

RW: I think the other condition of Orwell's later works was they had to be written by an ex-socialist. It also had to be someone who shared the general discouragement of the generation: an ex-socialist who had become an enthusiast for capitalism could not have had the same effect. The qualification one must make is that the composition of these writings predates the outset of the Cold War – he wrote *Animal Farm* during the period of maximum popularity of the Soviet Union in this country. There was an oppositional element in him which made him the first in the field.

The recruitment of very private feelings against socialism becomes intolerable by *Nineteen Eighty-Four*. It is profoundly offensive to state as a general truth, as Orwell does, that people will always betray each other. If human beings are like that, what could be the meaning of a democratic socialism? But this dimension of Orwell's writing is also a part of a very large form which has even deeper roots than the neutral observer. For the mode of an extreme distaste for humanity of every kind, especially concentrated in figures of the working class, goes back after all to the early Eliot – it was a mode of probably two successive generations and it has not yet exhausted itself. You can see it in Orwell's choice of the sort of working-class areas he went to, the deliberate neglect of the families who were coping – although he acknowledged their existence in the abstract – in favour of the characteristic imagery of squalor: people poking at drains with sticks. His imagination always and submissively goes to that. There is a powerful sense, which I think is theoretically very interesting, but difficult to understand, in which certain literary conventions really dictate modes of observation, not just of writing, although it's in the writing that the effective dictation comes and that what is taken as vivid and convincing and truthful is actually prescribed. In Orwell's Lancashire it is always raining, not because it often does or doesn't, but because it has to do so as a condition of convincing local detail of the North.

NLR: That convention could move, in certain cases, in the opposite direction. For example, the same themes of pervasive disgust can be found in the early Graham Greene. There is a remarkable comparative analysis of Greene and Orwell as novelists, in point of fact, in Terry Eagleton's *Exiles and Emigrés*. Yet if the initial sensibility was not dissimilar, the ideological conclusions were widely divergent – interestingly, on precisely the two questions of British patriotism and international communism. The mediation of a kind of Jansenism has something to do with Greene's development, of course.

RW: It is also that there was more to write Greene than to write Orwell. Because if you take Greene's writing after 1950, you are talking about a different kind of work. Who knows what kind of novel Orwell would have written if he'd turned up in Saigon or in Haiti, where Greene brings that convention to bear on an imperialist situation? We just don't know, and there isn't any point in speculating. A pathetic aspect of the literary world of the fifties and early sixties, in fact, was the imaginary competition to be the heirs of Orwell in the next generation.

NLR: Your book is very controlled and sympathetic in tone towards Orwell, through all its criticisms. Some of your comments now seem sharper. Have you altered your views on his work?

RW: I must say that I cannot bear much of it now. If I had to say which writings have done the most damage, it would be what you call the social patriotism – the dreadful stuff from the beginning of the war about England as a family with the wrong members in charge, the shuffling old aunts and uncles whom we could fairly painlessly get rid of. Many of the political arguments of the kind of labourism that is usually associated with the tradition of Durbin or Gaitskell can be traced to these essays, which are much more serious facts than *Animal Farm*. For all its weaknesses that still makes a point about how power can be lost and how people can be misled: it is defeatist, but it makes certain pointed observations on the procedures of deception. As for *Nineteen Eighty-Four*, its projections of ugliness and hatred, often quite arbitrarily and inconsequentially, onto the difficulties of revolution or political change, seem to introduce a period of really decadent bourgeois writing in which the whole status of human beings is reduced.

I would not write about Orwell in the same way now, partly because I have had more and more doubts about the character he invented. For example, there was no objective reason at all for the disgraceful attacks he made on pacifists or revolutionary opponents of the war in American periodicals, denouncing people here who were simply in his own position of three or four years before. The impression of consistent decency and honesty that Orwell gave went along with the invention of a character who comes up new in each situation, who is able to lose his whole past, and again be looking as the frank, disinterested observer who is simply telling the truth. When he does that to fellow socialists whose position he so recently shared, I can see the basis for a very much harder assessment of this kind of man and this kind of writing. The book was the last stage of working through a sense of questioning respect. I am bound to say, I cannot read him now: at every point it is these bad moves he made that stick in my mind.

READING 9

# On Morris: An Interview (1977)

## Editor's Introduction

Both in *The Highway* in 1956 and in *Culture and Society* in 1958, Williams found Morris's utopia almost as unsatisfactory as Orwell's dystopia. He repeats something of this criticism in the interview with *New Left Review* included below, for example when he describes Morris's treatment of the "discontinuity" between real world and fictional utopia as generating an "untenable" notion of "social simplicity." Interestingly, however, Williams also announces his intention here to look again at representations of utopian discontinuity in Morris, Wells, and subsequent sf. The tone is less than optimistic: Williams hopes to be able to revise his judgement on utopia, but nonetheless expects not to. The results of this inquiry would prove less predictable, however, than Williams anticipated.

## On Morris: An Interview (1977)

NLR: The other figure one wonders if you would still write about in anything like the same way is Morris. Your account of Morris is a very positive one. But one very much feels that there is no break in the texture of your attitude or treatment of Morris within the organization of the book. This has the subtle effect of reassimilating or neutralizing Morris, who is sandwiched between Ruskin and Mallock as if you are just proceeding from one equivalent author to another. Whereas what Morris really represents is the first time that this whole tradition centrally connects with the organized working class and the cause of socialism. That should surely have altered your presentation of him. There were, of course, important arguments afterwards and he did not say the last word on a number of critical questions. But he does occupy a special position, which the book does not exhibit to the reader.

RW: In terms of where he stands I entirely agree with the description you have just made. Morris represents the classic moment of the transvaluation of the tradition. There is a particular problem with him, however. He is rather an isolated figure, if not as wholly isolated as has often been made out. The organization of the book would have been quite different if there had been an alternative line of development following from him. But that did not happen. The confluence he achieved ought to have been much more productive than it was. It is very important to enquire why it was not. On the other hand, reading Edward Thompson's very spirited defence of Morris in the postscript to the new edition of his book on him, I don't find that I take a diametrically different view today of what Morris achieved in his writing as distinct from the crucial confluence that he represented – and the incentive he can still be to that kind of junction. I am trying to do some work at the moment on the introduction of historical break and discontinuity into fictional forms. This involves considering the status of utopian novels. So I will be looking again at Morris and Wells in those terms, as well as at subsequent attempts in science fiction. I would hope to be able to find, but I rather expect I shall not find, that I could revise my judgment of the quality of what follows the realization of discontinuity. Because what the representation of discontinuity typically produces is a notion of social simplicity which is untenable. The extent to which the idea of socialism is attached to that simplicity is counter-productive. It seems to me that the break towards socialism can only be towards an unimaginably greater complexity.

NLR: There is another dimension to Morris, however, besides *News from Nowhere* or *The Dream of John Ball*. You yourself quote a passage that Edward Thompson was to recall frequently, when in an extraordinary flash of historical imagination Morris conjured up something that was to be very much like the becalmed England of the Tory 1950s – when the workers would be "better treated, better organized, helping to govern themselves, but with no more pretence to equality with the rich, nor any more hope for it than they have now." You commented: "This insight into what has been perhaps the actual course of events since his death is a measure of Morris's quality as a political thinker." This must be one of the very few times in the book when you salute somebody for the quality of their political – as opposed to social or cultural – thinking. But you then immediately check the effect of it by going on: "Yet it was no more than an application under new circumstances, of the kind of appraisal which the century's thinking about the meanings of culture had made available." With these abstract phrases – "century" and "culture" – Morris is reintegrated. Their suggestion is that anybody who had absorbed the tradition could have made those predictions. In fact, to do so, Morris had to cross a class divide.

RW: The second sentence is clearly not true. It was not an application to different circumstances. Yet I think Morris had benefited from Ruskin's distinction between an alteration of relations and an alteration of conditions. That meaning had been provided, but Morris's use of it was a political break – you are right there.

PART THREE

# Learning from Le Guin: (Anti-) Postmodernism

READING 10

# Utopia and Science Fiction (1978)

## Editor's Introduction

This essay is clearly Williams's major theoretical statement on sf. Here, he expands on the notion, originally broached in *The Country and the City*, that sf represents a distinctly modern form of utopia and dystopia. There are four characteristic types of alternative reality, he argues: the paradise or hell, the positively or negatively externally altered world, the positive or negative willed transformation, and the positive or negative technological transformation. Sf, utopia, and dystopia are each centrally concerned with the "presentation of *otherness*," Williams continues, and thus depend on an element of discontinuity from "realism." But the discontinuity is more radical in non-utopian/non-dystopian sf, since the utopian and dystopian modes require for their political efficacy an "implied connection" with the real: the whole point of utopia or dystopia is to acquire some positive or negative leverage on the present. By contrast, other kinds of sf and fantasy are free to enjoy greater latitude in their relations to the real. The willed transformation and the technological transformation are therefore the more characteristically utopian or dystopian modes, because transformation – how the world might be changed, whether for better or worse – will normally be more important to utopia than otherness per se. Sf can and does deploy all four modes, but in each case drawing on "'science', in its variable definitions." Sf may be utopian or dystopian, and utopias and dystopias may be science-fictional, but the genres are analytically distinguishable, nonetheless, by virtue of the presence or absence of science (and technology).

Williams is now clear that utopia and dystopia are comparative rather than absolute categories, dealing respectively with "a happier life" and "a more wretched kind of life." Borrowing Miguel Abensour's distinction between "systematic" and "heuristic" utopias, that is, those focussed respectively on alternative organizational models and on alternative values, Williams casts new light on the old controversy between Edward Bellamy and William Morris. If Bellamy's *Looking Backward* had been an essentially systematic utopia, Williams observes, *News from Nowhere* is a "generous but sentimental heuristic transformation." Thus far, the argument runs much as in *Culture and Society*. The difference, however, is in the insistence on what is properly "emergent" in Morris: "the crucial insertion of the *transition* to utopia" as something "fought for." At this point, the heuristic becomes distinctly unsentimental. Much the same occurs in Wells, moreover, and it is in relation to these willed transformations to utopia, Williams continues, that the dystopias of Zamyatin, Huxley, and Orwell need be situated. Orwell's 1984 is neither more nor less plausible than Morris's 2003, he argues, but the latter's fictional revolution of 1952 is more plausible than either "because its energy flows both ways, forward and back." For Williams, this kind of openness – when the "subjunctive is a true subjunctive, rather than a displaced indicative" – powerfully calls into question "the now dominant mode of dystopia" represented paradigmatically in *Nineteen Eighty-Four*.

But this re-evaluation of Morris is not quite Williams's last word on utopia, for he also points to a parallel openness at work in a more immediately contemporary novel, Ursula K. Le Guin's *The Dispossessed*, which won the 1975 Hugo Award. Her anarcho-feminist Anarres is a getaway, rather than a transformation, he observes, but "an open utopia," nonetheless, "shifted, deliberately, from its achieved harmonious condition," thereby "depriving utopia of its classical end of struggle, its image of perpetual harmony and rest." In its very realism, this openness represents a "strengthening" of the utopian impulse, he continues, which "now warily, self-questioningly, and setting its own limits, renews itself."

# Utopia and Science Fiction (1978)

There are many close and evident connections between science fiction and utopian fiction, yet neither, in deeper examination, is a simple mode, and the relationships between them are exceptionally complex. Thus if we analyse the fictions that have been grouped as utopian we can distinguish four types: (a) *the paradise*, in which a happier life is described as simply existing elsewhere; (b) *the externally altered world*, in which a new kind of life has been made possible by an unlooked for natural event; (c) *the willed transformation*, in which a new kind of life has been achieved by human effort; (d) *the technological transformation*, in which a new kind of life has been made possible by a technical discovery.

It will of course be clear that these types often overlap. Indeed the overlap and often the confusion between (c) and (d) are exceptionally significant. One kind of clarification is possible by considering the negative of each type: the negative which is now commonly expressed as "dystopia." We then get: (a) *the hell*, in which a more wretched kind of life is described as existing elsewhere; (b) *the externally altered world*, in which a new but less happy kind of life has been brought about by an unlooked for or uncontrollable natural event; (c) *the willed transformation*, in which a new but less happy kind of life has been brought about by social degeneration, by the emergence or re-emergence of harmful kinds of social order, or by the unforeseen yet disastrous consequences of an effort at social improvement; (d) *the technological transformation*, in which the conditions of life have been worsened by technical development.

Since there can be no *a priori* definition of the utopian mode, we cannot at first exclude any of these dystopian functions, though it is clear that they are strongest in (c) and (d), perceptible in (b), and barely evident in (a), where the negative response to utopia would normally have given way to a relatively autonomous fatalism or pessimism. These indications bear with some accuracy on the positive definitions, suggesting that the element of transformation rather than the more general element of otherness, may be crucial. In the extension to the general category of science fiction we find:

(a) *The paradise or the hell* can be discovered or reached by new forms of travel dependent on scientific and technological (space-travel) or quasi-scientific (time-travel) development. But this is an instrumental function; the mode of travel does not commonly affect the place discovered. The type of fiction is little affected whether the discovery is made by a space voyage or a sea voyage. The place, rather than the journey, is dominant.

(b) *The externally altered world* can be related, construed, foretold in a context of increased scientific understanding of natural events. This also may be an instrumental function only; a new name for an old deluge. But the element of increased scientific understanding may become significant or even dominant in the fiction, for example in the emphasis of natural laws in human history, which can decisively (often catastrophically) alter normal human perspectives.

(c) *The willed transformation* can be conceived as inspired by the scientific spirit, either in its most general terms as secularity and rationality, or in a combination of these with applied science which makes possible and sustains the transformation. Alternatively the same impulses can be negatively valued: the "modern scientific" ant-heap or tyranny. Either mode leaves open the question of the social agency of the scientific spirit and the applied science, though it is the inclusion of some social agency, explicit or implicit (such as the overthrow of one class by another), that distinguishes this type from type (d). We must note also that there are important examples of type (c) in which the scientific spirit and applied science are subordinate to or simply associated with a dominant emphasis on social and political (including revolutionary) transformation; or in which they are neutral with respect to the social and political transformation, which proceeds in its own terms, or, which is of crucial diagnostic significance, where the applied science, though less often the scientific spirit, is positively controlled, modified, or in effect suppressed, in a willing return to a "simpler", "more natural" way of life. In this last mode there are some pretty combinations of very advanced "non-material" science and a "primitive" economy.

(d) *The technological transformation* has a direct relation to applied science. It is the new technology which, for good or ill, has made the new life. As more generally in technological determinism, this has little or no social agency, though it is commonly described as having certain "inevitable" social consequences.

We can now more clearly describe some significant relations between utopian fiction and science fiction, as a preliminary to a discussion of some modern utopian and dystopian writing. It is tempting to extend both categories until they are loosely identical, and it is true that the presentation of *otherness* appears to link them, as modes of desire or of warning in which a crucial emphasis is obtained by the element of discontinuity from ordinary "realism." But this element of discontinuity is itself fundamentally variable. Indeed, what has most to be looked at, in properly utopian or dystopian fiction, is the continuity, the implied connection, which the form is intended to embody. Thus, looking again at the four types, we can make some crucial distinctions which appear to define utopian and dystopian writing (some of these bear also on the separate question of the distinction of science fiction from older and now residual modes which are simply organizationally grouped with it):

(a) *The paradise and the hell* are only rarely utopian or dystopian. They are ordinarily the projections of a magical or a religious consciousness, inherently universal and timeless, thus commonly beyond the conditions of any imaginable ordinary human or worldly life. Thus the Earthly Paradise and the Blessed Islands are neither utopian nor science-fictional. The pre-lapsarian Garden of Eden is latently utopian, in some Christian tendencies; it can be attained by redemption. The medieval *Land of Cokaygne* is latently utopian; it can be, and was, imagined as a possible human and worldly condition. The paradisal and hellish planets and cultures of science fiction are at times simple magic and fantasy: deliberate, often sensational presentations of *alien* forms. In other cases they are latently utopian or dystopian, in the measure of degrees of connection with, extrapolation from, known or imaginable human and social elements.

(b) *The externally altered world* is typically a form which either falls short of or goes beyond the utopian or dystopian mode. Whether the event is magically or scientifically interpreted does not normally affect this. The common emphasis is on human limitation or indeed human powerlessness: the event saves or destroys us, and we are its objects. In Wells's *In the Days of the Comet* the result *resembles* a utopian transformation, but the displacement of agency is significant. Most other examples, of a science-fiction kind, are explicitly or latently dystopian: the natural world deploys forces beyond human control, thus setting limits to or annulling all human achievement.

(c) *The willed transformation* is the characteristic utopian or dystopian mode, in the strict sense.

(d) *The technological transformation* is the utopian or dystopian mode narrowed from agency to instrumentality; indeed it only becomes utopian or dystopian, in strict senses, when it is used as an image of *consequence* to function, socially, as conscious desire or conscious warning.

## "Scientific" and "Utopian"

No contrast has been more influential, in modern thought, than Engels's distinction between "utopian" and "scientific" socialism. If it is now more critically regarded, this is not only because the scientific character of the "laws of historical development" is cautiously questioned or sceptically rejected; to the point, indeed, where the notion of such a science can be regarded as utopian. It is also because the importance of utopian thought is itself being revalued, so that some now see it as the crucial vector of desire, without which even the laws are, in one version, imperfect, and, in another version, mechanical, needing desire to give them direction and substance. This reaction is understandable but it makes the utopian impulse more simple, more singular, than in the history of utopias it is. Indeed the variability of the utopian situation, the utopian impulse, and the utopian result is crucial to the understanding of utopian fiction.

This can be seen from one of the classical contrasts, between More's *Utopia* and Bacon's *New Atlantis*. It is usual to say that these show, respectively, a humanist and a scientific utopia:

that excellent perfection of all good fashions, humanitye and civile gentilnesse (*Utopia*, no pagination);

the end of our foundation is the knowledge of causes and secret motions of things and the enlarging of the bounds of human empire, to the effecting of all things possible (*New Atlantis* 321).

It can be agreed that the two fictions exemplify the difference between a willed general transformation and a technological transformation; that More projects a commonwealth, in which men live and feel differently, while Bacon projects a highly specialized, unequal but affluent and efficient social order. But a full contrast has other levels. Thus they stand near the opposite poles of the utopia of free consumption and the utopia of free production. More's island is a cooperative subsistence economy; Bacon's a specialized industrial economy. These can be seen as permanent alternative images, and the swing towards one or another, in socialist ideology as in progressive utopianism, is historically very significant. One might indeed write a history of modern socialist thought in terms of the swing between a Morean cooperative simplicity and a Baconian mastery of nature, except that the most revealing trend has been their unconscious fusion. Yet what we can now perceive as permanent alternative images was rooted, in each case, in a precise social and class situation. More's humanism is deeply qualified: his indignation is directed as much against importunate and prodigal craftsmen and labourers as against the exploiting and engrossing landlords; his social identification is with the small owners; his laws regulate and protect but also compel labour. It is qualified also because it is static: a wise and entrenched regulation by the elders. It is then socially the projection of a declining class, generalized to a relatively humane but permanent *balance*. Bacon's scientism is similarly qualified: the scientific revolution of experiment and discovery becomes research and development in an instrumental social perspective. Enlarging the bounds of human empire is not only the mastery of nature; it is also, as a social projection, an aggressive, autocratic, imperialist enterprise; the projection of a rising class.

*Nineteenth-Century Utopias*

We cannot abstract desire. It is always desire for something specific, in specifically impelling circumstances. Consider three utopian fictions of the late nineteenth century: Bulwer-Lytton's *The Coming Race* (1871); Edward Bellamy's *Looking Backward* (1888); William Morris's *News from Nowhere* (1890).

*The Coming Race* is at one level an obvious example of the mode of technological transformation. What makes the Vril-ya, who live under our Earth, civilized is their possession of Vril, that all-purpose energy source which lies beyond electricity and magnetism. Outlying underground peoples who do not possess Vril are barbarians; indeed the technology is the civilization, and the improvement of manners and of social relations is firmly based on it alone. The changes thus brought about are the transformation of work into play, the dissolution of the State and in effect the outlawing of competitive and aggressive social relations. Yet it is not, for all the obvious traces of influence, either a socialist or an anarchist utopia. It is a projection of the idealized social attitudes of an aristocracy, now generalized and distanced from the realities of rent and production by the technological determinism of Vril. In its complementary liberation of sexual and family relations (in fact qualified, though apparently emphasized, by the simple reversal of the relative size and roles of women and men) it can be sharply contrasted with the rigidities of these relations within More's humanism. Rut this is of a piece with the aristocratic projection. It is (as in some later fantasies, with similarly privileged assumptions) a separation of personal and sexual relations from those problems of care, protection, maintenance, and security which Vril has superseded. Affluence delivers liberation. By contrast the greed, the aggression, the dominativeness, the coarseness, the vulgarity of the surface world – the world, significantly, both of capitalism and of democracy – are easily placed. They are what are to be expected in a world without Vril and therefore Vril-ya. Indeed there are moments when Vril can almost be compared with Culture, in Matthew Arnold's virtually contemporary *Culture and Anarchy*. Arnold's spiritual aristocracy, his spiritual force beyond all actual classes, has been magically achieved, without the prolonged effort that Arnold described, by the properties of Vril. It is in each case desire, but desire for what? A civilizing transformation, beyond the terms of a restless, struggling society of classes.

What has also to be said, though, about *The Coming Race* is that its desire is tinged with awe and indeed with fear. The title introduces that evolutionary dimension which from this period on is newly available in utopian fiction. When the Vril-ya come to the surface they will simply replace men, as in effect a higher and more powerful species. And it is not only in his unVril humanity that the hero fears this. Towards the end he sounds the note that we shall hear so clearly later in Huxley's *Brave New World*: that something valuable and even decisive – initiative and creativity are the hovering words – has been lost in the displacement of human industry to Vril. This was a question that was to haunt the technological utopia. (Meanwhile, back in nineteenth-century society, an entrepreneur took his own short-cut. Inspired by Lytton he made a fortune from a beef extract called Bovril.)

Bellamy's *Looking Backward* is unquestionably a utopia, in the central sense of a transformed social life of the future, but it is in a significant way a work without desire; its impulse is different, an overriding rationalism, a determining total organization, which finds its proper institutional counterparts in the State-monopoly capitalism which is seen as the inevitable "next stage in the industrial and social development of humanity" (232) (the order of adjectives there is decisive.) That this forecast, rather than vision, was widely taken as an advocacy of socialism is indicative of a major tendency in Bellamy's period, which can be related to Fabianism but has also now to be related to a major current in orthodox Marxism: socialism as the next higher stage of economic organization, a proposition which is taken as overriding, except in their most general terms, questions of substantially different social relations and human motives. Morris's critique of Bellamy repeated almost exactly what is called the Romantic but is more properly the radical critique of utilitarian social models – that "the underlying vice [...] is that the author cannot conceive [...] anything else than the *machinery* of society" (*Political Writings* 250): the central point made in this tradition, from Carlyle's *Signs of the Times* onward. Morris's fuller response was his *News from Nowhere*, but before we look at this we should include a crucial point about the history of utopian writing, recently put forward by Miguel Abensour in his Paris dissertation "Formes de l'utopie Socialiste-Communiste."

*Systematic and Heuristic Futures*

Abensour establishes a crucial periodization in the utopian mode, according to which there is, after 1850, a change from the *systematic* building of alternative organizational models to a more open and *heuristic* discourse of alternative values. E.P. Thompson, discussing Abensour in *New Left Review*, 99 (1976), has interpreted this latter mode as the "education of desire." It is an important emphasis, since it allows us to see more clearly by contrast, how some examples of the mode of "willed social transformation" can be shifted, in their essence, to the mode of "technological transformation", where the technology need not be only a marvellous new energy source, or some industrial resource of that kind, but can be also a new set of laws, new abstract property relations, indeed precisely new *social machinery*. But then, when we have said this, and recognized the contrasting value of that more heuristic mode in which the substance of new values and relations is projected, with comparatively little attention to institutions, we have to relate the change to the historical situation within which it occurred. For the shift from one mode to another can be negative as well as positive. To imagine a whole alternative society is not mere model-building, any more than the projection of new feelings and relationships is necessarily a transforming response. The whole alternative society rests, paradoxically, on two quite different social situations: either that of social confidence, the mood of a rising class, which knows, down to detail, that it can replace the existing order; or that of social despair, the mood of a declining class or fraction of a class, which has to create a new heaven because its Earth is a hell. The basis of the more open but also the vaguer mode is different from either. It is a society in which change is happening, but primarily under the direction and in the terms of the dominant social order itself. This is always a fertile moment for what is, in effect, an anarchism: positive in its fierce rejection of domination, repression, and manipulation; negative in its willed neglect of structures, of continuity and of material constraints.

The systematic mode is, then, often a response to tyranny or disintegration; the heuristic mode, by contrast, seems often to be primarily a response to a constrained reformism.

It is then not a question of asking which is better or stronger. The heuristic utopia offers a strength of vision against the prevailing grain; the systematic utopia a strength of conviction that the world really can be different. The heuristic utopia, at the same time, has the weakness that it can settle into isolated and in the end sentimental "desire", a mode of living with alienation, while the systematic utopia has the weakness that, in its insistent organization, it seems to offer little room for any recognizable life. These strengths and weaknesses vary, of course, in individual examples of each mode, but they vary most decisively, not only in the periods in which they are written but in the periods in which they are read. The mixed character of each mode then has much to do with the character of the twentieth-century dystopias which have succeeded them. For the central contemporary question about the utopian modes is why there is a progression, within their structures, to the specific reversals of a Zamyatin, a Huxley, an Orwell – and of a generation of science-fiction writers.

*News From Nowhere*

It is in this perspective that we have now to read *News from Nowhere*. It is commonly diagnosed and criticized as a generous but sentimental heuristic transformation. And this is substantially right, of the parts that are made ordinarily to stick in the mind. The medievalism of visual detail and the beautiful people in the summer along the river are indeed inextricable from the convincing openness and friendliness and relaxed cooperation. But these are residual elements in the form: the Utopians, the Houyhnhnms, the Vril-ya would have found Morris's people cousins at least, though the dimensions of universal mutuality have made a significant difference. But what is emergent in Morris's work, and what seems to me increasingly the strongest part of *News from Nowhere*, is the crucial insertion of the *transition* to utopia, which is not discovered, come across, or projected – not even, except at the simplest conventional level, dreamed – but fought for.

Between writer or reader and this new condition is chaos, civil war, painful and slow reconstruction. The sweet little world at the end of all this is at once a result and a promise; an offered assurance of "days of peace and rest" (*News from Nowhere* 182), after the battle has been won.

Morris was strong enough, even his imagined world is at times strong enough, to face this process, this necessary order of events. But when utopia is not merely the alternative world, throwing its light on the darkness of the intolerable present, but lies at the far end of generations of struggle and of fierce and destructive conflict, its perspective, necessarily, is altered. The post-religious imagining of a harmonious community and the enlightened rational projection of an order of peace and plenty have been replaced, or at least qualified, by the light at the end of the tunnel, the sweet promise which sustains effort and principle and hope through the long years of revolutionary preparation and organization. This is a genuine turning-point. Where the path to utopia was moral redemption or rational declaration – that light on a higher order which illuminates an always present possibility – the mode itself was radically different from the modern mode of unavoidable conflict and resolution.

Morris's chapters "How the Change Came" and "The Beginning of the New Life" are strong and convincing. "Thus at last and by slow degrees we get pleasure into our work" (319). This is not the perspective of reformism, which in spirit, in its evasion of fundamental conflicts and sticking points, is much nearer the older utopian mode. It is the perspective of Revolution – not only the armed struggle but the long and uneven development of new social relations and human feelings. That they have been developed, that the long and difficult enterprise has succeeded, is crucial; it is the transition from dream to vision. But it is then reasonable to ask whether the achieved new condition is not at least as much rest after struggle – the relaxed and quiet evening after a long, hard day – as any kind of released new energy and life. The air of late Victorian holiday is made to override the complexities, the divergences, the everyday materialities of any working society. When the time-dreamer finds himself fading, as he looks in on the feast at the old church, the emotions are very complex: the comforting recall of a medieval precedent – "the church-ales of the Middle Ages" (398); the wrench of regret that he cannot belong to this new life; and then also, perhaps, for all the convinced assent to the sight of the burdens having been lifted, the impulse – and is it only unregenerate? – of an active, engaged, deeply vigorous mind to register the impression, though it is put into a voice from the future, "that our happiness even would weary you" (401). It is the fused and confused moment of different desires and impulses: the longing for communism, the longing for rest and the commitment to urgent, complex, vigorous activity.

## Conflict and Dystopia

When utopia is no longer an island or a newly discovered place, but our familiar country transformed by specific historical change, the mode of imagined transformation has fundamentally changed. But the historical agency was not only, as in Morris, revolution. It was also, as in Wells, some kind of modernizing, rationalizing force: the vanguard of Samurai, of scientists, of engineers, of technical innovators. Early rationalist utopias had, in the manner of Owen, only to be declared to be adopted; reason had that inevitability. Wells, though refusing popular revolution, belonged to his time in seeing agency as necessary, and there is a convincing match between the kind of agency he selected – a type of social engineering plus a rapidly developing technology – and the point of arrival: a clean, orderly, efficient and planned (controlled) society. It is easy to see this now as an affluent state capitalism or monopoly socialism; indeed many of the images have been literally built. But we can also, holding Morris and Wells together in our minds, see a fundamental tension within the socialist movement itself – indeed in practice within even revolutionary socialism. For there are other vanguards than those of Wells, and the Stalinist version of the bureaucratic Party, engineering a future which is primarily defined as technology and production, not only has its connections to Wells but has to be radically distinguished from the revolutionary socialism of Morris and of Marx, in which new social and human relations, transcending the deep divisions of industrial capitalist specialization, of town and country, of rulers and ruled, administrators and administered, are from the beginning the central and primary objective. It is within a complex of contemporary tendencies – of efficient and affluent capitalism set against an earlier capitalist poverty and disorder; of socialism against capitalism in either phase; and of the deep divisions, within socialism itself, between the reformist free-riders with capitalism, the centralizing social engineers, and the revolutionary democrats – that we have to consider the mode of dystopia, which is both written and read within this extreme theoretical and practical complexity.

Thus Huxley's *Brave New World* (1932) projects a black amalgam of Wellsian rationality and the names and phrases of revolutionary socialism in a specific context of mobile and affluent corporate capitalism. This sounds and is confused, but the confusion is significant; it is the authentic confusion of two generations of science fiction itself, in its powerful dystopian mode. "COMMUNITY, IDENTITY, STABILITY": this is the motto of the *Brave New World* State (1). It is interesting to track these ideals back into the utopian mode. Stability, undoubtedly, has a strong bearing; most of the types of utopia have strongly emphasized it, as an achieved perfection or a self-adjusting harmony. Huxley adds the specific agencies of repression, manipulation, pre-natal conditioning, and drugged distraction. Western science fiction has been prolific in its elaboration of all these agencies: the models, after all, have been close to hand. Stability blurs to Identity: the manufacture of human types to fit the stabilized model; but this, crucially, was never an explicit utopian mode, though in some examples it is assumed or implied. Variability and autonomy, within the generally harmonious condition, are indeed among the primary utopian features. But now, under the pressures of consumer capitalism and of monopoly socialism, the mode has broken. As in the later stages of realist fiction, self-realization and self-fulfilment are not to be found in relationship or in society, but in breakaway, in escape: the path the Savage takes, like a thousand heroes of late-realist fiction, getting out from under the old place, the old people, the old family, or like a thousand science-fiction heroes, running to the wastes to escape the machine, the city, the system.

But then the last and most questionable irony: the first word of the motto of this repressive, dominating, controlling system is Community: the keyword, centrally, of the entire utopian mode. It is at this point that the damage is done or, to put it another way, is admitted. It is in the name of Community, the utopian impulse, and in the names of communism

# Utopia and Science Fiction (1978)

(Bernard Marx and Lenina) that the system is seen as realized, though the actual tendencies – from the degradation of labour through an ultimate division and specialization to the organized mobility and muzak of planned consumption – rely for their recognition on a contemporary capitalist world. In his 1946 foreword Huxley continued his running together of historically contrary impulses but then, interestingly, returned to utopia, offering a third way beyond the incubator society and the primitive reservation: a self-governing and balanced community, little different in spirit from Morris's future society except that it is limited to "exiles and refugees", people escaping from a dominant system which they have no chance or hope of changing collectively. Utopia then lies at the far end of dystopia, but only a few will enter it; the few who get out from under. This is the path travelled, in the same period, by bourgeois cultural theory: from the universal liberation, in bourgeois terms, through the phase in which the minority first educates and then regenerates the majority, to the last sour period in which what is now called "minority culture" has to find its reservation, its hiding-place, beyond both the system and the fight against the system.

But then what is so strange is that this last phase, in some writing, returns to the utopian mode, throwing strange questions back to the whole prior tradition: questions which disturb the apparently simple grammar of desire – that desire for another place and another time which, instead of being idealized, can be seen as always and everywhere a displacement, but which can itself be transformed when a history is moving.

> Not in Utopia, subterranean fields,
> Or some secreted island, Heaven knows where!
> But in the very world, which is the world
> Of all of us, – the place where in the end
> We find our happiness, or not at all!
>     (Wordsworth, "French Revolution" 166)[1]

---

1    RW misquoted slightly.

Wordsworth's emphasis, it is true, can go either way: into revolutionary effort, when history is moving; into a resigned settlement when it goes wrong or gets stuck. The utopian mode has to be read, always, within that changing context, which itself determines whether its defining subjunctive mood is part of a grammar which includes a true indicative and a true future, or whether it has seized every paradigm and become exclusive, in assent and dissent alike.

For the same consideration puts hard questions to the now dominant mode of dystopia. Orwell's 1984 is no more plausible than Morris's 2003, but its naturalized subjunctive is more profoundly exclusive, more dogmatically repressive of struggle and possibility, than anything within the utopian tradition. It is also, more sourly and more fiercely than in Huxley, a collusion, in that the state warned against and satirized – the repression of autonomy, the cancellation of variations and alternatives – is built into the fictional form which is nominally its opponent, converting all opposition into agencies of the repression, imposing, within its excluding totality, the inevitability and the hopelessness which it assumes as a result. No more but perhaps no less plausible than Morris's 2003; but then, in the more open form, there is also Morris's 1952 (the date of the revolution), and the years following it: years in which the subjunctive is a true subjunctive, rather than a displaced indicative, because its energy flows both ways, forward and back, and because in its issue, in the struggle, it can go either way.

*New Heavens and Hells*

The projection of new heavens and new hells has been a commonplace in science fiction. Yet perhaps a majority of them, just because they are so often literally out of this world, are functions of fundamental alteration: not merely the intervention of altered circumstance, which in the type of the externally altered world is a minor mode of the utopian, but a basic recasting of the physical conditions of life and thence of its life forms. And then in most stories this is a simple exoticism, generically tied to the supernatural or magical romance. There is a range from casual to calculated fantasy, which is at the opposite pole from the hypothesized "science" of science fiction. Yet, perhaps inextricable from this genre, though bearing different emphases, there is a mode which is truly the result of a dimension of modern science: in natural history, with its radical linkages between life-forms and life-space; and in scientific anthropology, with its methodological assumption of distinct and alternative cultures. The interrelation between these is often significant. The materialist tendency of the former is often annulled by an idealist projection at the last, mental phase of the speculation; the beast or the vegetable, at the top of its mind, is still a human variation. The differential tendency of the latter, by contrast, is often an overriding of material form and condition: an overriding related to idealist anthropology, in which alternatives are in effect wholly voluntary. Yet it is part of the power of science fiction that it is always potentially a mode of authentic shift: a crisis of exposure which produces a crisis of possibility; a reworking, in imagination, of *all* forms and conditions.

In this at once liberating and promiscuous mode, science fiction as a whole has moved beyond the utopian; in a majority of cases, it is true, because it has also fallen short of it. Most direct extrapolation of our own conditions and forms – social and political but also immanently material – has been in effect or in intention dystopian: atomic war, famine, overpopulation, electronic surveillance have written 1984 into millennia of possible dates. To live otherwise, commonly, is to be other and elsewhere: a desire displaced by alienation and in this sense cousin to phases of the utopian, but without the specific of a connected or potentially connecting transformation and then again without the ties of a known condition and form. So that while the utopian transformation is social and moral, the science-fiction transformation, in its dominant Western modes, is at once beyond and beneath: not social and moral but natural; in effect, as so widely in Western thought since the late nineteenth century, a mutation at the point of otherwise intolerable exposure and crisis: not so much a new life as a new species, a new nature.

It is then interesting, within this largely alternative mode, to find a clear example of an evidently deliberate return to the utopian tradition, in Ursula K. Le Guin's *The Dispossessed* (1974). It is a return within some of the specific conditions of science fiction. The alternative society is on the moon of a far planet, and space-travel and electronic communication – to say nothing of the possibilities of the "ansible", that device for instantaneous space-wide communication developed from the theory of simultaneity – permit interaction between the alternative and the original society, within a wider interaction of other galactic civilizations. At one level the spaceship and the ansible can do no more, technically, than the sea voyage, the cleft in the underground cavern or, crucially, the dream. But they permit, instrumentally, what is also necessary for another and more serious reason: the sustained comparison of the utopian and the non-utopian options.

The form of the novel, with its alternating chapters on Anarres and Urras, is designed for this exploratory comparison. And the reason is the historical moment of this looking again at utopia: the moment of renewed social and political hope, of a renewed alternative social and political morality, in a context which has one variable from the ordinary origins of the utopian mode, that within the world in which the hope is being interestedly if warily examined there is not, or apparently not, the overwhelming incentive of war, poverty, and disease. When Morris's dreamer goes back from twenty-first to nineteenth century London the questions are not only moral; they are directly physical, in the evidently avoidable burdens of poverty and squalor. But when Le Guin's Shevek goes from Anarres to Urras he finds, within the place provided for him, an abundance, an affluence, a vitality, which are sensually overwhelming in comparison with his own moral but arid world. It is true that when he steps out of his privileged place and discovers the class underside of this dominant prosperity the comparison is qualified, but that need only mean that the exuberant affluence depends on that class relationship and that the alternative is still a shared and equal relative poverty. It is true also that the comparison is qualified, in the novel as a whole, by what is in effect a note that our own civilization – that of Earth, which in its North American sector Urras so closely and deliberately resembles – has been long destroyed: "appetite" and "violence" destroyed it; we did not "adapt" in time; some survivors live under the ultimate controls of "life in the ruins" (286–287). But this, strictly, is by the way. Urras, it appears, is not in such danger; Anarres remains a social and moral option, a human alternative to a society that is, in its extended dominant forms, successful. Yet it is among its still repressed and rejected that the impulse stirs, renewing itself, after a long interval, to follow the breakaway revolution, anarchist and socialist, which took the Odonians from Urras to a new life on Anarres. Shevek's journey is the way back and the way forward: a dissatisfaction with what has happened in the alternative society but then a strengthened renewal of the original impulse to build it. In two evident ways, then, *The Dispossessed* has the marks of its period: the wary questioning of the utopian impulse itself, even within its basic acceptance; the uneasy consciousness that the superficies of utopia – affluence and abundance – can be achieved, at least for many, by non-utopian and even anti-utopian means.

The shift is significant, after so long a dystopian interval. It belongs to a general renewal of a form of utopian thinking – not the education but the learning of desire – which has been significant among Western radicals since the struggles and also since the defeats of the 1960s. Its structures are highly specific. It is a mode within which a privileged affluence is at once assumed and rejected: assumed and in its own ways enjoyed, yet known, from inside, as lying and corrupt; rejected, from in close, because of its successful corruption; rejected, further out, by learning and imagining the condition of the excluded *others*. There is then the move to drop out and join the excluded; a move to get away, to get out from under, to take the poorer material option for a clear moral advantage. For nothing is more significant, in Le Guin's contrasted worlds, than that Anarres, the utopia, is bleak and arid; the prosperous vitality of the classical utopia is not there but in the existing society that is being rejected. This is a split of a major kind. It is not that Anarres is primitivist: "they knew that their anarchism was the product of a very high civilization, of a complex diversified culture, of a stable economy and a highly industrialized technology" (81). In this sense, the modification of Morris is important; it is clearly a future and not a past, a technically advanced rather than a simplified form. But it is significantly only available in what is in effect a waste land; the good land is in the grip of the Urrasti dominance. It is then in effect the movement that Huxley imagined, in his 1946 foreword. It is not the transformation, it is the getaway.

Yet it is a generous and open getaway, within the limited conditions of its waste-land destination. The people of Anarres live as well, in all human terms, as Morris's cooperators; mutuality is shown to be viable, in a way all the more so because there is no abundance to make it easy. The social and ethical norms are thus at the highest point of the utopian imagination. But then there is a wary questioning beyond them: not the corrosive cynicism of the dystopian mode, but a reaching beyond basic mutuality to new kinds of individual responsibility and, with them, choice, dissent, and conflict. For this, again of its period, is an open utopia: forced open, after the congealing of ideals, the degeneration of mutuality into conservatism; shifted, deliberately, from its achieved harmonious condition, the stasis in which the classical utopian mode culminates, to restless, open, risk-taking experiment. This is a significant and welcome adaptation, depriving utopia of its classical end of struggle, its image of perpetual harmony and rest. This deprivation, like the waste land, may be seen as daunting, as the cutting-in of elements of a dominant dystopia. But whereas the waste land is voluntary deprivation, by the author – the product of a defeatist assessment of the possibilities of transformation in good and fertile country – the openness is in fact a strengthening. Indeed it is probably only to such a utopia that those who have known affluence and known with it social injustice and moral corruption can be summoned. It is not the last journey. In particular it is not the journey which all those still subject to extreme exploitation, to avoidable poverty and disease, will imagine themselves making: a transformed this-world, of course with all the imagined and undertaken and fought-for modes of transformation. But it is where, within a capitalist dominance, and within the crisis of power and affluence which is also the crisis of war and waste, the utopian impulse now warily, self-questioningly, and setting its own limits, renews itself.

READING 11

# The Tenses of Imagination (1978)

## Editor's Introduction

This essay was originally presented in lecture form at the University of Wales, Aberystwyth. It takes up and elaborates on some of the issues raised for Williams by Le Guin's *The Dispossessed*. At an important stage in certain kinds of future story, Williams observes, "a writer sits and *thinks*; assembles and deploys variables." This is so, moreover, even when "the factors are only partly known" and their interaction "is quite radically uncertain." Such is the case with *The Dispossessed*, he continues, for here there is evidence "of deliberate and sustained thought about possible futures." His point is that Le Guin's thinking is deliberate and sustained, rather than "sentimental," in Abensour's terms, and directed toward the possible, rather than the "untenable." What had been a moment only in Morris – essentially chapters XVII and XVIII of *News from Nowhere* – thus informs the whole life of Le Guin's "Odonian" utopia.

Williams's interest in Le Guin warrants three further observations. First, it should be apparent that this enthusiasm for "realistic" utopias and utopian "realism" clearly rehearses his earlier sympathy for "space anthropology." In 1956, he had conceived the latter as quite distinct from utopia and dystopia. By 1978, however, he had come to realize that utopian plausibility requires something very much like it. It is a truism, but nonetheless true, that Le Guin's Hainish novels exhibit an extraordinary richness of precisely such "anthropological" detail, in their treatment of myth and language, kinship, child-rearing, and so on. If that is perhaps less true of *The Dispossessed* than of *The Left Hand of Darkness*, *The Word for World is Forest* or *The Telling*, it is still clearly this very quality which makes Anarres so believable. Second,

Williams's sense of what was different about *The Dispossessed* interestingly prefigures what Sargent, Baccolini, Moylan, and others would later write about the "critical dystopias" of late twentieth-century sf (Sargent 7; Baccolini; Moylan, *Scraps of the Untainted Sky* 183–199).

Third, we should note that, unlike *News from Nowhere* or "A Story of the Days to Come" – or indeed Gethen in *The Left Hand of Darkness* – Anarres is unambiguously feminist, if not unambiguously utopian. This is not to suggest that its textual politics are somehow either "ideal" or "correct." There are good arguments to be made against the specific content of its anarcho-feminism. Hence, Samuel R. Delany's conclusion that its excitement lay in "the book's ambition more than its precise accomplishments" (308), a view much echoed elsewhere, for example, in Moylan, who judged it "an important, if flawed, critical utopia" (*Demand the Impossible* 120). The point, however, is not that *The Dispossessed* was some kind of perfectly realized feminist novel, but only the more obvious one that its politics were expressly and explicitly feminist in a way that had not been true of *The Left Hand of Darkness*. This matters if only because Williams's own sexual politics had often been anything but feminist. As one former student, Morag Shiach, wryly observed: "Feminists can find much of use to them in the work of Raymond Williams; they cannot, however, find many women" (51). In his later years, however, Williams had at least begun to make more sympathetic noises: in *Politics and Letters*, for example, he conceded that it had been both a political weakness and an intellectual failing "not to confront the problem" of gender (150); and in *Towards 2000*, he would include feminism amongst his resources of hope. No doubt, the wider feminist movement had itself compelled some of this belated attention. It is possible, however, that Odonian Anarres played some small part of its own.

# The Tenses of Imagination (1978)

Imagination has a history. There are changing and conflicting interpretations of what it is and of its value. Imagination also has a structure, at once grammatical and historical, in the tenses of past, present and future.

Commonsense appears to predicate that it is bad to lack imagination but almost as bad to have or use it too much. This follows from the complex history of the idea. The negative senses are strong and early in English: "full of imagination, of dreads" (1390); "conjecture and ymaginacion" (1460). This is the idea of a mental conception of something not present to the senses, but there was always uncertainty whether this should be valued as vision or dismissed as fantasy. The Latin root word had at first a simple physical sense, the making of images or likenesses; it is linguistically related to the idea of "imitating." It developed a later sense of picturing things to oneself, and it is there that the double judgment starts. As in English in 1576: "they accounted his undoubted divinations madde imaginations." Or as in the lines of *A Midsummer Night's Dream*:

> The lunatic, the lover, and the poet
> Are of imagination all compact.

One sees devils, the next sees beauty where there is none, the next "gives to airy nothing a local habitation and a name", This last sense of "creative imagination" has come through very strongly. It is now one of the two main positive senses, the other being connected with a capacity for sympathy and understanding in the ability to "imagine", to "realize", someone's else situation. Yet in context the "strong imagination" has "tricks", summoning but often mistaking the objects of joy or fear.

The ambiguous valuation has persisted, in spite of attempts on the one hand to distinguish and distance "imagination" from mere "fancy" and on the other hand to distinguish both from "reality" and "facts." "Fabricating images without any foundation in reality is distinguished by the name of imagination", Kames wrote in 1762. "Imagination," Darwin wrote in 1871, "is one of the highest prerogatives of Man. By this faculty he unites, independently of the will, former images and ideas, and thus creates brilliant and novel results." But "facts and not imagination", almost everyone seemed to say, if the occasion suited.

It is not surprising that so powerful and universal a process should have been so variously interpreted. Moreover, there is no simple way of resolving the ambiguity: much that is valuable has been imagined, and much that is worthless and dangerous. Yet at a different level it may be possible to make some different distinctions. In the course of my own work I have often been struck by the varying tenses of imagination. The sense of imagination as working on the past to create some new present is familiar in Darwin's concept and more widely, over a range from associationist psychology to psychoanalysis. The apparently opposite grammatical sense, rooted in ideas of divination but also given different and more rational bases, turns imagination towards the future, towards foreseeing what will or could happen. At the same time one of the strong current positive senses is essentially involved with the present: having enough imagination to understand what it is like to be in some other contemporary condition: bereaved, unemployed, insane.

These are everyday uses and are all important. But in the processes of writing, the considerations and then the actual practices seem to me to be different, and they are different also according to whether the directive tense of the writing is past, present or future. Writers have related in varying ways to the everyday definitions: to the processes of combining images and ideas to create something brilliant and novel; to the process of imagining, down to fine detail, what could happen, given this selection of characters and circumstances; and to the processes of empathy, to be able to write of a condition not directly experienced. All these are involved in different kinds of writing, but there is also a major conflict of ideas, in the long argument about whether imagination, in any of these kinds, produces or can produce things more real than what is ordinarily observable, or whether these are specific processes for "realizing" – embodying in communicable form – what is already, at other levels, undoubtedly real. There is also the popular bypassing of this problem in the idea that imagination creates autonomous objects of art, which have their own rather than some other reality.

## The Tenses of Imagination (1978)

I have thought about these problems, in theory and in practice, but the problems of actual work seem to me quite different. I can give examples only from my own writing, though I think – or imagine – that I notice them also in the work of others. They would not be problems of the same kind if I could believe, like most of my contemporaries, that I am sitting here alone doing the work. I am in fact physically alone when I am writing, and I do not believe, taking it all in all, that my work has been less individual, in that defining and valuing sense, than that of others. Yet whenever I write I am aware of a society and of a language which I know are vastly larger than myself: not simply "out there", in a world of others, but here, in what I am engaged in doing: composing and relating. And if this is so at what can be seen as one end of the process, it seems to be equally true at the other: what is usually defined as what we are "writing about." Many writers talk of researching their fiction, not only for historical novels but for contemporary stories and plays. Even tax inspectors will sometimes make an allowance for travel to get what they nicely call "copy." I can't be sure, but while I have often visited places and people and asked questions, and also looked things up, this has usually seemed quite separate from writing. Even the ideas and experiences you think you are taking to the blank page come out differently, again and again, as you go through the actual practice, which is one of intense and locally isolated concentration and yet, at the same time, as I have experienced it, a condition of active presence – assisting and resisting – of the wider forces of a language and a society.

I have tried to understand this after the work has been done. For example my "Welsh Trilogy" – *Border Country*, *Second Generation* and *The Fight for Manod* – has a simple structure of past, present and future. This covers the actual periods of the action; a succession of fathers and sons; even the forms of transport that are among the most evident social relations. Yet I could not get *Border Country* right until it was more than the past – the period of *my* childhood. I had to make that past present in the fully independent and contemporary figure of a father: in fact, as it turned out, two fathers, to make an inherited choice of directions actual. But then this was eventually accessible because it was a lived past. For the sequence during the General Strike I could go to my father's direct memories and to the documents he had kept. Yet I had then to invent episodes which activated the sequence, as distinct from what can happen in memories – especially prepared memories, *memoirs* – when what is there is the summary product. There is then also the process – obvious but quite hard in practice – of seeing this happening to a young man rather than to the old man who is telling you about it. Yet still, while the voice is there, the past has this living connection.

It is proving very different in the trilogy I am now writing, on a vastly greater timescale, following a place and its peoples through very long changes: what I think of as historical rather than as period novel-writing. Its only living connections are the physical presence of the mountains in which and under which so many different kinds of life have been lived, and the physical inheritors of all these lives, who are however *not* historically aware of them, whose memories are recent and whose projections, beyond those memories, are usually (not through their fault; it is what has passed for education) vague and wrong. My wife and I have done long research for these novels: research in archaeology and history and in exploration. It has often proved possible to find a real and surprising base: a different physical landscape, different and yet precise kinds of work and living.

Yet what is then involved in making people move and speak on that base – people "like ourselves" when the point is so often that they are at once very like and very unlike, and differently so as the real history of the place develops: is that imagination? I suppose it must be; it certainly feels like it, not least in its practical surprises, in what has actually got onto the page. Yet much of the time it is as if prolonged thinking about what I have called the base, especially when this is done, far away from books, on the actual ground, however altered, where it all happened, is not imagination in that inventive sense at all, though of course one is literally inventing. It feels, rather, like some kind of contact, and not irrationally so; like some authentic information, stressing every syllable of that word. Then later of course you have to check up and see if you got the discoverable facts right or at least not wrong: facts that are the condition but only the condition of these other lives that you think you have begun to feel move.

I was recently trying to compare this with what at first sight seems most different from it: the experience of writing a consciously contemporary novel, begun in Oxford on a city much like Oxford, with its places and kinds of work and kinds of people all around me. "Kinds of people": that was where I hesitated and then took the experience across. For if you read the novel *Second Generation* back, from the finished product – and this is the normal procedure for most people who write about what they call imaginative works – you can see a fairly clear set of social relationships, positive and negative, between the car factory and the university in a single city, and these relationships as embodied in people who, however sharply individualized, are social figures of that set of relationships: liberal don and working-class graduate student; shop steward and his politically and intellectually ambitious wife; the non-political home-centred worker and his family-centred wife. I am forcing myself to describe them in these abstract ways, as a way of facing the problem that this is how they might or even should be construed when in conscious practice nothing of that kind of thinking happened at all. Of course I was strongly aware of what I have been calling the base: the strong social, economic and cultural contrasts between the people around the car factory and the people around the university. At an important level I sought to inform myself more fully about the kinds of life being lived: visiting the car factory and talking to people who worked there as well as more consciously observing the university and political circles in which I had a more connected presence. But still there, in an actual city and in an immediate present, this base was only fully relevant at an early and then at a late stage of the writing: preparation and checking, one might say, though each process is more complicated than that. Indeed it was not so very different, in that available actuality, from the later situation in a much more distant, relatively unknown past. But then how can this be so?

I can say only that what seems to happen is the emergence of a structure of feeling. This is a phrase I have used in analysing works written by others, when I know little or nothing of their making but only what has been made. It is a difficult phrase and idea, but it comes much nearer the experience than any other I know. For I remember being preoccupied, before either the car factory or the university was there as material for writing, with that extension of the father-son relationship which comes through as a movement of generations. I was engaged by the experience which I once tried to describe as having, simultaneously, a loved physical father and a quite different "social father", who in a time of exceptional social and especially educational mobility was taking on many of a real father's functions: passing on knowledge and experience and judgments and values in this differently constituted and discontinuous social situation. Father and son, tutor and student: the relationships are in different dimensions but both, in these circumstances, are real and can become confused.

The simpler structure of feeling of *Border Country*, within a relatively more stable world which had nevertheless been brought to a point of radical choice of values and ways to live, was at once connected and suddenly much more complicated, and the complication soon settled in the figure of the mother: intellectually ambitious but without her son's apparently defined place and role. That mother, necessarily, invoked another mother, so that Kate and Myra were there with Harold and Robert Lane and Arthur Dean. And then what happened was what writers often describe, that certain characters and situations were being strongly felt, and the base which was there both before and after them was where they lived rather than where they were lived from.

Perhaps that has to happen, if the people are to come through, but I am not persuaded by some reductive accounts of the process, in which persons, "individuals", simply materialize, in a creative alchemy, any more than I am persuaded by the theoretically opposite reductive accounts, in which the writer reads the real structure of the society and then sets figures to it: types who are then personalized. What I have called the structure of feeling seems to me different from either kind of account. It is strongly felt from the beginning, in the way that important actual relationships are felt, but also it is a structure and this, I believe, is a particular kind of response to the real shape of a social order: not so much as it can be documented – though it ought never, I think, to contradict the documentation – but as it is in some integrated way apprehended, without any prior separation of private and public or individual and social experience.

Moreover, so far as I can understand it, this process is not distillation or novel association; it is a formation, an active formation, that you feel your way into, feel informing you, so that in general and in detail it is not very like the usual idea of imagination – "imagine if ...", "imagine that ..."

## The Tenses of Imagination (1978)

– but seems more like a kind of recognition, a connection with something fully knowable but not yet known.

There must, all the same, be a radical difference in how this happens as it relates on the one hand to societies in which you are living and then to other societies which are at some significant difference in time. I have known this difference, in obvious ways, in trying to approach a kind of life in which, for example, the land was not known and named but was being explored, or in which very different kinds of primary relationship were decisive: the kind of hunting group or family, for example, in which people were close and loving but where the need to abandon a crippled boy or to be pressed, by custom and scarcity, to female infanticide had to be felt not only as alien and distant but as *recognized* in actual people and situations. Perhaps across such distances it is not possible, yet I have not so far found it so. I know that I am getting beyond my own life, as those structures of feeling form, but in a lesser degree that was also what was happening even when writing about contemporary life in a known place. Either past or present, in their ordinary and reasonable temporal senses, seems to have to go through this other process before, as we say, people begin to move and speak. There may be a very general idea of what one is doing, but all the active and detailed formation seems to happen somewhere else. People may call the results "imagination", and if the connection really happens "imaginative", but this is where the matter of tense comes in again, for something very different is involved if a writer tries to "imagine" the future: to "project" a future, as it is often put.

I am fascinated by the forms of "future fiction", just as much as by that other large area of "science fiction" – the very best of it anyway – in which what I see happening is a structure of feeling formed as some alien life and environment. Often this stands out more sharply than the structure of feeling, even a very similar structure, which in the course of writing has been saturated in known and recognizable and connecting detail: our everyday, which can seem and sometimes be the whole object, and is then so different from that distant and surprising and discontinuous "science fiction" world. I have no direct experience of making that kind of work, though I respect its obviously "imaginative" reach. But I have now twice – in *The Fight for Manod* and in *The Volunteers* – set novels ahead of their time of writing: in one case more as a plan, in the other case – deliberately and discontinuously – as an action.

I may be wrong but I found in these two very different cases that something much nearer the ordinary idea of imagination was directly involved. I mean that at some important stage, in work with the future tense, a writer sits and *thinks*; assembles and deploys variables; even constructs what in secular planning are called "scenarios", in the interplay of this and that projected factor, when even the factors are only partly known – their degree of development can be variably estimated – and when their interaction – bringing this factor up, fading that down – is quite radically uncertain. It can of course be argued, and in many cases demonstrated from actual works, that the structures which are projected and realized are usually no more than reproductions of existing structures in externally altered circumstances – the trivial case of those American stories in which Planet Earth encounters aliens through a President and corporations in Washington and New York is only an example of hundreds of more serious cases. Even some of the more surprising futures, in Huxley and Orwell for example, can be shown to rest on striking *interpretations* of the present, from which countervailing or mitigating factors are simply excluded: a negative present, you might say, rather than a positive future.

But beyond reproduction and interpretation there do seem to be cases – Le Guin's *The Dispossessed* is an example – in which there is evidence both of deliberate and sustained thought about possible futures and then, probably both preceding and succeeding this, the discovery of a structure of feeling which, within the parameters of that thought, is in its turn a form of recognition. In *The Fight for Manod* I tried to include some of the relevant thinking and argument about a possible future, but without any convention of cut-off from the present. The whole point of that novel was the relation between necessary and desirable plans for the future and at once the ways in which they get distorted and frustrated and the even more complex ways in which they relate to what is already lived and known and valued. In *The Volunteers* I used a degree of cut-off from the present, to get an action in which both received and abstract values were tested without the familiar context of supporting and reliable institutions embodying them: a possible near future, I then thought, and with whatever variation of date and detail, I am not yet persuaded it was other than closely possible.

In any real future tense, then, what we call imagination seems more like the usual accounts of it than in either present or past tenses. We speculate, we project, we attempt to divine, we figure. The actual writing that goes with that dimension is in its turn distinctive: more general; more immediately accessible to ideas; often more angular and more edged; relatively low in the kind of saturation by detailed and unlooked-for experiences so common and ordinarily so valued in the other tenses. I do not want to turn a contrast of kinds into some order of merit. Each kind of writing does quite different work. But if that is a recognizable kind of imagination – over a range from the secular and political to the solidly traditional and the surprisingly private visions and divinations – there is a problem in using not just the same word but the same concept, pointing to the same general process, in the other tenses. The problem is already there, however, in the everyday range of the word. The mental concept of something not present to the senses, which corresponds to future-writing and to many kinds of fantasy, coexists in the language with the sense of empathy, of feeling our way into a situation which in a general way we know but which we can come to know as it were from the inside – a sense which I think is not far from the idea of discovering and being moved by a structure of feeling within what is already nominally and even carefully known. Yet if the word can be applied to either process, the real processes are still different, and the key difference, as it matters in writing, seems to me essentially a matter of real tense.

There are periods in a culture when what we call real knowledge seems to have to take priority over what is commonly called imagination. In our own image-conscious politics and commerce there is a proliferation of small instrumental professions which claim the sonorous titles of imagination and creativity for what are, when examined, simple and rationalized processes of reproduction and presentation. To know what is happening, in the most factual and down-to-earth ways, is indeed an urgent priority in such a world. A militant empiricism claims all; in a world of rearmament and mass unemployment seems rightly to claim all. Yet it is now the very bafflement and frustration of this militant empiricism, and especially of the best of it, that should hold our attention. It can quickly identify its enemies among the hired image-makers, the instrumental projectors of the interests of wealth and power. But now, very clearly, there are other deeper forces at work, which perhaps only imagination, in its full processes, can touch and reach and recognize and embody. If we see this, we usually still hesitate between tenses: between knowing in new ways the structures of feeling that have directed and now hold us, and finding in new ways the shape of an alternative, a future, that can be genuinely imagined and hopefully lived. There are many other kinds of writing in society, but these now – of past and present and future – are close and urgent, challenging many of us to try both to understand and to attempt them.

READING 12

# Beyond Actually Existing Socialism (1980)

## Editor's Introduction

This essay is an extended review, written by Williams for the *New Left Review*, of the first English translation of Rudolf Bahro's *Die Alternative. Zur Kritik des real existierenden Sozialismus*. Bahro wrote *Die Alternative* from inside Communist East Germany, partly as a response to the Russian invasion of Czechoslovakia in 1968. He smuggled the manuscript out to the West, where it was published in 1977. He was arrested more or less immediately and imprisoned as a Western spy until 1979, when he was released and deported. Bahro's leftist critique of Eastern Communism is both a premonition of the left opposition that would eventually bring down the regime and a precursor of the Green politics that would later challenge the Social Democratic Party's dominance over the West German Left. Bahro himself became a founder member of the German Green Party in 1980, but resigned only five years later in protest against the party's growing electoralism. In his last years, he was increasingly associated with what is sometimes dismissed as Green fundamentalism. He was diagnosed with cancer in 1995, possibly a result of the radioactive contamination of his manuscripts by the East German State Security, and died in 1997.

Like Herbert Marcuse and others in the Western New Left, Williams was overwhelmingly sympathetic to Bahro's politics. Interestingly, Williams's judges Bahro's own self-declared utopianism "unlikely." This is so, it immediately becomes clear, because Williams considers Bahro's vision both "practical and possible." "Bahro is not a utopian," he writes, but rather someone who "thinks through, in unusually sustained detail, the processes of transformation of conditions and needs." This is itself something very close to his own procedures in *The Long Revolution*. Close too, we might now add, to their eventual resumption and extension in *Towards 2000*. But if practicality alone distinguishes Bahro's and Williams's alternatives from utopianism, then what if they, too, prove impractical, as they surely have, at least to date? Bahro's claim that "utopian thought has a new necessity" might then be more persuasive than Williams allows.

## Beyond Actually Existing Socialism (1980)

"Communism is not only necessary, it is also possible." The quiet words carry a major historical irony. For what has now to be proved, before an informed and sceptical audience, is indeed possibility. And this not only in the reckoning of strategic or tactical chances, which in these dangerous years carry as much fear as hope. Where the proof really matters is at another level, where intention and consequence, desire and necessity, possibility and practice, have already bloodily interacted. Thus we are no longer in any position to cry great names or announce necessary laws, and expect to be believed. The information and the scepticism are already too thoroughly lodged at the back of our own minds. Strategy and tactics can still be played from the front, but the greatest unknown quantity in any of their moves is again possibility. The condition of shifting any of it beyond the parameters of a desperate game is possibility in the hardest sense: not whether a new human order might, in struggle, come through, but whether, as a condition of that struggle, and as the entire condition of its success, enough of us can reasonably believe that a new human order is seriously possible.

It has, after all, been widely believed before. It has, nevertheless, been widely believed. We can choose either of these ways of putting it, without much effect. The tenses of past and of an implied present lead us only into known conditions and known difficulties. Yet with most future tenses now comes at best a familiar scepticism, at worst a conventional hopelessness.

Possibility, seriously considered, is different. It is not what with luck might happen. It is what we can believe in enough to want, and then, by active wanting, make possible. Specifically, for socialists, after defeats and failures, and both within and after certain profound disillusions, it is not recovery or return but direct, practical possibility. Of course not practical or possible within the reduced terms of the existing order: possibility as a resignation to limits. Possibility, rather, as a different order, which no longer from simple assumptions, or from known discontents and negations, but on our own responsibility, in an actual world, we must prove.

## Bahro's Alternative in Eastern Europe

The quiet words come at the end of Rudolph Bahro's important book, *The Alternative in Eastern Europe* (453). Their full effect depends on their position, for what is most remarkable about Bahro's work is that while its first part covers familiar ground, in an analysis of "the non-capitalist road to industrial society", and its second part important ground, in an "anatomy of actually existing" socialist societies, its third part, over two hundred pages, begins from an insistence that "today utopian thought has a new necessity" and yet proceeds to something very unlike utopianism, indeed to a relatively detailed outline of a practical and possible communist society.

It is a very significant moment in socialist thought. We can fall back on the irony that, within a nominally socialist or communist society, its author was at once put in prison. This is an irony which cannot be compounded by the success of the book in the West, in the spirit of that romantic notion which Brecht identified, with Galileo's *Discorsi* crossing the frontier in a closed coach. The fact is that either in Eastern or Western Europe, of course under different local conditions, the challenge which Bahro is making must immediately encounter and engage – for that is its whole purpose – the fixed institutional and ideological habits of "actually existing socialism." Bahro chose this awkward phrase, after much hesitation, to describe the non-capitalist societies of Eastern Europe. But it has also to be applied, again noting our different conditions, to the institutions, ideologies and programmes of majority West European socialism, including its Communist Parties. It makes an important difference that our comrades in Eastern Europe are not, like us, confronting an entrenched and still powerful capitalist order. It means that they can look, already, along a different road. Yet in practice, like us, only look. Any actual generation of effective possibility faces as many, if different, obstacles, on either side of the line. But then at the same time it is true that effective movement, anywhere, will assist every other struggle.

This possible community of purpose, through what is certain to be a long, difficult and uneven effort, is the most heartening effect of Bahro's work. It is already significant that it allows us to move beyond the defensive, qualified solidarity with what has been defined, in Eastern Europe, as dissidence; to move beyond it, moreover, by distancing ourselves, in a more specific solidarity, from the anti-communism which can so readily exploit more limited positions. In one sense Bahro's work joins what has been already, for a generation, a marginal dissidence within Western socialism, but then the fact that it was written from within a non-capitalist society, with close day-to-day experience of its actual workings, and moreover from within a profound attachment to Marxism and to communism, makes a crucial difference. What it prevents, above all, is any complacent continuation of those perspectives of majority Western socialism which still, over a range from social democrats to communists, share with the countries of Eastern Europe certain common definitions of the nature of a socialist economic order, adding only, but often rhetorically, that in addition to this there should be substantially greater civil and political liberties.

For that is the depth of the challenge, and of the call to possibility: "Humanity must not only transform its relations of production, but must also fundamentally transform the overall character of its mode of production, i.e. *the productive forces as well* [...] it should consider its perspective as not bound to anyone historically inherited *form* of development and satisfaction of needs, or to the world of products that is designed to serve these" (261–262).

Thus a communist perspective of general emancipation has to be sharply distinguished from those governing perspectives, East and West, which in their primary emphasis on the "organization of production", in the special form of growth of existing *kinds* of production, and in their consequent emphasis on social relations and social welfare as dependent on the stage this has reached, have made and are making of socialism a would-be higher form of capitalism. Against this, Bahro puts a communist emphasis: "Not a growth in production, but cultural revolution – as the present form of *economic* emancipation is the means finally to dissolve the capitalist structure" (265–266).

## Meanings of Cultural Revolution

It is really only now, seeing Bahro's work written within an explicit and central Marxist perspective, that we can find ways of bringing together the apparently different emphases and concerns of those movements, in different parts of the world, which have identified themselves as working for "cultural revolution." I can remember, for example, the sneering use of the phrase to mark off the early New Left. Our use of "culture" to designate a central process and area of social and political struggle was at best identified (as significantly, later, was the Prague Spring) as the emergence of a group of intellectuals with special interests in "the superstructure", having nothing much or at all to say to the organized working class in its continuing material struggles at "the base." But then no sooner had this dismissive or marginalizing description got into general currency than, to everyone's surprise, the same phrase, "cultural revolution", became known as a description of the most remarkable political movement of the twentieth century: the sustained (and of course confused) attempt, in People's China, to define new priorities and alter actual and foreseen political relations, trying to make new forms of popular power within and where necessary against the received shapes of a socialist economic order. Now again, as the phrases settle, and as those particular historical moments have passed, an East European communist, writing from inside his experience of actually existing socialism, chooses the same phrase, "cultural revolution", to describe his central emphasis on the revolutionary way forward, for the achievement of communism.

Is this some accident of a phrase? There are differences, evidently, in these ideas and movements, but they are not necessarily greater than the radical differences of social conditions within which they were mounted. When these have been taken into account, what comes through is a line of division within Marxist theory and within socialist practice: a line which must now be more clearly drawn.

The central theoretical point is this. All Marxists share the belief that social being determines consciousness. The main conclusion that is ordinarily drawn from this is that we cannot change social being by changing consciousness; we must, on the contrary, change consciousness by changing social being. This conclusion is then stabilized as a contrast and opposition between "idealist" and "materialist" theory and practice, and, typically, the proponents of "cultural revolution" are assigned to the former: "culture" is the "sphere of consciousness." But what has then happened is that consciousness has been separated from the "sphere of social being", characteristically in the form of abstracting "the superstructure" from "the base." Work in the latter is then materialist; in the former either idealist or at best "voluntarist."

"Conservatives in both systems raise a hue and cry about voluntarism. But this only gives it away how much they fear changes, or at the very least do not want to lead and take responsibility for them. We must bear in mind that it is a social body in its *subjective capacity* that has economic laws, and not the other way round." "Even mechanical materialists today have an inkling that the 'growing role of the subjective factor' involves something quite different from the mere conscious execution of historical laws. Marxism has always claimed that being can determine consciousness precisely to determine being *anew*" (256).

There is room for argument about the relation of either of these emphases to a single system called "Marxism." But Bahro's emphasis is the common factor in the propositions of "cultural revolution." Consciousness is no longer the mere product of social being but is at once a condition of its practical existence and, further, one of its central productive forces.

This theoretical distinction can be said to be permanent. It is and has been made and practised in widely different social formations. But at the centre of Bahro's argument is a specific interpretation of conditions in modern industrial societies, where the production and reproduction of ideas and of intellectual practices have become and are becoming, at a growing rate, inherent in wide areas of the basic labour processes and in the general social order. Thus a fundamental form of the division of labour, between mental and manual operations, is being at once practically eroded and yet, in the forms of a class-based social order or of an apparently new order which is continuous with this in its mode of production though in other respects discontinuous, is still being practically imposed.

To put the point again theoretically: change in a mode of production can not occur only on the basis of a change in *relations* of production – as in the removal of capitalist owners of the means of production and their replacement by State planning authorities or public boards, where as a matter of fact even the relations of production have not necessarily been more than abstractly altered – but must also involve change in the *forces* of production, which are never only manual or mechanical but are also (and now increasingly) intellectual means. Thus a cultural revolution, by contrast with other social programmes, is directed towards the general appropriation of all the real forces of production, including now especially the intellectual forces of knowledge and conscious decision, as the necessary means of revolutionizing the social relations (determination of the use of resources; distribution and organization of work; distribution of products and services) which follow from variable forms of control of and access to all the productive forces. A cultural revolution is then always practically centred on the areas and processes of knowledge and decision, each ineffective without the other. In going beyond those changes in the relations of production which are practicable, especially at the distributive level, within persistent inequalities in control of and access to the underlying productive forces – changes which have been both partly achieved and programmatically projected in social-democratic and in "actually existing socialist" formations – cultural revolution – but then, in effect, any full revolution – works for those more general (and necessarily connected) changes which, in changing the whole mode of production, would be at once the processes and the conditions of a general human emancipation.

*"Mature Industrialism"*

It may be relatively easy to accept such definitions, at their usual level of generality. But we are speaking, in our conditions, among informed and sceptical people. The factor of information, uneven and incomplete as in all cases it must be, is at once the problem and the opportunity of contemporary socialist argument. Indeed the scepticism and worse with which such argument is now widely met is the inevitable consequence of failure to recognize this qualitatively new level of information (a failure which those listening to the arguments can now, in the forms of rhetorical replication, local opportunism, large promise and practical evasiveness, so quickly identify). At the same time, and more fundamentally (for it is here that the refusal of socialism is generated) there is a self-protecting and eventually indulgent habit of resigned but knowing acquiescence in the central reality of the existing mode of production: a widespread conclusion that information and argument have little or no purchase on the range of actual decisions; that it is then "all talk." It is then not only against its declared enemies – the existing owners, controllers and distributors of privileged knowledge and decision – but also against the cultural consequences, in long experience and habituation, of this decisive element of the mode of production itself – sceptical subordination, compensatory marginal avoidances, in Bahro's terms, *subalternity* – that the cultural revolution sets out to act. That is why, always vulnerably but still deliberately, it sets *possibility* as its central challenge.

But "possibility" can then acquire a utopian tinge. Indeed a familiar form of Marxism stands especially ready to confront it. Possibility is the future – the Sunday after next. Social democracy, in its late and most resigned forms, has of course settled to saying that "when we have got the economy right" we can go on to "the things we all want", but meanwhile [...] in this mode of production, produce. Yet in remarkably similar ways, many Marxist arguments, and the settled practices of "actually existing socialism", offer the same message: "when we have achieved plenty, which is a condition of communism"; "when we have caught up with the West." It is especially against such positions and practices, with their very serious social

## Beyond Actually Existing Socialism (1980)

and political consequences in the relations between socialist formations and actual working people, that Bahro develops his arguments.

His central point applies equally in the East and in the West, though for historical reasons, of uneven development, it is not new in "Western socialism" even if it has been effectively forgotten. Thus it is widely believed that communism, or full socialism, will be possible only when the productive forces have "matured." But, "given the present structure of industrial societies in both formations, the productive forces will never become mature, despite and precisely on account of their technical dynamic. Yet even today those countries that first set out on the industrial-capitalist road are those materially closest to socialism. Nowhere is the *beginning* of the transformation more pressing than it is there. But it is also nowhere more hard. And neither the less developed nor the underdeveloped peoples can afford to wait for them" (125).

"The industrial-capitalist road", but we must then make distinctions. It is not new in Marxist thought, though it has not often been emphasized, that the *capitalist* mode of production, for deep internal reasons, can *never* become mature. Since it has become dominant, in one area after another, it has been uncontrollably disturbing and restless, reaching local stabilities only almost at once to move away from them, leaving every kind of social and technical debris, disrupting human continuities and settlements, moving on with brash confidence to its always novel enterprises. And the real reason for this is that it is not, finally, a mode of *production*, in any primary sense. In its developed forms it is centred not on social production but on the reproduction of capital and the maximization of profit, which impose quite different priorities.

But what then of the linkage with what is now commonly called "industrialism"? For historical reasons the theoretically distinguishable types – "capitalism" and "industrialism" – are virtually impossible to disentangle, in advanced capitalist societies. It is then very striking to find Bahro extending the point to an "industrial society" in a non-capitalist order. The local reason he offers, in the fact of the "technical dynamic", is not in itself convincing. Maturity, whatever that might be, or in more practical terms a non-disruptive continuity of production, ought certainly to be able to include a series of quite extensive technical changes, while these are governed by the needs of social production rather than by the priorities of capital. Bahro's later reason, that the non-capitalist and ex-colonial economies are in many ways determined by the forms and pressures of industrial capitalism elsewhere, is more convincing. But the most important eventual point of the analysis is to show that what has to be overcome, for any general emancipation, is not only "capitalism", in the important but limited sense of minority ownership of the means of production, but that wider mode, in which the scale and complexity and technical redivisions of labour characteristic of modern industrial enterprises are central factors. And then the deep obstacles of this wider mode are the facts of the appropriation, expropriation, at many levels of general social and working processes, of skills, effective knowledge and powers of practical decision. It is against this expropriation that the cultural revolution, much wider than that against the more immediately recognizable features of capitalism, is directed.

But there are also other reasons for insisting that the capitalist mode of production, and its non-capitalist simulacra, can never become mature. These reasons are historical. First, that the successful struggles against political and economic imperialism are already altering, and seem certain to alter further, the access to cheap raw materials and controlled markets on which the most successful phases of advanced capitalism depended. Second, that within the advanced capitalist societies, economic and technical solutions, of a rationalizing and modernizing kind, are already, in structural unemployment, in consequent market, credit and service difficulties, and in the political disruption of settled social (national and regional) formations, moving very rapidly *away from* rather than towards maturity. Third, and decisively, that the now evident crises of resources, and of the unwanted side-effects of several central productive processes, are combining to set *material* limits to what has been, not only in ideology but in its central dynamic, a limitless expansion. The combined effect of these reasons is what now makes communism necessary. But given the exceptional dangers and difficulties of any real alteration of priorities and of any effective alternative construction, the question is still: is it possible?

## "Surplus Consciousness"

Bahro sees the way through in one of his most memorable but also arguable concepts: that of the contemporary production of "surplus consciousness." He defines this as "an energetic mental capacity that is no longer absorbed by the *immediate* necessities and dangers of human existence and can thus orient itself to more distant problems" (257).

There is obviously some truth in this, as in any local comparison of the lives of most workers between, say, the mid-nineteenth and the late twentieth centuries. Something very important is then being indicated. But on any wider historical scale it can be reasonably argued that this "surplus consciousness" is at once a cultural and a material variable. There is no unilinear progression of "free consciousness", but on the contrary a highly variable and always complex relation between this sphere of mental possibility and the local imperatives of specific modes and types of production. And because this is so we cannot rest on the essentially quantitative notion of a "surplus." For the consciousness and energy that are available beyond the immediately necessary tasks are not simple quanta; they are and must be related to the forms of consciousness and energy expended and generated in the primary tasks. Of course this correction must not be extended to the absurd point reached in an opposite tendency in Marxism, in which there is *no* free consciousness (except, ambiguously, at the level of theory) but only the labyrinthine monopoly of a totalized ideology. Yet there can be no simple reliance either on the mere fact of a "surplus", and Bahro is much more convincing when he goes on to recognize this by distinguishing, usefully, between "compensatory" and "emancipatory" uses of this "surplus": that is, between drives to possession, consumption and power, which can be seen as partial substitutes for any certain and equitable share in human needs, and those other non-exploitative orientations towards self-realization and the collective realization, recognition, of the essential qualities of others.

The cultural revolution is then for *the conditions of* the emancipatory and against *the need for* the compensatory activities. (This distinguishes Bahro, as a Marxist theorist, from the strictly "moralist" version of a comparable argument, in which the shift is seen only as internal and suasive.)

But then this is not really the appropriation of a surplus. Indeed the very sharp rise in every kind of "compensatory" activity – a process now central to advanced capitalist production itself – not only reminds us of the obstacles but should force us to review, much more carefully than has been common in most branches of criticism of "consumer" society, the relatively simple initial categories. It is not only that the argument (more commonly the sermon or the tirade) can slip very quickly into asceticism or into revived forms of cultural ethno-centrism. It is, more fundamentally, that human emancipation is intrinsically, and as a matter of principle, more diverse than *any* philosophical definition of emancipatory transformation. Utopia, that is to say, as a singular noun, is not an emancipatory concept; indeed it is often and at its best frankly compensatory.

*A Long Revolution*

In fact Bahro is not a utopian; that is the most important quality of his book. He thinks through, in unusually sustained detail, the processes of transformation of conditions and needs. This was for me a remarkable experience, in that it came through, quite personally, as another version of the project of *The Long Revolution*. When Bahro comes to summarize his "perspectives for general emancipation" I find myself back in those years and the kinds of thinking that followed from them. A redivision of labour; unrestricted access to general education; a childhood centred on the capacity for development rather than geared to economic performance; a new communal life based on autonomous group activities; socialization (democratization) of the general process of knowledge and decision. Moreover "there is neither the hope nor the danger that these goals [...] can be achieved 'too quickly'. A society cannot be taken by surprise or with a coup d'etat. [...] The question is rather to create first of all the political and mental conditions [...]" (275).

It is then not at all a question of who said what when. The project is too widely shared and too essentially collaborative for any of that. But it remains remarkable that there should be this convergence, within such different conditions, and then the irreplaceable and quite novel merit of

*Beyond Actually Existing Socialism (1980)*

Bahro's work is that he has defined this project from close practical experience of an "actually existing socialism." What was then already outlined in communications, in education and in communal self-management is radically strengthened by proposals in economic planning, in factory organization and in the "problem-solving collectives" of technical and scientific work. The problems of political organization, within such perspectives, are again convergently but in each case incompletely seen. What has then to be thought through (for the details of Bahro's arguments and proposals must simply be read) is an interlocking set of questions which, beyond the exhilaration of the realization of convergence, remain as real difficulties: the true difficulties of possibility.

*Self-Management*

The case for self-management, in every kind of social and economic activity, has often been made, and in some important cases has been endowed with practical detail. It is the indispensable objective of any movement to achieve (for it is not really to recover) the powers and faculties of effective knowledge and decision. Moreover, while Bahro is writing from an "existing socialist" experience, in which, at least internally, there are not the implacable barriers of direct monopoly and finance capitalism, we have to notice that in our own blocked and bleak situation the most active social forces have already arrived at this point. In various kinds of community organization, and especially those around schools, housing, transport and hospitals, a vigorous if usually local collective activity is already widespread. Many kinds of "voluntary" organization (the conventional description throws an ironic light on the true character of the dominant order) already engage kinds of collective activity and self-organization which offer repeated evidence of practical possibility. In work the growing practice of factory occupations is not always limited to protest but is producing some notable examples of counter-planning; this is also, if intermittently, widespread in education. In some strikes there have been remarkably vigorous instances of direct collective organization and – as in the flying pickets – initiative.

It remains true, of course, that all such examples compose only a minority experience, when set against the predominant experience of frustrated energy and initiative within blocked bureaucratic and hierarchical organizations. It has also to be said that most such actions are defensive protests, often at a very late stage, rather than fully constructive. But then it is not only that all such practices are the necessary means of learning the new and difficult skills of autonomous organization: something that is also happening, again vigorously, in the alternative and oppositional collectives. It is also that the limited character of the available and developing modes reminds us, sharply, of the next and decisive theoretical barrier that has to be crossed.

For if it is becoming clear that the best democratic and socialist way of running organizations is through regular and informed collective decision-making, it should be at once equally clear, and especially to socialists, that this principle cannot be limited to specific enterprises and communities. Indeed there is even some danger that the growing belief in existing and commonly foreseen forms of community politics and workers' control will actually hide from us the more difficult problems of the general framework within which, necessarily, they must be practised. It is here, with Bahro, that we arrive at the hitherto intractable concepts and realities of Party, State and Plan.

*Party, State and Plan*

There is a powerful socialist tradition, almost equally reinforced by both Bolshevism and Fabianism, which whether or not it has been modified by ideas of local democracy arrives at the problems of the general framework with firm ideas of a unitary general authority. In modern "communist" practice this authority has been the Party, as the projected will and interest of the working class. Bahro's analysis of this, in its actual development into monopoly and repression, can be debated, historically, since his reference to conditions of external pressure and deformation, and of immediate "backwardness", is insufficient, as indeed he later argues, to account for its remarkable and ideologically defended persistence. And we can join the argument here from our own experience, since in relatively much more favourable conditions the dominant socialist perspective is again the unitary party and the state plan. It is true that in the West this is modified by the substantial practices of (relatively) open elections and of the "mandate." But what election and mandate are still intended to deliver is "the party in government" with its central plan. When this in practice interlocks with the existing and relatively unaltered framework of the capitalist state it is already suspect and invariably deceptive. But then there is equally no reason to believe, from the experience of Eastern Europe, that any simple removal of capitalist property relations is sufficient to alter the realities of monopoly state power and the imposed authority of the plan; indeed it may lead directly to them. It is then on this common site, if under radically different conditions, that the cultural revolution must be waged, and as something more than a series of local options.

The first area to contest, as Bahro convincingly recognizes, is that of the plan. It is obviously necessary that within any effective political community (and in modern material conditions this is unlikely to be small) basic allocations of resources and conditions of distribution have to be affirmed. The concept of the socialist "plan" competes, here, with the (always in practice qualified) imperatives of the capitalist market. It is commonly supported by the paired notions of "public interest" and "rationality", which together are held to compose "socialism." But then the whole point is that public interest and rationality, which are general human conditions and processes, have been theoretically and practically appropriated by a centrally directive mechanism. In any actual case of "public interest" the reality (and not only in class societies) is only rarely unitary; it is almost always in practice a *relativity* of interests, variable from instance to instance and through time. The exercise of "rationality" is then in its turn a more complex and variable process than any conceivable amalgam of "expert" inquiries and directions. Yet at the same time it is clearly not possible in any complex society to make rational decisions without very advanced effective knowledge.

It is then a good test of where any socialist stands, in this matter of cultural revolution, to see how he reacts to the proposal that in any issue requiring general decision there should *never be less than two* independently prepared "plans." For this goes to the heart. It is not just the practical point that we have had more than enough experience of expert plans which turned out to be wrong (the switches from coal to oil, and from rail to road, are only the most obvious examples). It is, more fundamentally, that the preparation of at least two plans, while fulfilling the necessary conditions of effective and where necessary specialist knowledge, provides, in its practical alternatives, genuine conditions for the actual as distinct from the appropriated exercise of public interest and rationality. Moreover it is inherent in the requirement of detailed and practicable alternatives that decision is neither appropriated nor mandated but is each time actively and generally made.

We are only now beginning to learn, with notable assistance from Bahro, at once the genuine difficulties and the practical possibilities of so radically new a social order. And then nothing is to be gained by underestimating the complexity of such decision-making, or the long period of active learning and informed participation which would be necessary to make it effective. But it is not only, theoretically, that this is the way to cultural revolution: a way drawing on the only actual social forces which are capable of achieving general emancipation. It is also that the material means of such complex, informed and relatively rapid decision-making are becoming increasingly available in modern communications technology, which indeed it must be one of the first conditions of cultural revolution to direct for this rather than (as now mainly) for existing marketing uses. Practicable institutions and procedures, in many different areas of reference and at varying levels of formality, directly corresponding to the nature and effect of the decisions, are now indeed within our material capacity. The main thrust must then be towards political and educational practice of the many kinds necessary to give them substance; to make them *possible*.

It is then necessary to consider the relations between such new kinds of decision-making and our received notions of "representation" and of "party." It might be said that in the West we already have such alternatives and procedures of choice, in competing parties and plans. Yet the combined practices of representation and of parties conceived in its terms radically limit – and often seem meant to limit – democratic procedures. It is not only that representatives, in such conditions, are not in theory or practice bound by the kinds of reporting back and *specific* instruction which would make general opinions and wishes regularly effective. It is much more that the theory of representation offers an all-purpose and generalized substitute for the specific, diverse and shifting interests of what are always diverse individuals and groups. Indeed in this it resembles, though under some qualifying controls, the explicit "substitutionism" of the would-be monopoly party which "represents" the working class, not by taking its instructions or even consulting it, but by the kinds of ideological appropriation which Bahro so vividly describes. It is customary to contrast such "totalitarian" parties with the "democratic" parties of the West, yet these are only different forms of appropriation of popular information and decision. The means of this appropriation, in the West, is the procedure of electoral mandate, on an unsortable bundle of plans and policies, which delivers some years of monopoly of power. This form of "representation" inherently generalizes and preempts what is always in practice a sequence of specific, variable and often unforeseeable decisions, of which the direct *presentation* would be a wholly different political practice from all-purpose and appropriated *representation*.

Of course individuals and groups must combine and find resolutions as and where specific interests and decisions interact. But these, though they may at any time take the immediate form of parties, are properly alliances, blocs, coalitions, always specifically formed and necessarily open to change, rather than the fixed "representative" parties which now appropriate these active processes. It is indeed at this level that we might be said to be already in the first phase of a cultural revolution. For it is evident that the traditional delivery of representative blocks of all-purpose votes, which then monopolize and exhaust the political process, is relatively rapidly breaking down. Yet the forms of movement beyond it, in what are called "single-issue campaigns", are distrusted even by those who have moved into them, against the existing appropriations and exclusions. Out of habit, it would seem, they look to forms of influence which would in practice incorporate them into parties of an existing kind, when the real lesson of their experience is that they are early forms of a movement towards conditions of direct and specific public decision-making, to which, without mediation and beyond appropriation, their interests and campaigns can be directly and associatively addressed. For they are already, in embryo, those forms of "collectives of associated individuals" which are rightly seen by Bahro as the fibres of a communist society. Their diversity and specificity, now experienced, within the dominant appropriation, as disadvantages, are in fact an early (if of course incomplete, indeed fragmentary) realization of that principle of "the association of individuals into unions in which they pursue the various specific purposes that make up the process of their social life" which Bahro, following Marx, addresses as the only basis for general emancipation (440).

What the cultural revolution is then really proposing is a radical recasting of the old problem of the relations between special interests and the general interest. It has of course to find means of negotiating such relations, but it starts from the position that all existing institutions and procedures of the "general interest" are in fact falsifications, either in the arbitrary definitions of a dominant class, or in those more complex procedures of representation in which the "general interest" is a negative appropriation deployed against each "special interest" in turn, the only means of ascertaining the true general interest in relation to any actual special interest, by direct consultation and specific popular decision, having been systematically excluded. In these false systems, the lines of communication and of decision, which have been directly appropriated, flow from "top" to "bottom" as a matter of course. The cultural revolution, by contrast, seeks a system in which there are still indeed many levels of generality – including levels of elected delegate assemblies – and in which decisions and relevant information necessarily move from the more local and specific to the more general, extensive and indeed in these senses determining, but in which, because the lines of communication and decision now flow the other way, "individuals are equally and simultaneously present at all levels of subjective interest" (440).

*What a Society Produces*

Yet the scepticism and impatience which such proposals now commonly induce, even among those whose own definitions of a desirable form of society already lead them in such directions, have to be directly faced. For in both East and West, if in different ways, a potentially lethal combination of abstract desire and practical cynicism seems now to be overtaking actual majorities, as a consequence not only of repeated disappointments but of the (in itself correct) identification of their causes as systematic: an unbearable state of mind in itself, where no alternative is really believed in, and quickly convertible either to violent reaction or to projection of the systematic failure to the human species and order – a projection which even the waiting formulae of religion can only temporarily hold.

The urgency of cultural revolution then hardly needs to be argued. But though it has necessarily to be attempted in every area of social existence, there are good reasons for believing, with Bahro, that the decisive engagement will be with the problems of "the economy." Yet it is clear that the form of this engagement, as distinct from the now dominant and preoccupying "programmes for economic survival", has to begin in some new and still unfamiliar ways. Thus when we speak of plans and programmes, which are undoubtedly necessary, we have first to challenge the alienated logic of a capitalist order and its non-capitalist derivatives. In his detailed discussions of economic planning and factory organization Bahro is at his best, not only because of his relevant experience, but because his central beliefs are then so directly connected.

The point reaches deeply back into theory, but of course emerges every day as practice. It is centred on the question of what a society needs to produce. Within the alienated logic this is necessarily defined, even by many socialists, in the quantitative terms of necessary objects. Plans and targets are then derived, and collective production is organized, throughout, in these habitually alienated terms. Consciousness, individuality, the social order itself, are then seen as by-products of this necessary production.

Against this logic, the cultural revolution insists, first, that what a society needs, before all, to produce, is as many as possible conscious individuals, capable of all necessary association. Thus not only is "the plan" differently conceived from the beginning. It is in fact now the only developed response to the changed conditions of material production, in which quantitative results are relatively easily achieved, at the level of objects, but are still given their residual priorities over other general human interests and developments. Thus the material task which requires the work of sixty is developed, by capitalist logic, to the point where it requires the work of only six, and the other fifty-four become, in that deeply significant term of the current alienation, "redundant." In an alternative logic, there would be the choice, from the beginning, of associating more workers than are necessary, at any particular material stage, so that within the labour process itself there is room for other kinds of relationship and reflection, or of so redistributing necessary working time that other kinds of activity and relationship become the emancipatory centre rather than the compensatory margin of social life. It is of course clear that any such plan requires, absolutely, abolition of the current imperatives of capital, which exerts its quantitative dominance at just these points. And it is then deeply encouraging that, even within capitalist conditions, some trade unions are now moving strongly, if still in limited ways, towards these objectives, while at a more practical level (though still as often negative as positive) more and more people are actually treating work in such ways, as far as they can, of course to the outrage of all existing types of controller. What then urgently matters is the generalization, extension and where necessary conversion of these existing tendencies, with the now conscious rather than defensive or shamefaced purpose of remaking the working order. For, so far from being impractical, the positive and conscious pursuit of these aims is now the only practical alternative to a new stage of division of humanity into the engaged and the redundant.

What this really involves, as a central task of the cultural revolution, in its necessary alteration of the nature of the productive forces, is a practical redefinition of the nature of "work." For while, within the inevitable material limits and within the rational decisions of a society seeking genuine economic maturity, the necessary material tasks can undoubtedly be performed in less total time, any effective response to more general human needs, in care and relationships, and in knowledge and development, is in one sense genuinely limitless, and will make demands on our energies which are at the very opposite pole from a relaxed and unchallenging utopia. Indeed, these now equally basic needs, as we can already glimpse from their pressures at the end of the old logic – pressures which seem actually to be increasing in conditions of advanced commodity development –

## Class

We have then to consider, finally, the relations between these definitions and perspectives of the cultural revolution and the most general received definitions and perspectives of revolutionary socialism. For many reasons, the problem of these relations is centred in the concept of class. Bahro scandalized many people, and not only the dogmatists against whom he was mainly arguing, with his vigorous assertion that "the working class" is "an inapplicable concept in proto-socialist society" (183–202). Some distinctions have then to be made. In his analysis of a rhetoric of "the working class" as a cover for practical appropriation and repression in Eastern Europe Bahro is on relatively firm ground. Clearly any adequate definition of the social situation of wage-workers in non-capitalist economies requires a whole new analysis. But then he both extends and has been taken by others to extend this specific problem to a very wide and (it must be said) very familiar critique of the Marxist idea of the proletariat and its revolutionary possibilities. The trouble with this part of his argument is that there is a recurrent slippage between consideration of the working class in non-capitalist and capitalist societies. As a result, while making some new points about a partly new situation, he drifts, not without some hesitations, into a familiar identification of the "technical intelligentsia" – the most advanced sector of the "collective worker" – as the leading edge of the cultural revolution. This conclusion is best understood within the specific difficulties of Eastern European societies, but, whatever may be its truth or plausibility there, it would be disastrous if in the West the idea of cultural revolution were given this kind of social location.

It is of course true that modern intellectual workers – no longer to be defined only by traditional intellectual occupations, but as very widely integrated into industrial, distributive and informational processes – are likely to be specially alerted to the facts of appropriation of effective knowledge and powers of decision by the existing social order. Precisely because in their own situations they have some real access to unmediated knowledge, and are in a privileged position to observe and understand many of the actual processes of mediation and control and decision, they are potentially and often actually at the leading edge of effective (if usually localized) social criticism. And then it is not only that such groups can contribute (are already in some areas notably contributing) to the cultural revolution; it is also that the outcome of theoretical and practical struggles within such groups will have a major effect on the chances of effective socialist directions.

Yet it is obvious that at any time a significant proportion of such workers are, with whatever local dissatisfactions, elements of the very process of appropriation itself. Their practical enlistment into *new forms* of appropriation is then the most likely initial direction of any radical break. This is why, though necessarily on the basis of rigorous new analysis, socialists committed to the idea of cultural revolution have still to find common cause – and by learning as much as by teaching – with those who are *most* subject to appropriation, who alone have fully objective interests in its ending.

It can be readily shown that "the working class" has changed, sometimes very radically, in modern productive and distributive conditions. Its mere invocation is indeed often, as Bahro argues, a protection against thought. But the major elements of these changes need not only be interpreted as the disintegration of the "classical proletariat"; they can be interpreted also as a profound (and for the existing social order, dangerous) instability. It is not only, though it is crucially, the factual rise in expectations. It is also that the erosion of the old crude division between mental and manual labour has, partly through an extended educational system but at a rising rate within certain labour processes and their consequent problems of management, reached deep into the general class of wage-earners. The coexistence of such expectations and such erosion with the still firmly sustained imperatives of capital or of "the plan" is then profoundly unstable, and incentives to challenge the existing appropriation of effective knowledge and decision-making are undoubtedly increasing, especially in conditions of structural industrial change. The practice of such challenges will require alliance with radical sectors of the "technical intelligentsia", but the main social forces to identify, sustain and carry them through must, for both structural and ideal reasons, come from these working majorities.

Yet one of the advantages of the idea of cultural revolution, as it reaches beyond the area of immediate industrial property relations, is that it identifies wide groups who are subject to the appropriation of knowledge and effective decision but who are structurally different from the old or the new working class. The outstanding case is that of women, who as workers share one kind of subjection but who more generally, as women, are still profoundly subject to kinds of appropriation deeply rooted in the whole mode of production (and especially the appropriation of their full, as distinct from wage-earning productive forces). The cultural revolution, as distinct from incentives and reforms to permit their inclusion in "the plan", will be deeply sited among women or it will not, in practice, occur at all.

The final major structural area is that of local communities, in their diverse and complex relations with the larger administrative units which increasingly appropriate even their local powers, and in their now critical relations with the large and brutal sweeps of capital relocation and the disruptive imposition of what, from the level of the appropriation, are seen as mere infrastructures. Nowhere now is there more active need and potential to challenge the fundamental appropriation of decision-making by the existing social order.

*Conclusion*

Thus, albeit in some new as well as some continuing forms, a socialist cultural revolution has still to be rooted in potential majorities which can, by their own organization and activity, become effective majorities. The principle of cultural revolution offers an outline of ways in which there can be both effective association and new forms of negotiation beyond specific associations. In this assertion of possibility, against all the learned habits of resignation and scepticism, it is already a definition of practical hope. Beyond that, it seems now to be the only way forward in a situation of very general and very dangerous unsettlement, where the taking of direct responsibility is not just an attractive idea but probably the only means of survival. We can agree that it will be long, hard, contentious and untidy – its criterion of success, for as far as we can see, being a possible majority of successes over its many failures. We can also be sure, in the West as certainly as in the East, that while many of its forms will be extensive and pervasive there will be certain decisive confrontations, with very powerful opposing forces, which will all too sharply remind us that we are attempting cultural *revolution* and not some unimpeded process of social growth. But what will get us through such confrontations, and in some important cases into them, is not only association and organization; it will be also what we can call, with Bahro, the "material force of the idea": the production and the practice of possibility.

READING 13

# Resources for a Journey of Hope (1983)

## Editor's Introduction

*Towards 2000* is neither a literary utopia nor sf, and Williams himself would almost certainly have denied that it was a political utopia. But it is, as the title suggests, an exercise in radical futurology. In this extract, Williams coins the term "Plan X" to describe the "new politics of strategic advantage" characteristic of the late-capitalist political economy. This is what we have since learned to name as "globalization," the politics of the World Trade Organization and the International Monetary Fund, the World Bank and the World Economic Forum. Williams's own description of "X Planning" remains startlingly prescient: "their real politics and planning," he writes, are centred on "an acceptance of the indefinite continuation of extreme crisis and extreme danger." Against this, he pits the labour movements, but not the labour parties, which merely "reproduce the existing definitions of issues and interests," and also the new social movements – the peace movement, the ecology movement, the feminist movement, and the movement of "oppositional culture" – his additional "resources for a journey of hope" beyond capitalism. A quarter of a century later, the analysis stands up surprisingly well, though the X Planners have proven stronger, and the opposition weaker, than Williams hoped. As Francis Mulhern observed, *Towards 2000* remains "actual and exemplary" in its "commitment to the renewal of rational historical imagination" (115).

# Resources for a Journey of Hope (1983)

*I*

It is usually taken for granted that to think about the future, as a way of changing the present, is a generous activity, by people who are not only seriously concerned but also, in those familiar adjectives, forward-looking, reforming, progressive. All the good ideas are on this side; all the bad or disappointing practice on the other. There is a question of how far we can go on with this easy assumption. As things now are, all the good ideas, and especially the ways in which they connect or might connect with how people are actually living, have to be rigorously re-examined.

Yet there is also another check to the assumption. It used to be taken for granted that the opposing forces were not themselves forward-looking: that they were, in those equally familiar adjectives, conservative, regressive, reactionary. Many of them indeed still are, but we misread the current situation if we rely on this easy contrast. There is now a very important intellectual tendency, with some real bases in political power, which is as closely concerned with thinking and planning the future as any reforming or progressive group. Within this tendency the signals are not being jammed but are being carefully listened to. Yet there is then the deliberate choice of a very different path: not towards sharing the information and the problems, or towards the development of general capacities to resolve them. What is chosen instead, intellectually and politically, is a new hard line on the future: a new politics of strategic advantage.

I call this new politics "Plan X." It is indeed a plan, as distinct from the unthinking reproduction of distraction. But it is different from other kinds of planning, and from all other important ways of thinking about the future, in that its objective is indeed "X": a willed and deliberate unknown, in which the only defining factor is advantage. It is obvious that this has connections with much older forms of competitive scheming and fighting, and with a more systematized power politics. There are all too many precedents for its crudeness and harshness. But what is new in "Plan X" politics is that it has genuinely incorporated a reading of the future, and one which is quite as deeply pessimistic, in general terms, as the most extreme readings of those who are now campaigning against the nuclear arms race or the extending damage of ecological crisis.

The difference of "Plan X" people is that they do not believe that any of these dangerous developments can be halted or turned back. Even where there are technical ways they do not believe that there are possible political ways. Thus while as a matter of public relations they still talk of solutions, or of possible stabilities, their real politics and planning are not centred on these, but on an acceptance of the indefinite continuation of extreme crisis and extreme danger. Within this harsh perspective, all their plans are for phased advantage, an effective even if temporary edge, which will always keep them at least one step ahead in what is called, accurately enough, the game plan.

The first obvious signs of Plan X politics were in the nuclear arms race, in its renewal from the mid-1970s. It was by then clear to everyone that neither staged mutual disarmament (the professed ultimate aim) nor any stable strategic parity (the more regular political ratification) could be achieved by the development of radically new weapons systems and new levels of overkill. Many sane people called these new developments insane, but within Plan X thinking they are wholly rational. For the real objective is neither disarmament nor parity, but temporary competitive advantage, within a permanent and inevitable danger.

There were further signs of Plan X in some of the dominant responses to the rise in oil prices. Other groups proposed a reduction in energy consumption, or a reduction in dependence on oil, or negotiations for some general stability in oil and other commodity prices. Plan X people think differently. Their chosen policy is to weaken, divide and reduce the power of the oil producers, whatever the long-run effects on supply, so that a competitive advantage can be retained. To argue that this cannot be a lasting solution is to miss the point. It is not meant to be a lasting solution, but the gaining of edge and advantage for what is accepted, in advance, as the inevitable next round.

Again, Plan X has appeared recently in British politics. As distinct from incorporating the working class in a welfare state, or of negotiating some new and hopefully stable relationship between state, employers and unions (the two dominant policies of post-1945 governments), Plan X has read the future as the certainty of a decline in capitalist profitability unless the existing organizations and expectations of wage-earners are significantly reduced. Given this reading, Plan X operates not only by ordinary pressures but where necessary by the decimation of British industrial capital itself. This was a heavy and (in ordinary terms) unexpected price to pay, but one which had to be paid if the necessary edge of advantage was to be gained or regained. Again many sane people say that this policy is insane, but this is only an unfamiliarity with the nature of Plan X thinking. Its people have not only a familiar hard drive, but one which is genuinely combined with a rational analysis of the future of capitalism and of its unavoidable requirements.

In this kind of combination, Plan X people resemble the hardest kinds of revolutionary, who drive through at any cost to their perceived objectives. But the difference of Plan X from revolution is that no transformed society, no new order, no lasting liberation seriously enters these new calculations, though their rhetoric may be retained. A phase at a time, a decade at a time, a generation at a time, the people who play by Plan X are calculating relative advantage, in what is accepted from the beginning as an unending and unavoidable struggle. For this is percentage politics, and within its tough terms there is absolute contempt for those who believe that the present and the future can be managed in any other way, and especially for those who try to fudge or qualify the problems or who refuse the necessary costs. These wet old muddlers, like all old idealists, are simply irrelevant, unless they get in the way.

Does it need to be said that Plan X is dangerous? It is almost childish to say so, since it is, in its own terms, a rational mutation within an already existing and clearly foreseeable extremity of danger. There is often a surprising overlap between the clearest exponents of Plan X and their most determined political opponents. The need for constant attention to the same kinds of problem, and for urgent and where necessary disturbing action in response to them, is a common self-definition by both groups. The difference, and it ought to be fundamental, is that Plan X is determined solely by its players' advantage. Any more general condition is left deliberately undefined, while the alternative movements see solutions in terms of stable mutual advantage, which is then the principle of a definable and attainable general condition: the practical condition which replaces the unknown and undefined X.

If we put it in this way the general choice ought to be simple. Yet we are speaking about real choices, under pressures, and we have then to notice how many elements there are, in contemporary culture and society, which support or at least do not oppose Plan X. Thus the plan is often presented in terms of national competitive advantage: "keeping our country a step ahead." In these terms it naturally draws on simple kinds of patriotism or chauvinism. Any of its damaging consequences to others can be mediated by xenophobia, or by milder forms of resentment and distrust of foreigners. Very similar feelings can be recruited into the interests of a broader alliance, as now commonly in military policy. Again, at a substantial level, there is a deep natural concern with the welfare of our own families and our own people. That they at least should be all right, come what may, inspires extraordinary effort, and this, in certain conditions, can appear as Plan X. Moreover, from the long experience of capitalist society, there is a widespread common sense that we have always to look to our own advantage or we shall suffer and may go under. This daily reality produces and reproduces the conditions for seeing Plan X as inevitable. It has then made deep inroads into the labour movement, which was basically founded on the alternative ethic of common wellbeing. When a trade union argues for a particular wage level, not in terms of the social usefulness of the work but, for example, in terms of improving its position in the "wages league table", it is in tune with Plan X.

There are also deeper supporting cultural conditions. Plan X is sharp politics and high-risk politics. It is easily presented as a version of masculinity. Plan X is a mode of assessing odds and of determining a game plan. As such it fits, culturally, with the widespread habits of gambling and its calculations. At its highest levels, Plan X draws on certain kinds of high operative (including scientific and technical) intelligence, and on certain highly specialized game-plan skills. But then much education, and especially higher education (not only in the versions that are called business studies) already defines professionalism in terms of competitive advantage. It promotes a deliberately narrowed attention to the skill as such, to be enjoyed in its mere exercise rather than in any full sense of the human purposes it is serving or the social effects it may be having. The now gross mutual flattery of military professionalism, financial professionalism, media professionalism and advertizing professionalism indicates very clearly how far this has gone. Thus both the social and cultural conditions for the adoption of Plan X, as the only possible strategy for the future, are very powerful indeed.

At the same time Plan X is more than anyone of these tendencies; it is also more than their simple sum. To emerge as dominant it has to rid itself, in practice, whatever covering phrases may be retained, of still powerful feelings and habits of mutual concern and responsibility, and of the very varied institutions which support and encourage these. Moreover, to be Plan X, it has to be more than a congeries of habits of advantage, risk and professional play. This is most evident in the fact that its real practitioners, still a very small minority, have to lift themselves above the muddle of miscellaneous local tendencies, to determine and assign genuine major priorities. At the levels at which Plan X is already being played, in nuclear-arms strategy, in high-capital advanced technologies (and especially information technologies), in world-market investment policies, and in anti-union strategies, the mere habits of struggling and competing individuals and families, the mere entertainment of ordinary gambling, the simplicities of local and national loyalties (which Plan X, at some of its levels, is bound to override wherever rationally necessary) are in quite another world. Plan X, that is to say, is by its nature not for everybody. It is the emerging rationality of self-conscious elites; taking its origin from the urgent experiences of crisis-management but deliberately lifting its attention from what is often that mere hand-to-mouth behaviour. It is in seeing the crises coming, preparing positions for them, devising and testing alternative scenarios of response, moving resources and standbys into position, that it becomes the sophisticated Plan X.

To name this powerful tendency, and to examine it, is not to propose what is loosely called a conspiracy theory. There are many political conspiracies, as we eventually learn when at least some of them are exposed, usually after the event. Elements of Plan X are inherently conspiratorial.

But we shall underestimate its dangers if we reduce it to mere conspiracy. On the contrary, it is its emergence as the open common sense of high-level politics which is really serious. As distinct from mere greedy muddle, and from shuffling day-to-day management, it is a way – a limited but powerful way – of grasping and attempting to control the future. In a deepening world crisis, it is certain to strengthen, as against an older, less rational, less informed and planned politics. But then the only serious alternative to it is a way of thinking about the future, and of planning, which is at least as rational and as informed in all its specific policies, and which is not only morally much stronger, in its concern for a common wellbeing, but at this most general level is *more* rational and *better* informed. For the highest rationality and the widest information should indicate a concern for common well-being, and for stable kinds of mutual general interest, as the most practical bases for particular wellbeing and indeed for survival.

## II

This is where the real political problems start. We can begin by trying to assess the actual and immediately potential resources for any radical changes of direction. Two sectors are at once apparent. There is now a growing body of detailed professional research, most of it dependent on the still expanding scientific community, in the key areas of ecology, alternative technologies and disarmament. There is also a rapidly growing movement of specific campaigns, most visible in the peace movement and in ecological initiatives but also extending over a very wide social and cultural range. Here, certainly, are actual and immediately potential resources for radically new kinds of politics.

Yet it has to be recognized that in some ways these are two very different groups of people. In some of their forms of activity they are quite distinct and unconnecting. Thus much of the most useful scientific work is directed, as if it were still orthodox research, at existing political leaders or generalized public opinion. Because by current definitions much of it is "not political", but rather an objective assessment of physical facts, there is a tendency to resist its involvement with the simplifications of politics or with the street cries and emotionalism of demonstrations. Again, by their own best values, many of the campaigns are concerned primarily with forms of public witness and protest, with direct personal involvement in opposition to some evil, or with the growth of immediate relationships of an alternative kind. They can then be generalized, by some of their representatives, as movements of conversion, analogous to early religious movements, and as such disdainful both of what is seen as mere intellectualism and of the whole system of organized politics.

These differences have to be recognized. Yet the most remarkable fact about both the peace and the ecology movements of recent years has been their relative success in combining scientific information, at quite new levels of practical development, with the direct action, in witness and exposure, of both small-group protests and huge public demonstrations. This is never either an easy or a stable combination, but in the degree it has practically reached, in many countries, it is already a new political factor.

A similar kind of combination has been evident in the most recent phases of feminism. There is now a remarkable and growing body of distinctively feminist scholarship and argument, shifting our intellectual perspectives in many fields, while at the same time there has been a major expansion of supportive groups and initiatives, as well as sharp public and private challenges to old dominative and subordinating habits. This degree of combination is relatively stable, resting as it does on more immediate identities and bondings than are available in the peace and ecology movements. At the same time, as is evident from the quality of the intellectual work, the specific directions of what is called "the women's movement", but is more often an association of distinctive movements with different bases and intentions, are still being formed and are subject to crucial interactions with other forms of political organization, many of these not yet resolved.

It would be possible to project, from these humane and growing movements – peace, ecology and feminism – an immediately potential and effective political majority. Yet the general situation is not really like that. The potential cannot reasonably be doubted. It is the immediacy that is the problem. There is now a major risk that there will be a jump from this sense of potential, centred in the reasonable belief that these movements represent the deepest interests of large human majorities, to an option of indifference towards all other organized and institutionalized political and social forms. The jump seems irresistible, time and again, as we look from these dimensions of concern and possibility to the mechanical thinking and manoeuvring practice of most of these forms for most of their time. Yet this is still not a jump that can be reasonably made, especially by some loose analogy with early religious movements or with heroic minorities whose objective time will come. That option should already have been rejected in the experiences of the sixties, even if there were not such clear intellectual arguments against it.

For it is not only in the movements of peace, ecology and feminism that the shift has begun. It is also in the vigorous movement of what is called an alternative culture but at its best is always an oppositional culture: new work in theatre, film, community writing and publishing, and in cultural analysis. But what has been learned very clearly in all this work, and in new kinds of political and ideological analysis, is that the relations between small-group initiatives and potentials and a dominant system are at the very centre of the problem. It is there that we have learned how new work can be incorporated, specialized, labelled: pushed into corners of the society where the very fact that it becomes known brings with it its own displacements. It is possible here also to persist as a minority, but in the cultural system as a whole it is soon clear that the central institutions are not residual – to be disregarded, for their often residual content, until the emergent minority's time has come – but are dominant and active, directing and controlling a whole connected process towards which it is impossible to be indifferent. And if this is true of the cultural system, it is even more strongly true of the general social and political system which the institutionalized forms control and direct.

At the practical centre of this problem are the existing political parties. For it is clear that at all effective levels it is towards such parties that the system now directs us. Yet it is equally clear that the central function of these parties is to reproduce the existing definitions of issues and interests. When they extend to new issues and interests, they usually lead them back into a system which will isolate, dilute and eventually compromise them. If there is one thing that should have been learned in the years since 1945, it is this. Indeed in Britain, where in the early 1960s the popular cause of nuclear disarmament was entrusted to an apparently welcoming Labour Party, only then to sink without trace, for some fifteen years, at either effective popular or institutional levels, the lesson has been very sharp and should be unmistakeable. Moreover, it is not of a kind that can be reversed by the now systematic apologias for such events, assigning merely local and proximate causes and assuring everyone that it is bound to be different next time. In their present forms the parties are practically constituted to be like this. They absorb and deflect new issues and interests in their more fundamental process of reproducing and maximizing their shares of the existing and governing dispositions.

It need not stay like this. For comparable in importance to the growth of new issues and movements is a steady withdrawal of assent to orthodox politics by what is in all relevant societies a sizeable minority of a different kind, and in some societies an already practical majority. Thus except in conditions of unusual stability, which are not going to be there, the pressures on existing political forms and institutions will in any case become irresistible. It is because one likely outcome of these pressures is a harsh movement beyond the now familiar forms, into new and more open kinds of control and repression, that there can be no jump to any kind of indifference to the institutions. On the contrary, just because there will be so many pressures of a negative, cynical and apathetic kind, it is essential that the carriers of the new and positive issues and interests should move in on the institutions, but in their own still autonomous ways.

This point has special reference to the institutions of the labour movement. It is clear that these began, in all or most of their original impulses, beyond the terms of what were then the governing definitions. They were genuine popular responses, slowly built over generations, to changes in the social and economic order which were at least as fundamental as those which we are now beginning to experience. Yet any comparative measure of degrees of change has to be assessed also in two further scales. First, the relative speed of current transfers of employment beyond the societies in which the institutions were shaped, and the interaction of this with internally generated structural unemployment. Second, the basic orientation of the institutions to predominantly male, predominantly stable, and above all nationally-based and nationally-conceived economic processes.

In both these respects the existing institutions have become not only insufficient but at certain key points actually resistant to new kinds of issue. The new issues of peace and of feminism have been included in certain ways: the former as a commitment to nuclear disarmament, but characteristically of a "unilateral", nationally-based kind; the latter as a limited responsibility to women workers as trade unionists, but largely omitting, in theory and especially practice, response to the wider critique of hierarchy and dominance. The relative indifference of the institutions to the new cultural movements is notorious. Their confidence in their sets of received ideas keeping new kinds of thinking at a distance ratified by the disdain for "intellectuals" and "academics" which they share with their capitalist masters – has ensured that at the broadest public levels they have been losing the decisive intellectual arguments. In relation to the ex-colonial world, the political affiliations of an earlier epoch have been sustained but there has been a radical unwillingness to face the consequences of the contemporary domination of the international economic order by capitalist trading forms within which, from positions of advantage, their own "labourist" economic policies and assumptions are still based.

It is possible and necessary to believe that substantial changes can be made, on each of these issues, in the general direction of the existing institutions. Yet by their nature this cannot be done by any form of intellectual affiliation to them. On the contrary, the only relevant approach is one of challenge. This is especially important in what is often the most urgent practical area, that of elections. There is an orthodox electoral rhythm in the society as a whole. But there is also a rhythm of radical thought, in which periods of intense activity on the decisive long-term issues are punctuated by silences, compromises, evasions, expressions of meaningless goodwill and artificial solidarity, which are thought appropriate because an election is imminent. It is not only that much of this is in any case vanity. What a radical minority does or does not do in these large spectacular events, dominated by the deployment of competitive leaderships, is not in practice very important. But what is much more serious is the practical surrender of the real agenda of issues to just that version of politics which the critique has shown to be deceptive and is offering to supersede.

There are some elections which are genuinely decisive: especially some which it is important not to lose, with all the evident consequences of some reactionary or repressive tendency being strengthened. Specific decisions to be electorally active in these terms are entirely reasonable. There are also some rarer occasions when an election can be much more positively worked for, because it contains the probability of some coherent advance. But even in these cases there can be no intellectual affiliation to the adequacy of the processes themselves, and no defensible temporary pretence that they are other than they are. The challenging move towards the existing institutions, which can be effectively made only if there are already alternative institutions and campaigns on a different issue-based orientation, is in no way reducible to elections, or even to party programmes and manifestos. The central approach is always to the actual people inside them, but then on the same terms as the much wider approach to the significant number of people who are at their edges or who are leaving or have left them.

This approach, by definition, has to be in good faith, candid, open to learn as well as to teach: in all those real senses comradely. But we should now have reached the end of a period in which campaigners and intellectuals acquired the habit of going as petitioners or suppliants, touched by guilt or by an assumed deference to so much accumulated wisdom. There is hardly anything of that kind to go to any longer, and any of it that is genuinely wise will not require deference or sidelong flattery. If it is indeed the case, as now seems likely, that the most the existing institutions can do, in their fixed terms, is conduct losing defensive battles, then much deeper loyalties are in question, in the survival and welfare of actual people.

*III*

The toughest element in all the changes that will need to be made is in the economy. It is significant that the new movements are active and substantial in almost every area of life except this. It is as if everything that was excluded by the economic dominance and specializations of the capitalist order has been grasped and worked on: in the real issues of peace, of ecology, of relations between men and women, and of creative artistic and intellectual work. Movements of a new kind race ahead in these areas, with new bodies of argument and action. But meanwhile, back in the strongholds of the economic order itself, there are not only the dominant institutions and their shadow subordinates. There are, for most of the time, most of the people.

Thus it has been possible to move relatively large numbers of people on popular versions of the issues of disarmament, protection of the environment, the rights of women. There is then an apparent asymmetry between these real advances and persistent majorities of a different kind: conservative (in more than one party); nationalist; consumerist. Some people make desperate attempts to prove that this is not so, seizing on all the exceptions, all the local breaks, all the local resistances. But while these must of course be respected, there is no real point in pretending that the capitalist social order has not done its main job of implanting a deep assent to capitalism even in a period of its most evident economic failures. On the old assumptions it would have been impossible to have four million people unemployed in Britain, and most of our common services in crisis or breaking down, and yet for the social order itself to be so weakly challenged or political support for it so readily mobilized. Yet that is where we now are.

It is then no time for disappointment or recrimination. All that matters is to understand how this can happen, and this is not in fact difficult. All the decisive pressures of a capitalist social order are exerted at very short range and in the very short term. There is a job that has to be kept, a debt that has to be repaid, a family that has to be supported. Many will fail in these accepted obligations after all their best efforts. Some will default on them. But still an effective majority, whatever they may do in other parts of their minds or in other areas of their lives, will stick in these binding relations, because they have no practical alternative. The significance of predominantly middle-class leadership or membership of the new movements and campaigns is not to be found in some reductive analysis of the determined agencies of change. It is, first, in the fact of some available social distance, an area for affordable dissent. It is, second, in the fact that many of the most important elements of the new movements and campaigns are radically dependent on access to independent information, typically though not exclusively through higher education, and that some of the most decisive facts cannot be generated from immediate experience but only from conscious analysis.

What is then quite absurd is to dismiss or underplay these movements as "middle-class issues." It is a consequence of the social order itself that these issues are qualified and refracted in these ways. It is similarly absurd to push the issues away as not relevant to the central interests of the working-class. In all real senses they belong to these central interests. It is workers who are most exposed to dangerous industrial processes and environmental damage. It is working-class women who have most need of new women's rights. The need for peace in which to live and to bring up our families is entirely general. But then it is a consequence of the social order that, lacking the privileges of relative social distance and mobility, or of independent (often publicly funded) access to extended learning, the majority of employed people – a significantly wider population than the working-class in any of its definitions – have still primarily to relate to short-range and short-term determinations.

Even the issues that get a widening response are marginalized as they encounter this hard social core. Moreover what is repeatedly experienced within it, and has been put there to be experienced, is a prudence, a practical and limited set of interests, an unwillingness to be further disturbed, a cautious reckoning and settling of close-up accounts. Whatever movement there may be on issues at some distance from these local and decisive relations, there is no possibility of it becoming fully effective until there are serious and detailed alternatives at these everyday points where a central consciousness is generated. Yet it is at just these points, for historically understandable reasons, that all alternative policies are weakest.

*IV*

The hard issues come together on two grounds: the ecological argument, and changes in the international economic order. There are times when all that seems to flow from these decisive issues is a series of evident and visible disadvantages, losses of position, to the employed majorities in the old industrial economies. Some campaigners still race ahead, on defensible grounds of universal need or justice. But they can hardly then be surprised that they are not followed. Indeed what often happens is that their proposals soon become even more unrealistic. There is at times an indiscriminate rejection of all or most industrial production, supported by some option for local crafts or for subsistence agriculture. It is not that these are unavailable ways of life. It is that they are unavailable as whole ways of life for the existing populations of urban industrial societies. The association of such wholly unrealistic proposals with the central critique of industrial-capitalist society is then either an indulgence or a betrayal. It can still be either of these when it is accompanied by talk of an imminent moral conversion.

The means of livelihood of the old industrial societies will in any case change; are indeed already changing. But there is then need for more qualified, more rational and more informed accounts. The intellectual problem, however, is that while certain principles can be established, all actual policies have to depend on new and difficult audits of resources, which must by definition be specific. We can look first at the principles, but their full practical bearings cannot be set down except in this place and that, by this enquiry and that, in a sustained and necessarily negotiated process.

The principles that matter are as follows. First, we have to begin, wherever we can, the long and difficult movement beyond a market economy. Second, we have to begin to shift production towards new governing standards of durability, quality and economy in the use of non-renewable resources. Third, and as a condition of either of the former, we have to move towards new kinds of monetary institutions, placing capital at the service of these new ends.

These principles are very general, but some specific cases look different in their light. Thus, if we begin the movement beyond a market economy, it is by no means inevitable, as the capitalist order now threatens, that many or even most industrial assembly processes should be moved out of the old economies. Nor is it inevitable that transformation-manufacturing processes should be similarly moved out. On the contrary, the decisions about any of these would be subject to a different kind of accounting.

The most obvious new reference point would be the relation of any of these processes to indigenous resources. It is only the capitalist accounting of cheap labour elsewhere that is exporting many kinds of assembly. On the other hand, processes which centrally depend on the import of major raw materials would be among the first to be transferred to those economies which could radically improve their own livelihoods by their own indigenous manufacturing and processing. There would doubtless be exceptions and anomalies, as these long shifts were negotiated, but if the principle of moving beyond the market economy is taken seriously such shifts have to be made. They can be accounted as losses in the old industrial economies, as many of them would necessarily be. But there can be corresponding gains, not only in some productive transfers to new advanced technologies, developed in relation to actual indigenous resources, but also in the retention of many kinds of assembly and manufacture which would otherwise, by the operations of the now dominant global market, be transferred elsewhere. They often become a false priority in those other societies, which could better determine alternative kinds of development from their own resources and needs. It follows, inevitably, that equitable kinds of mutual protection would then have to be negotiated, as alternatives to the destructive interventions which the market, following only its own criteria, would otherwise quickly impose.

Again, in the new emphases on durability, reclamation, maintenance and economy of resources, there are some immediate losses that would have to be negotiated. A significant part of current production is oriented by the market towards relatively early obsolescence and replacement, and many jobs depend on these cycles. Yet it is only the false accounting of the market system that makes reclamation now economically marginal, and it is probable that in many processes the result of the different emphases would be a broadly comparable area of work but with many quite basic real savings. The examples of badly-made and short-term houses, furniture, toys, cars and a whole range of everyday equipment are already clear, from our experience as users. There have been sharp declines in quality over a range even of genuine short-term goods, from bread to ironmongery. The market pressures for cheap standardized production based on minimal adequacy and early replacement have distorted the common sense of a whole economy. In certain sectors of the market, of a relatively privileged kind, this lesson has already been learned and there has been a movement towards greater quality and durability, avoiding the selling routines and devices of the "mass" market. But to generalize this would mean gaining control over the central production processes, rather than the best that is now, within market terms, foreseen, of extending the "quality" market. This is not, except in a very few areas, a return to "crafts." On the contrary, it is mainly a redirection of available and new advanced technologies to the priorities of production rather than the priorities of marketing. A wholly unreasonable proportion of technical development has been assigned to improvements in marketing – now the leading edge of the whole system – rather than to the improvements in production – durability, quality, economy – which will be centrally necessary in the material conditions which lie ahead of us.

There can be no changes of these kinds unless there is a successful challenge to the monetary institutions which, centred on a financial rather than a material world, and predominantly oriented to short-term profit, now sustain what should be seen as obsolescent economies. A large part of contemporary capital is now socially generated, through taxation, savings, insurance and pension funds, over and above the direct capitalist generation through surplus value. It should then be axiomatic that these are subject to direct social controls, for investment in a different kind of economy. But it is very doubtful if this can be achieved by any of the older socialist methods, and especially by procedures of state centralization. The most promising way forward is through a combination of new kinds of auditing of resources, within self-determining political areas, with a related auditing of available monetary resources of these kinds. Instead of the existing and uninviting alternatives of state or corporate appropriation, there should be a linked process, democratically discussed and determined, of the actual planning of physical investment and the allocation of funds. Production and service decisions should be determined by locally agreed needs, and monetary investment similarly determined by local retention of its own self-generated funds. In the long and complex negotiations towards this radically alternative system there would undoubtedly have to be arrangements for transfers between relatively advantaged and disadvantaged areas.

This process, structurally very similar to the complex negotiation of income transfers in quite new conditions of employment, will be the central political problem of the coming generations. But it has only to be compared with the predictable results of the existing alienations and appropriations of capital, and of the consequent dislocations and widening inequalities within and between societies, to stand out as necessary, and to generate the will to find new procedures.

All these changes would be occurring within the radical changes in working habits already discussed. The market economy, left to itself, will continue to produce massive redundancies, including of whole societies, which it has not the least chance of regulating and compensating by any orthodox political means. At the same time, in its current dominance, it is inducing fatalism by its ideological insistence that its processes, and its alone, are "economic." In fact, through the linked development of shorter working time and of new schemes of education and retraining, and through the new procedures of locally audited decisions on the kinds of work undertaken, there is every chance of making, even in very diverse and sometimes unfavourable circumstances, stable and equitable economies in which all necessary work is reasonably shared. Genuine labour-saving in certain kinds of production could be linked with a necessary expansion in all the caring services – themselves typically labour-intensive and relatively economical in resources and especially imported resources. But this can happen only if there are new kinds of linkage between production and expenditure, cutting out the institutions that now appropriate and distribute them by their own alienated priorities. What could be a major opportunity for easing the strains of work without discarding large numbers of people will be seized only if this kind of commitment to a directly determined social order, rather than to either corporate capitalism or a centralized socialist command economy, begins to grow from a popular base.

It is here that the assessment of political resources for so different a social order is at its most critical point. There is really only one sector in which these alternative kinds of thinking and planning can be effectively developed, and that is in the trade unions and professional associations. Many kinds of expert help – scientific, technical and economic – will be needed. But none of it can happen, in the necessary practical ways, unless trade-union organization, now typically oriented to corporate-capitalist and national scales, becomes more flexible in two new directions: first in direct relations with effective smaller-scale political communities; and second, in extended relations with the international labour movement.

There are already some signs of such developments. But there is bound to be a long and difficult transition from the existing kinds of state-centred and industry-centred organizations and priorities. The signs of change, understandably, are occurring in crisis-hit enterprises – as in the alternative production plans of the Lucas Aerospace shop stewards – or in areas which already have some distinctive political identity and have been especially hard hit by the current depression – Scotland, Wales, London, the English North-East. The political problem is to extend and generalize these early shifts of direction, beyond the emergencies which now govern them, until there is a labour movement of a new kind, determined to take direct responsibility for the organization of work and resources, and capable of taking such responsibility, through new kinds of open and qualified research and planning.

In fact the extension of the trade-union movement to workers in some of the most complex areas of technology, management and finance offers a real possibility of this kind of cooperative transformation. At every level this would be very different from the reproductive and defensive strategies which are still dominant. These old strategies, excluding broader public considerations or merely projecting them to an incompetent all-purpose political party, now hold the movement back from the real work it has to do.

It is in what will happen in this central economic area that the future of the social order will be determined. Once there is significant movement here, the alternative movements and campaigns which can alone make general sense of the kind of society which an alternative economic order must serve will move into a radically different set of political relationships and possibilities.

## V

What is now beginning to emerge, to support these changes, is at least the outline of a unified alternative social theory. This involves three changes of mind.

First, as I argued in my analysis of the industrial revolution, the connection between the forces and the relations of production has to be restated. It is evidently false to abstract the forces of production, as in technological determinism. But it is equally false to abstract the relations of production, as if they were an independent variable. It is no longer reasonable to believe, as in most modern forms of socialism, that these can be independently altered or transformed. On the contrary, what is at issue within both the forces and the relations of production is a set of alternatives at a more fundamental level of decision. The dominant version has been a basic orientation to the world as available raw material. What has been steadily learned and imposed is a way of seeing the world not as life forms and land forms, in an intricate interdependence, but as a range of opportunities for their profitable exploitation. It is then true that this has been most damaging within a capitalist economy, in its relentless drives for profit and for the accumulation of capital. But this cannot reduce the argument to one against the property and wage forms of capitalism. If that were true, we would have no way of explaining the continuing appropriation and exploitation of the world as raw material in the "communist" or "actually existing socialist" economies.

The necessary new position is that this orientation to the world as raw material necessarily includes an attitude to people as raw material. It is this use and direction of actual majorities of other people as a generalized input of "labour" which alone makes possible the processes of generalized capital and technology. Thus the drive to use the earth as raw material has involved, from the beginning, the practical subordination of such majorities by a variety of means: military, political, economic, ideological. The system of capitalist property and wage relations is only one such form. Slavery and serfdom preceded it. Modern forms of the mobilization and direction of labour can succeed it. In any of these cases, what is most at issue is the basic orientation itself, in which relations to other people and to the physical world have changed and developed in a connected process, within which the variations are important but neither absolute nor, in our present situation, decisive.

It is clear from our material history that what we can now see as a basic orientation was developed through several critical stages, each increasing its practical effects. Its first stage can be seen in the complex of changes which are summarized as the Neolithic and Bronze Age Revolutions, in which, with the development of farming, stockbreeding and metalwork, decisive interventions in a constituted nature were successfully made. Yet this stage, which was indeed the appropriation and transformation of certain life forms and land forms as raw material, was still highly selective and coexisted with other forms of social and natural orientation. We can see this very clearly if we compare it with the last stages of this orientation, through which we are now living. In the development of much more powerful technologies, and in their capture by a class which defined its whole relationship to the world as one of appropriation, what was once selective and guided by conscious affinities with natural processes has been replaced by a totalitarian and triumphalist practice in which, to the extent that it succeeds, there is nothing but raw material: in the earth, in other people, and finally in the self.

The early interventions in a constituted nature were, in the strict sense, new means of livelihood. It has taken a very long time to transform these reasonable intentions and practices to the stage at which we now find ourselves. There has been a remarkable increase in such means of livelihood but *as part of the same process* (which we are now in a position to observe) a remarkable increase also in forms of death and destruction. Each part of the process is beyond the terms of a constituted nature.

It is then tempting to try to revert, if only in principle, to a stage before these conscious interventions. But this is neither possible nor necessary. We are now in a position where we can monitor our interventions, and control them accordingly. We can select those many interventions which support and enhance life, in continuing ways, and reject those many other interventions which have been shown to be damaging or to involve the reasonable possibility of damage. This is the central ecological argument. But it can only prevail if we unite it with the political and economic argument, in ways that then change what we have become used to as politics and economics. For it is the ways in which human beings have been seen as raw material, for schemes of profit or power, that have most radically to be changed. Some of these changes are already inscribed in the deepest meanings and movements of democracy and socialism. But not all of them are, and the exclusions now limit and even threaten to destroy these two most hopeful forces of our world.

What is most totalitarian about the now dominant orientation is its extension beyond the basic system of an extraction of labour to a practical invasion of the whole human personality. The evidence of treating people as raw material is not to be gathered only in accounts of wages and conditions, or of real absolute poverty, serious and often grave as these are. It is present also in an area which has been conventionally excluded from both politics and economics. It is quite clear, for example, in those sexual attitudes and practices which have been correctly identified, principally by feminists, as treating people as "sex objects." There is now a major interpretation of sexual relationship as finding, in another person, the raw material for private sensations. This has been profitably institutionalized in pornography, but there are much more serious effects in the actual physical treatment of others, with women and children especially vulnerable.

Failure in such versions of relationship is wholly predictable since relationship is precisely an alternative to the use of others as raw material. But what is most totalitarian about this failure is that it extends not only to the cruel punishment of others, who indeed in these terms cannot yield the lasting satisfactions that are sought, but also to the cruel punishment of self: in alcoholism, in addiction to damaging drugs, in obesities and damaging asceticisms. For the very self is then only raw material in the production of sensations and identities. In this final reach of the orientation, human beings themselves are decentred.

Thus there are profound interconnections in the whole process of production – that version of relations with others and with the physical world – to which the now dominant social orders have committed themselves. The way forward is in the neglected, often repressed but still surviving alternative, which includes many conscious interventions in a constituted nature but which selects and directs these by a fundamental sense of the necessary connections with nature and of these connections as interactive and dynamic. This can emerge, in practice, only if it is grounded in a conception of other people in the same connected terms. But this is where the intellectual difficulties of uniting the ecological and economic arguments, in a new kind of politics, are most evident. This brings us to the second necessary change of mind.

The concept of a "mode of production" has been a major explanatory element of the dominant social orders through which we have been living. It has enabled us to understand many stages of our social and material history, showing that the central ways in which production is organized have major and changing effects on the ways in which we relate to each other and learn to see the world. But what has now to be observed is that the concept itself is at some important points a prisoner of the social orders which it is offering to analyse. It has been most successful and enlightening in its analysis of capitalism, and this is not accidental, for in its own conceptual form it seized the decisive element of capitalism: that this is a mode of production which comes to dominate both society as a whole and – which is less often stressed – the physical world. The eventual inadequacy of the concept is then that it has selected a particular historical and material orientation as essential and permanent. It can illuminate variations of this orientation, but it can never really look beyond it. This fact has emerged in the most practical way, in that the great explanatory power of Marxism, where this concept has been most active, has not been accompanied by any successful projective capacity. For all that follows from one mode of production is another, when the real problem is radical change, in hard social and material terms, in the idea of production itself.

Thus it is not surprising to find that Marx shared with his capitalist enemies an open triumphalism in the transformation of nature, from the basic orientation to it as raw material. He then radically dissented from the related and cruel uses of people as raw material, and looked for ways in which they could organize to transcend this condition and control production for themselves. This is his lasting and extraordinarily valuable contribution. Yet in basing his thought on an inherited concept of production – one which is in no way a necessary outcome of the most rigorous historical materialism – Marx was unable to outline any fully alternative society. It is not only the attempts and failures to find such alternatives, in the name of such thinking however diluted or distorted, which confirm this conclusion. The problem and the obstacle are in the concept itself.

For the abstraction of production is a specialized and eventually ideological version of what is really in question, which is the form of human social relationships within a physical world. In his justly influential idea of "man making himself" Marx seized one specialized moment which connected with the developed processes he was observing in his own time: the intervention in nature to transform it as new means of livelihood: that is, to *produce*. Yet "man" – actual men and women – had been "making themselves", developing their social and material skills and capacities, long before this specialized and conscious intervention. Living within a constituted nature, in the hunting and gathering societies, they had already developed high social and technical skills. The long subsequent shift, through successive stages of intervention and production, altered both nature and people but was nevertheless in some major respects continuous with that earlier human phase. The sense of a connection with constituted nature was still the ground of the most successful innovations, in that selective breeding of plants and animals which positively depended on continuing interactive observation. It is in the major interventions we now class as technological – from metal working to modern chemistry and physics – that the sense of transforming intervention is strongest, but all these, in practice, at their most useful, have similarly depended on continuing interactive observation, within both a physical and a social world. It is then only at the point when these processes are abstracted and generalized as "production", and when production in this sense is made the central priority over all other human and natural processes and conditions, that the mode of intervention – at once material and social – becomes questionable. The decisive question is not only about intervention – "production" – itself, but about its diverse practical effects on nature and on people.

It is this which social analysis based only on a "mode of production" prevents us from seeing or from taking seriously. For, just as capitalist production, in practice, attempted to substitute itself for the broader and more necessary principle of human societies in a natural world, so this concept, in theory, attempted to substitute itself for the broader bases of human social and material activities. It was common to see human history before such specialist interventionist production as a mere prehistory; almost in effect pre-human. What has now to be seen, at this most intense stage of the isolation and dominance of interventionist production, spreading rapidly over the entire planet and beyond it, is another stage of prehistory, or, better, a second but now concluding stage of history, as active but also as limited as that which preceded it.

For the consciousness of the possibilities of intervention, which inaugurated that phase of history which connects to our own time, is now, at a point of great danger, being succeeded by a new consciousness of its full effects. They are at once its real and sustainable advantages and its at first inextricable recklessness and damage to people and to the earth. It is in this new consciousness that we again have the opportunity to make and remake ourselves, by a different kind of intervention. This is no longer the specialized intervention to produce. The very success of the best and most sustainable interventions has made that specialized and overriding drive containable. Where the new intervention comes from is a broader sense of human need and a closer sense of the physical world. The old orientation of raw material for production is rejected, and in its place there is the new orientation of livelihood: of practical, self-managing, self-renewing societies, in which people care first for each other, in a living world.

A third change of mind follows, when we have replaced the concept of "society as production" with the broader concept of a form of human relationships within a physical world: in the full sense, a way of *life*. This change appears in one special way, in the current movement beyond the specialization and contrast of "emotion" and "intelligence." It is understandable that people still trapped in the old consciousness really do see the new movements of our time – peace, ecology, feminism – as primarily "emotional." Those who have most to lose exaggerate this to "hysterical", but even "emotional" is intended to make its point. The implied or stated contrast is with the rational intelligence of the prevailing systems. In reaction to this there is often a great business of showing how rational and intelligent, in comparable ways, the campaigns themselves are. Moreover, and increasingly, this is true. But a crucial position may then be conceded. For it is in what it dismisses as "emotional" – a direct and intransigent concern with actual people – that the old consciousness most clearly shows its bankruptcy. Emotions, it is true, do not produce commodities. Emotions don't make the accounts add up differently. Emotions don't alter the hard relations of power. But where people actually live, what is specialized as "emotional" has an absolute and primary significance.

This is where the new broad concept most matters. If our central attention is on whole ways of life, there can be no reasonable contrast between emotions and rational intelligence. The concern with forms of whole relationship excludes these specialized and separated projections. There are still good and bad emotions, just as there are good and bad forms of rational intelligence. But the habit of separating the different kinds of good from each other is entirely a consequence of a deformed social order, in which rational intelligence has so often to try to justify emotionally unacceptable or repulsive actions.

The deformed order itself is not particularly rational or intelligent. It can be sharp enough in its specialized and separated areas, but in its aggregates it is usually stupid and muddled. It is also, in some of its central drives, an active generator of bad emotions, especially aggressiveness and greed. In its worst forms it has magnified these to extraordinary scales of war and crime. It has succeeded in the hitherto improbable combination of affluent consumption and widespread emotional distress.

Informed reason and inquiry can explore these complex forms, but it is not surprising that the strongest response to them has appeared at the most general "emotional" levels. Before any secondary reasons or informed intelligence can be brought to bear, there is an initial and wholly reasonable reaction, carrying great emotional force, against being used, in all the ways that are now possible, as mere raw material. This response can develop in several different directions, but where it is rooted in new concepts, now being steadily shaped, and in many kinds of relationship – forms of genuine bonding which are now being steadily renewed and explored – it is already generating the energies and the practical means of an alternative social order.

It can then make a difference that this alternative is being clarified theoretically. The central element is the shift from "production" to "livelihood": from an alienated generality to direct and practical ways of life.

These are the real bases from which cooperative relationships can grow, and the rooted forms which are wholly compatible with, rather than contradictory to, other major energies and interests. They are also, at just this historical stage, in the very development of the means of production, the shifts that most people will in any case have to make.

## VI

It is reasonable to see many dangers in the years towards 2000, but it is also reasonable to see many grounds for hope. There is more eager and constructive work, more active caring and responsibility, than the official forms of the culture permit us to recognize. It is true that these are shadowed by the most general and active dangers. They are shadowed also by the suspicion – which the official culture propagates but which also comes on its own – that as the demonstration disperses, as the talk fades, as the book is put down, there is an old hard centre – the reproduction of a restricted everyday reality – which we have temporarily bypassed or ideally superseded but which is there and settled and is what we have really to believe.

Two things have then to be said. First, that the objective changes which are now so rapidly developing are not only confusing and bewildering; they are also profoundly unsettling. The ways now being offered to live with these unprecedented dangers and these increasingly harsh dislocations are having many short-term successes and effects, but they are also, in the long term, forms of further danger and dislocation. For this, if we allow it, will be a period in which, after a quarter of a century of both real and manufactured expectations, there will be a long series of harshly administered checks; of deliberately organized reductions of conditions and chances; of intensively prepared emergencies of war and disorder, offering only crude programmes of rearmament, surveillance and mutually hostile controls. It is a sequence which Plan X can live with, and for which it was designed, but which no active and resilient people should be content to live with for long.

Secondly, there are very strong reasons why we should challenge what now most controls and constrains us: the idea of such a world as an inevitable future. It is not some unavoidable real world, with its laws of economy and laws of war, that is now blocking us. It is a set of identifiable processes of *realpolitik* and *force majeure*, of nameable agencies of power and capital, distraction and disinformation, and all these interlocking with the embedded short-term pressures and the interwoven subordinations of an adaptive commonsense. It is not in staring at these blocks that there is any chance of movement past them. They have been named so often that they are not even, for most people, news. The dynamic moment is elsewhere, in the difficult business of gaining confidence in *our own* energies and capacities.

I mean that supposing the real chances of making a different kind of future are fifty-fifty, they are still usually fifty-fifty after the most detailed restatement of the problems. Indeed, sometimes, in one kind of detailed restatement, there is even an adverse tilt. It is only in a shared belief and insistence that there are practical alternatives that the balance of forces and chances begins to alter. Once the inevitabilities are challenged, we begin gathering our resources for a journey of hope. If there are no easy answers there are still available and discoverable hard answers, and it is these that we can now learn to make and share. This has been, from the beginning, the sense and the impulse of the long revolution.

READING 14

# *Nineteen Eighty-Four* in 1984 (1984)

## Editor's Introduction

Williams's third and final account of Orwell's dystopia is developed in this essay, which was first published as an afterword to the second edition of *Orwell* and as a separate article in *Marxism Today*. He begins by observing that the novel has three distinct layers: an "infrastructure," where the hero-victim moves through a degraded world in search of a better life; a "structure of argument" concerning the nature of the fictional society; and a "superstructure" of fantasy, satire, and parody which renders this society ludicrous and absurd. Williams's main interest was in the second layer, which he saw as comprising three main themes: the division of the world into super-states; their internal organization along totalitarian lines; and the crucial significance to the latter of media manipulation through "thought control." He is clear, as he had not been in the book's first edition, that these societies have "developed beyond both capitalism and socialism" and that the novel is not therefore "anti-socialist." Indeed, he requotes exactly the same passage from the Auto Workers Union letter, so as to insist that: "This is a much harder position than any simple anti-socialism or anti-communism."

Not that Williams is uncritical of *Nineteen Eighty-Four*. Rather, he subjects it to much the same mode of analysis as that in *The Country and the City*: comparing Orwell's projections, as developed in the novel and in political essays, with the real world that eventuated in the post-Second World War period. Unitary super-states did not emerge, Williams points out, only superpowers and their attendant military alliances; the arms race between these superpowers generated affluence and technological innovation, rather than the stagnation and poverty envisaged by Orwell; and the superpowers were often resisted, both by local tradition in the metropolitan heartlands and by national-liberation movements in the former colonial periphery. More fundamentally, what Orwell had most failed to anticipate was the "spectacular capitalist boom," which falsified "virtually every element of the specific prediction." Here, Williams revisited his own earlier charge that Orwell had "specialized" the argument about totalitarianism to the socialist tradition. Here, however, he adds the important and paradoxical parenthesis: "by his own choice, though he protested against it." If this still seems not quite right – where exactly was the choice? – it does suggest a more developed sense of Orwell's political vision.

Williams quotes extensively from Orwell's 1946 essay on James Burnham – which he ignored in the first edition of *Orwell* – so as to situate the novel in a very precise politico-intellectual context. Like Burnham, Orwell believed capitalism finished; unlike Burnham he hoped to see it replaced by democratic socialism, but like Burnham he also acknowledged the strong possibility that quasi-socialist rhetoric would be used to legitimize the "managerial revolution" and bureaucratic dictatorship. Burnham anticipates this prospect with some relish, Orwell with much fear. Hence, the latter's insistence, both with and against Burnham, that: "the question is whether capitalism, now obviously doomed, is to give way to oligarchy or to true democracy" (*Collected Essays, Journalism and Letters* Vol. 4, 198). This, then, was for Williams Orwell's crucial mistake: to have imagined capitalism already beaten and, hence, the central issue as that between different "socialisms." As it turned out, the real "question" would be that of a resurgent capitalism, re-legitimized by post-war affluence and radically oligarchic in its own later responses to the renewed depression and unemployment of the last quarter of the century. What really survives, Williams concludes, is "Orwell's understanding of propaganda and thought control," even though the thought-controllers are press lords and film magnates rather than totalitarian ideologues.

In effect, Williams pitted his own futurology against Orwell's, *Towards 2000* against *Nineteen Eighty-Four*. Williams's stress on "national and international monetary institutions" and "their counterparts in the giant paranational corporations" seems right, not only as an account of how late capitalism actually works, but also as a way into understanding why *Nineteen Eighty-Four* seems dated, for example, by comparison with Huxley's *Brave New World*. From *Alien* and *Blade Runner*, through cyberpunk, to Kim Stanley Robinson and David Cronenberg, the most persuasive near-future sf of the late twentieth and early twenty-first centuries has taken, as its central thematic, precisely that collusion between state power and transnational corporate-media capital, which Williams targeted fictionally in *The Volunteers* and politically in *Towards 2000*.

Williams also turns Orwell's essay on Burnham against the novel in what would turn out to be his own last word on dystopia. He repeats the earlier argument that, in its very hopelessness, *Nineteen Eighty-Four* killed hope; that its warnings against totalitarianism are themselves so totalitarian that, "in the very absoluteness of the fiction," it becomes "an imaginative submission to its inevitability." But he adds that Orwell himself rejected precisely this kind of submission before power in Burnham. "Burnham never stops to ask why people want power," Orwell wrote, because he assumes that power hunger "is a natural instinct that does not have to be explained." This is O'Brien's answer to Winston in Room 101, Williams comments, the only answer available anywhere in the novel. But there "*are* reasons," Williams continues, "as outside the fiction Orwell well knew," reasons which must be sought for and distinguished, the good from the bad, the better from the worse, so as to avert the brute cynicism of Burnham's attempt "to discredit all actual political beliefs and aspirations." Williams's last reading of *Nineteen Eighty-Four* is clearly richer than its predecessors: it combines a more developed understanding of the novel's workings as a text with an expanded sense of its socio-political and intertextual contexts. But his suspicion of radical dystopia remains essentially unchanged.

## *Nineteen Eighty-Four* in 1984 (1984)

It was never at all likely that any actual society, in 1984, would much resemble the hellhole of Orwell's novel. He was in any case not making that kind of prediction:

> I do not believe that the kind of society I describe necessarily *will* arrive, but I believe (allowing of course for the fact that the book is a satire) that something resembling it *could* arrive (*Collected Essays, Journalism and Letters* Vol. 4, 564).

The qualification is important. He had written earlier:

> this is a novel about the future – that is, it is in a sense a fantasy, but in the form of a naturalistic novel. That is what makes it a difficult job – of course as a book of anticipations it would be comparatively simple to write (*Collected Essays, Journalism and Letters* Vol. 4, 378).

This difficulty of the form needs emphasis, as we try in his arbitrarily dated year to reassess his vision. The form is in fact more complex than the combination, in his terms, of "fantasy" and "naturalistic novel." For there is a third element, most clearly represented by the extracts from the notorious Book and by the appendix on "The Principles of Newspeak." In the case of the Book, especially, the method of the writing is that of argument: the historical and political essay.

There are then in effect three layers in the novel. First, an infrastructure, immediately recognizable from Orwell's other fiction, in which the hero-victim moves through a squalid world in a series of misunderstandings and disappointments, trying and failing to hold on to the possibility – as much a memory as a vision – of a sweeter kind of life. Second, a structure of argument, indeed of anticipations, in the extracts from the Book and in some of the more general descriptions of the actual society. Third, a superstructure, including many of the most memorable elements, in which, by a method ranging from fantasy to satire and parody, the cruelty and repression of the society are made to appear at once ludicrous and savagely absurd.

The three levels are of course interconnected, though, as he recognized, imperfectly. The figure of the hero-victim is connected because at the centre of his memory or vision is an idea of truth, which the social order is determined to destroy. The everyday squalor is more generally connected, in the argument that the state of perpetual war has been instituted to keep people poor, but also as a bitter reversal of the normal condition of the authoritarian Utopia, in which material plenty is commonplace. Similarly, the most bizarre elements of the superstructure – the spy telescreen, Newspeak, the memory hole, the Two Minutes Hate, the Anti-Sex League – are satirical projections of the state of mind of the central social order:

> I believe [...] that totalitarian ideas have taken root in the minds of intellectuals everywhere, and I have tried to draw these ideas out to their logical consequences (*Collected Essays, Journalism and Letters* Vol. 4, 564).

As for the passages of argument, Orwell strongly resisted a suggestion from an American publisher that they should be abridged.

> It would alter the whole colour of the book and leave out a good deal that is essential (*Collected Essays, Journalism and Letters* Vol. 4, 544).

He made the same point in commenting on a draft blurb from his English publisher:

> It makes the book sound as though it were a thriller mixed up with a love story, & I didn't intend it to be primarily that. What it is really meant to do is to discuss the implications of dividing the world up into "Zones of influence" (I thought of it in 1944 as a result of the Teheran conference), & in addition to indicate by parodying them the intellectual implications of totalitarianism (*Collected Essays, Journalism and Letters* Vol. 4, 519–520).

It is then from Orwell's own sense of the book that we can find support for taking this central structure of argument, this element of reasoned anticipation, as important. Moreover it is above all with this central structure that a re-reading in 1984 should be primarily concerned.

This is so in spite of some formal difficulties, which can be briefly noted. Writing under great difficulties, because of his illness, Orwell undoubtedly had problems in integrating these levels of argument. This is especially clear in the fact that the essay on "The Principles of Newspeak" had to be put in as an appendix, though some of it is a more developed version of the description and examples he had included in the main narrative. It is one of Orwell's liveliest essays, but there is a problem of position, caused by its attachment to the story. Thus within the first two pages Orwell veers between a position as historian of Ingsoc and Newspeak –

> It is with the final, perfected version, as embodied in the Eleventh Edition of the Dictionary, that we are concerned here (*Nineteen Eighty-Four* 312).

– and a position as contemporary essayist, contemplating the horrible projection –

> Newspeak was founded on the English language as we now know it, though many Newspeak sentences, even when not containing newly created words, would be barely intelligible to an English speaker of our own day (313).

This kind of uncertainty, in fact soon overcome by the interest of the examples, is repeated in a more serious way in the extracts from the Book. On the one hand, as will be shown, they are very close to some of Orwell's own political thinking at the time, and even closer to some of his more obvious sources. They are in any case presented as from the secret Book of the underground opposition, the Brotherhood, and as written by the reviled Goldstein. On the other hand, like so much else that at first sight appears hopeful and trustworthy, they are eventually presented as elements of the Party's total deception. The Inner Party torturer O'Brien says:

> "I wrote it. That is to say, I collaborated in writing it. No book is produced individually, as you know."
> "Is it true, what it says?"
> "As description, yes. The programme it sets forth is nonsense." (274)

The intricacies of deception and betrayal, and of the deliberate confusion of truth and lies, are at this point so great that it is futile to ask which version Orwell intended readers to believe. What matters much more is that the extracts are there – whatever the plausibility of their use in an already complete trap – because Orwell wanted to set out, in a consecutive argument, his ideas of how the world was going and could go. The narrative status of the Book becomes important only when we compare his fictional projections, in the extracts and in the more general story, with what he was writing in the same years without these special problems of form.

Three themes predominate in this central structure on which, at the level of ideas, the book is founded. First, there is the division of the world into three super-states, which in shifting alliances are in a state of limited but perpetual war. Second, there is the internal tyranny of each of these states, with a specific version of the relations between social classes and a detailed presentation of a totalitarian society which has been developed beyond both capitalism and socialism. Third, there is the exceptional emphasis on the control of a society through ideas and means of communication: backed up by direct repression and torture but mainly operating through "thought control."

These three themes need to be considered in detail, both in Orwell's presentation of them and in the actual history to which they offer to relate. It is especially important to consider all three, and to see how Orwell thought of them as essentially interrelated. Ironically, however, it is only possible to consider them, with the seriousness that he expected, if we isolate them, temporarily, from the actual structure of the novel, and, in a more permanent way, from the resonance which, since its publication, has surrounded it.

It would be possible, for example, to run a silly kind of checklist on the projections. Is there an Anti-Sex League? Is there a two-way telescreen for spying on people in their homes? Is there a statutory Two Minutes Hate? No? Well then it just shows, as some said at the time, that the book is a wild kind of horror-comic, or at best stupidly exaggerated. But these are elements of the parodic superstructure. The structure then? Yet in the predominant political resonance which has surrounded the novel we do not even have to look at these arguments, because their proof is already given in the real world. "This is where socialism gets you." "This is where it has already got, in Russia and Eastern Europe." But Orwell was quick to separate himself from this interpretation, which accounted for much of the early success of the book and which is still offered as if it were beyond question.

> My recent novel is NOT intended as an attack on Socialism or on the British Labour Party (of which I am a supporter) but as a show-up of the perversions to which a centralized economy is liable and which have already been partly realized in Communism and Fascism (*Collected Essays, Journalism and Letters* Vol. 4, 564).

"*Partly* realized", in the social orders directed by Stalin and Hitler. The full perversions are shown as going further. Moreover the easy response, to put down the book and look East, where "it is all already happening", should be checked by Orwell's emphasis:

> The scene of the book is laid in Britain in order to emphasize that the English-speaking races are not innately better than anyone else and that totalitarianism, *if not fought against*, could triumph anywhere (564).

The point is more than one of local correction, against the use and abuse of the novel during the cold war. It is central to Orwell's arguments that what is being described, in its main tendencies, is not only a universal danger but a universal process. That is the true source of his horror. If the novel is absorbed into the propaganda of this or that state, as a basis for hating and fearing an enemy state, against which there must be preparation for war, there is the really savage irony that a citizen of Oceania, in 1984, is thinking as he has been programmed to think, but with the reassurance of the book to tell him that he is free and that only those others are propagandized and brainwashed. Orwell was offering no such reassurance. He saw the super-states, the spy states, and the majority populations controlled by induced ideas as the way *the world* was going, to the point where there would still be arbitrary enemies, and names and figures to hate, but where there would be no surviving faculty of discovering or telling the truth about *our own* situation: the situation of any of us, in any of the states and alliances. This is a much harder position than any simple anti-socialism or anti-communism. It is indeed so hard that we must begin by examining what he took to be its overpowering conditions, leading first to the super-states and to limited perpetual war.

## II

*Nineteen Eighty-Four* is so often quoted as a vision of the worst possible future world that it may seem odd to say that in at least one respect Orwell notably underestimated a general danger. It is not often remembered that in the novel a war with atomic bombs has been fought in the 1950s. There are not many details, though it is mentioned that an atomic bomb fell on Colchester. This is one of several instances in which, read from the actual 1984, the novel can be clearly seen as belonging to the 1940s. Orwell was quick to comment on the importance of the new weapon. He wrote in *Tribune* in October 1945 that it was dangerous mainly because it made the strong much stronger; its difficult manufacture meant that it would be reserved to a few powerful societies that were already heavily industrialized. "The great age of democracy and of national self-determination" had been "the age of the musket and the rifle." Now, with this invention,

> we have before us the prospect of two or three monstrous super-states, each possessed of a weapon by which millions of people can be wiped out in a few seconds, dividing the world between them (*Collected Essays, Journalism and Letters* Vol. 4, 25).

This is not only the outline of the world of *Nineteen Eighty-Four*. It is also an intelligent recognition of the actual power of the new weapons. Yet still, after this, he included in his story a war with atomic weapons after which, though with its own kinds of horror, a relatively recognizable land and society survived. This is no discredit to Orwell. Again and again it has been almost impossible to imagine the true consequences of an atomic *war*, as distinct from the one-sided use of the bomb which has been the only actual event. Indeed there has been a familiar kind of *doublethink* about nuclear weapons, in which it is simultaneously if contradictorily known that they would lead to massive and in many cases absolute destruction and yet that, with sufficient political determination, of whatever kind, they could be absorbed and survived.

The idea of an atomic war in the 1950s was common enough in the middle and late 1940s. It was seen as virtually inevitable, once more than one state possessed atomic bombs, by several writers and especially by James

Burnham, about whom Orwell wrote two substantial essays in the years in which he was writing *Nineteen Eighty-Four*. Orwell began his novel in August 1946 and completed the first draft in November 1947. His essay "Burnham and the Managerial Revolution" was published in May 1946 and "Burnham and the Contemporary World Struggle" in March 1947. The essays are full of the themes of the novel, and there are several close correspondences between them and the fictional extracts from the Book. On the other hand there are significant differences between Orwell's discriminating discussions of Burnham's theses and the relatively simplified presentation of closely comparable ideas in the Book.

Thus Burnham's argument in *The Struggle for the World* is that the United States, while in sole possession of the atomic bomb, should move to prevent any other nation ever acquiring it. Orwell comments that "he is demanding, or all but demanding, an immediate preventive war against Russia", and indeed such proposals, to be preceded by ultimatum like demands to abandon "communism" or "world-communism", were directly made by others. Against such arguments, Orwell in the later essay hoped that there would be more time than Burnham had supposed: "perhaps ten years, but more probably only five" (*Collected Essays, Journalism and Letters* Vol. 4, 363, 360). If there was indeed more time there would be better political directions than an American world order and an anti-communist crusade. He added that "the more the pessimistic world-view of Burnham and others like him prevails, the harder it is for such [alternative] ideas to take hold" (371).

It is strange now, when Burnham has been largely forgotten, and when *Nineteen Eighty-Four* is so much better known than Orwell's essays, to retrace the formation of the "pessimistic world-view" of the novel. We can look again at the idea of the dominant superstates. In the novel it is as follows:

> The splitting up of the world into three great super-states was an event which could be and indeed was foreseen before the middle of the twentieth century. With the absorption of Europe by Russia and of the British Empire by the United States, two of the three existing powers, Eurasia and Oceania, were already effectively in being. The third, Eastasia, only emerged as a distinct unit after another decade of confused fighting (*Nineteen Eighty-Four* 192–193).

This is more or less directly taken from Burnham:

> Burnham's geographical picture of the new world has turned out to be correct. More and more obviously the surface of the earth is being parcelled off into three great empires, each self-contained and cut off from contact with the outer world, and each ruled, under one disguise or another, by a self-elected oligarchy (*Collected Essays, Journalism and Letters* Vol. 4, 25).

The idea is now so familiar, from the novel, that some effort is needed to realize the strangeness of Orwell's assertion, at that date, that the picture "has turned out to be correct", and, further, that the empire nearest home – the American/British of the fictional Oceania is, like the more frequently cited Soviet empire, "ruled [...] by a self-elected oligarchy."

The next stage in Orwell's development of the idea, while he was in the middle of writing his novel, follows from his definition of three political possibilities: a preventive war by the United States, which would be a crime and would in any case solve nothing; a cold war until several nations have atomic bombs, then almost at once a war which would wipe out industrial civilization and leave only a small population living by subsistence agriculture; or

> That the fear inspired by the atomic bomb and other weapons yet to come will be so great that everyone will refrain from using them. This seems to me the worst possibility of all. It would mean the division of the world among two or three vast super-states, unable to conquer one another and unable to be overthrown by any internal rebellion. In all probability their structure would be hierarchic, with a semi-divine caste at the top and outright slavery at the bottom, and the crushing out of liberty would exceed anything that the world has yet seen. Within each state the necessary psychological atmosphere would be kept up by complete severance from the outer world, and by a continuous phony war against rival states. Civilizations of this type might remain static for thousands of years (*Collected Essays, Journalism and Letters* Vol. 4, 424).

This is, in effect, the option taken by the novel, though an intervening and less damaging atomic war has been retained from earlier positions. In his directly political writing, at this time, Orwell saw an alternative to all three dangers: the building of "democratic Socialism [...] throughout some large area [...] A Socialist United States of Europe seems to me the only worth-while political objective today" (425). But in the perspective of the fiction this is entirely absent.

Obviously we must ask, in 1984, why none of Orwell's three (or four) possibilities has occurred. Yet we must do this soberly, since we shall not be released from any of the dangers he and others foresaw by the mere passage of a fictional date. It is not, in some jeering way, to prove Orwell wrong, but to go on learning the nature of the historical developments which at his most serious he was trying desperately to understand, that we have to ask what he left out, or what he wrongly included, in his assessment of the world-political future.

First we have to notice that what came through, in this period, were not unitary super-states or empires but the more complex forms of military superpowers and primarily military alliances. There are times, especially as we listen to war propaganda, when we can suppose that the Burnham/ Orwell vision has been realized, in the monolithically presented entities of "East" and "West", and with China as the shifting partner of either. But the full political realities have turned out to be very different. There is, for example, a coexistent and different hierarchy of *economic* power, with Japan and West Germany as major forces. In significantly different degrees in "East" and "West", but everywhere to some extent, old national forms have persisted and continue to command the loyalty of majorities, though also in every such nation, including those of "the West", there is a significant minority who are conscious agents of the interests of the dominant power in the military alliance.

At the same time, in ways that Orwell could not have foreseen, these elements of political autonomy and diversity – within very narrow margins in the Warsaw Pact, within broader margins in NATO which contains most kinds of political state from liberal democracies to military dictatorships – are radically qualified by the nature of modern nuclear-weapons systems. The atomic war of *Nineteen Eighty-Four* is damaging but not disastrous; in fact it is made to precipitate the "perpetual limited war" which is a central condition of the novel, in which the superstates are unconquerable because their rulers cannot risk atomic war. The war actually being fought, with its distant battles and its occasional rockets, belongs technologically to the 1940s. But then it is not only that the effects of atomic war have been underestimated; it is that the military and political consequences of a relative monopoly of nuclear weapons have turned out to be quite different from anything that Orwell and most others supposed.

> Suppose – and really this is the likeliest development – that the surviving great nations make a tacit agreement never to use the atomic bomb against one another? Suppose they only use it, or the threat of it, against people who are unable to retaliate? In that case we are back where we were before, the only difference being that power is concentrated in still fewer hands and that the outlook for subject peoples and oppressed classes is still more hopeless (*Collected Essays, Journalism and Letters* Vol. 4, 25).

Between the powers that have acquired atomic weapons there has been neither formal nor tacit agreement never to use the weapons against one another. On the contrary, the predominant policy has been one of mutual threat. Within this policy there has not, as Orwell thought, been technical stagnation, but a continual enlargement and escalation of weapons systems, each typically developed under an alleged threat of the superiority of the other side. And these have now reached the point at which national autonomies, within the alliances, contradict in one central respect the technical requirements of the most modern systems, which require instant response or even, some argue, preventive first use, if the other power is not to gain an early and overwhelming advantage.

It would be easy to argue from this, yet again, that the Burnham/Orwell kind of super-state, with the necessary unitary command, is inevitable, as a product of the new weapons. But to move to that kind of super-state, for all its strategic advantages, would be to provoke major political problems – especially, for example, in Western Europe – which would endanger and probably break the now fragile compromise between surviving political autonomies and loyalties and the military-strategic alliance which has been superimposed on them. Thus Britain, in 1984, both is and is not, in Orwell's phrase, Airstrip One. It is dense with its own and foreign air and missile bases but it is also – and crucially, by a majority, is valued as – an independent political nation. To force the question to the point where it would have to be one thing *or* the other would bring into play all the forces which Orwell recognized in his essays but excluded from the novel. For the agents of paranational military and economic planning Britain has become, in a true example of Newspeak, the UK or Yookay. But for the peoples who live on the actual island there are more real and more valued names and relationships and considerations.

It is in the exclusion of even these traditional elements of resistance to what might seem a logical new order that Orwell, in the novel though usually not in the essays, went most obviously wrong. But there is an even larger error in the exclusion of new forces of resistance: most notably the national-liberation and revolutionary movements of what he knew as the colonial world. The monopoly of nuclear weapons, in the major industrialized states, has not prevented major advances towards autonomy among the "subject peoples" whose condition he predicted as more hopeless. This is the peculiar unreality of the projection, that the old world powers, newly grouped into super-states, are seen as wholly dominant, and that the rest of the world is merely a passive quarry of minerals and cheap labour. Again, however, what has actually happened is complex. There have been political liberations in this vast area that Orwell reduced to passivity, but there is a limited sense in which what he foresaw has happened: not in superstate wars for its control, but in a complex of economic interventions, by paranational corporations which have some of the technical attributes of super-states; of political interventions, manoeuvres and "destabilizations"; of exceptionally heavy arms exports to what in the worst cases become client states; and of military interventions, in some cases, where heavy and bloody fighting still excludes the use or threat of use of the nuclear weapons which in the perspective of the 1940s had seemed decisive for either conquest or blackmail.

Thus there has been, in one sense, the "perpetual war" that Orwell thought likely, but it has been neither of a total nor of a phoney kind. The complex political and economic forces actually engaged have prevented the realization of the apparently simple extrapolations from technical necessity or political ambition. It is sometimes hard to say, at this world-political level, whether the real 1984 is better or worse than the projected Nineteen Eighty-Four. It is more complex, more dynamic, more uncertain than the singular nightmare. Many more people are free or relatively free than the projection allowed, but also many more people have died or are dying in continuing "small" wars, and vastly more live in danger of annihilation by nuclear war. The rationed and manipulated shortages of the projection have been succeeded by an extraordinary affluence in the privileged nations, and by actual and potential starvation in extending areas of the poor world. It is then not for showing danger and horror that anyone can reproach Orwell. If there is to be reproach, it is for looking so intently in one direction, with its simplified and easily dramatized dangers, that there is an excuse for not looking at other forces and developments which may, in the end, prove to be even more disastrous.

## III

"War is Peace" is one notable chapter of the Book. As a comment on a perpetual and normalized *state* of war its details may be wrong but its feeling is right. "We are the peace movement," a British Government minister said recently, supporting the next phase of rearmament.

"Ignorance is Strength" is the other main chapter. This eventually describes the purposes and methods of thought control, but it begins with an analysis of the social structure of the super-states, based on a sort of historical-political theory:

> Throughout recorded time, and probably since the end of the Neolithic Age, there have been three kinds of people in the world, the High, the Middle and the Low. They have been subdivided in many ways, they have borne countless different names, and their relative numbers, as well as their attitude towards one another, have varied from age to age: but the essential structure of society has never altered. Even after enormous upheavals and seemingly irrevocable changes, the same pattern has always reasserted itself [...] (*Nineteen Eighty-Four* 209).

It is at points like this that the status of the Book, in relation to Orwell's own thinking, is most problematic. Many examples could be quoted to show that he understood history as change rather than this abstract recurrence. The point is relevant again when the Book asserts:

> No advance in wealth, no softening of manners, no reform or revolution has ever brought human equality a millimetre nearer (210).

This is, as written, such obvious nonsense that the status of the whole argument becomes questionable. If this were really true, there would be no basis for calling Ingsoc a "perversion"; it would be yet one more example of an inevitable, even innate process.

Clearly Orwell did not believe this, and neither did the author or the authors of the Book, a page or two on. For what is there argued is that while in earlier periods, because of the stage of development of the means of production, "inequality was the price of civilization", in the twentieth century "human equality had become technically possible" with the development of "machine production." However, just at that point, "all the main currents of political thought" stopped believing in equality and became authoritarian.

This level of argument is so perverse that one could indeed believe that O'Brien had written it. But more significantly it is an imperfect composition of three incompatible kinds of argument: one from Orwell, one from Burnham and one from Marx. The Marxist proposition of the unavoidable relations between the stages of development of the means of production and the formation of class societies, with the orthodox communist gloss that fully developed machine production would at last make equality possible, is unmistakably present. The Orwell argument or reservation that much talk of this kind, among its actual representatives, is just a cover for a new authoritarian conspiracy, ending capitalism but then even more thoroughly repressing and controlling the working class, is also evident. But the really discordant element, though it becomes dominant, is from Burnham. As Orwell summarizes him in the first essay:

> Every great social movement, every war, every revolution, every political programme, however edifying and Utopian, really has behind it the ambitions of some sectional group which is out to grab power for itself [...] So that history consists of a series of swindles, in which the masses are first lured into revolt by the promises of Utopia, and then, when they have done their job, enslaved over again by new masters (*Collected Essays, Journalism and Letters* Vol. 4, 210).

In the essay Orwell circles hesitantly and intelligently around these crude propositions. He even comments:

> He [...] assumes that the division of society into classes serves the same purpose in all ages. This is practically to ignore the history of hundreds of years (211).

And he goes on from this to the Marxist proposition, repeated in the Book, on the relation of class society to methods of production.

At the level of Orwell's direct arguments, then, the eventual emphasis of the Book is a known simplification. But it is the combination of this simplification with his own, often reasonable, reservations and suspicions about socialists or nominal socialists who are really authoritarians which determines the social structure of *Nineteen Eighty-Four*. His own contribution is then more specific than Burnham's. Burnham had foreseen a "managerial revolution." As Orwell summarizes:

> Capitalism is disappearing, but Socialism is not replacing it. What is now arising is a new kind of planned, centralized society which will be neither capitalist nor, in any accepted sense of the word, democratic. The rulers of this new society will be the people who effectively control the means of production: that is, business executives, technicians, bureaucrats and soldiers, lumped together by Burnham under the name of "managers." These people will eliminate the old capitalist class, crush the working class, and so organize society that all power and economic privilege remain in their own hands. Private property rights will be abolished, but common ownership will not be established (*Collected Essays, Journalism and Letters* Vol. 4, 192).

This is not, in any full sense, how things have actually turned out, though there are elements that are recognizable. But Orwell did not call the new social order Ingmana; he called it Ingsoc. Burnham's prediction, and the wider argument of which it is a relatively simple instance, pointed as clearly to Fascism and the Corporate State, or to what is now called a managed, interventionist post-capitalism, as to an authoritarian communism. It was Orwell who specialized it to a development within the socialist tradition, which it was also betraying. We can then, in 1984, only properly assess the prediction if we pull back to its full context.

In one way it is easy to understand Orwell's narrowing specialization. Fascism, when he was writing, had just been militarily defeated. Capitalism, he assumed, was finished and deserved to be finished. What then mattered was which kind of socialism would come through, and since his option was for democratic socialism what he had mainly and even exclusively to oppose was authoritarian socialism.

> The real question is not whether the people who wipe their boots on us during the next fifty years are to be called managers, bureaucrats or politicians: the question is whether capitalism, now obviously doomed, is to give way to oligarchy or to true democracy (*Collected Essays, Journalism and Letters* Vol. 4, 198).

This makes strange reading in 1984, especially if *Nineteen Eighty-Four* is there to tell us to concentrate our attention on Ingsoc and the Party. It is true that within the countries of what is now called "actually existing socialism" this is broadly how it has turned out. Indeed the only correction we have to make, in that area, is that "the Party", in that singular ideological sense, has proved to be less significant than the actual combination of technicians, bureaucrats and soldiers which the political monopoly of the Party makes possible and legitimizes. It was significant during the Solidarity crisis in Poland that the different fractions of this hitherto effective ruling group were shown, under pressure, to have crucially variable interests, and more generally the idea of the monolithic Party has been shown to be false by a continuing series of internal dissensions and conflicts. However, that "actually existing socialism" is still the prime case (though closely followed by the "nationalized" or "publicly owned" industries of the capitalist democracies) of the prediction that "private property rights will be abolished, but common ownership will not be established."

This does not mean, however, that the Orwell prediction of oligarchy has to be specialized, as in the novel, to "Oligarchical Collectivism." There are and for a long time have been many other forms of oligarchy. The most important modern form depends on the centralization of effective political and economic controls. This has been associated with state versions of socialism, and indeed, ironically, Orwell conceded and approved this association:

> Centralized control is a necessary pre-condition of Socialism, but it no more produces Socialism than my typewriter would of itself produce this article I am writing (*Collected Essays, Journalism and Letters* Vol. 4, 36).

But so far from this idea of a centralized socialism being a modern perversion, or likely to lead to it, it is in fact an old kind of socialism, of the period of the Fabians as much as of the Bolsheviks, and it has been increasingly rather than decreasingly challenged by new socialist ideas of decentralized politics and economic self-management. Orwell, in that sense, is behind even his own time.

Yet this is still to specialize the argument about oligarchy to socialism, when what has really undermined the basis of Orwell's prediction has been the phenomenal recovery of capitalism, which he had seen as "doomed." The spectacular capitalist boom from the mid-1950s to the early 1970s falsified virtually every element of the specific prediction. The real standard of living rose for many millions of working people. The main socialist movements, in the old industrial societies, moved steadily towards a consensus with the new, affluent, managed capitalism. Political liberties were not further suppressed, though their exercise became more expensive. The main motor of the boom, in an extraordinary expansion of consumer credit, was a new predominance of financial institutions, which gained in power at the expense of both political and industrial forces. When the boom ended, in depression and the return of mass unemployment, a new oligarchy was plainly in view. The national and international monetary institutions, with their counterparts in the giant paranational corporations, had established a both practical and ideological dominance which so far from being shaken by the first decade of depression and unemployment was actually reinforced by it. These were the actual forces now "wiping their boots on us", in the old industrial societies and the new ex-colonial countries alike. Internally and externally they had all the features of a true oligarchy, and a few people, at least, began to learn that "centralization" is not just an old socialist nostrum but is a practical process of ever-larger and more concentrated capitalist corporations and money markets. State power, meanwhile, though trying to withdraw from its earlier commitments to common provision for social welfare, has increased at military levels, in the new weapons systems, and in its definitions of law and order and of security (backed up by some intensive surveillance). Thus it is an obvious case of *doublethink* when the radical Right, now in power in so many countries, denounce the state at the level of social welfare or economic justice but reinforce and applaud the state at the level of patriotic militarism, uniform loyalty, and control over local democratic institutions. To hear some of the loudest of these double-mouthed people is to know what is meant, in Newspeak, by a *doubleplusgood duckspeaker.*

But then what about the *proles*? Here again the prediction was quite wrong, though there are a few disillusioned people thinking it might have been right. For the key feature of the new capitalist oligarchy is that it has not left "eighty-five per cent of the population" to their own devices. On the contrary, it has successfully organized most of them as a market, calling them now not "proles" but "consumers" (the two terms are equally degrading). It is true that there is massive provision, by the newspapers and other media of the oligarchy, of the semi-pornography and gambling and mechanical fiction which the Party was supposed to provide. (This, incidentally, is one of Orwell's interesting errors about Soviet communism, where the Party has exercised its ideological controls *against* these mainly "Western" phenomena.) But the real controls are different. A straight contract between disciplined wage-labour and credit-financed consumption was offered and widely accepted. Even as it became unavailable to the many millions who in depression became, in that cruel oligarchic term, "redundant", its social and political hold, as the essence of any social order, was at first barely disturbed. Indeed the ideological response of the oligarchy was to act to make the contract more secure: by disciplining the trade unions which represent an independent element in its bargaining, beyond oligarchic control; and by identifying as public enemies, in its newspapers, dissenting political figures: not the "proper official Opposition" but the "unofficial" Reds, Wreckers, Extremists, who in good *Nineteen Eighty-Four* style are seen as either mad or guilty of *thoughtcrime.*

*IV*

It would be surprising if one kind of oligarchy could succeed, for long, in using the features of another to distract attention from its own. Yet *Nineteen Eighty-Four*, in 1984, is being primarily used for just this purpose, ironically by some of the same propaganda methods which it exposes and attacks. Because what Orwell wanted to show as a universal tendency became attached (by his choice, though he protested against it) to the practice of socialism, any anti-socialist movement can exploit it, even in ways which confirm its own deepest warnings. It is one thing for dissident and oppositional groups in Eastern Europe to say, as some of them do, that *Nineteen Eighty-Four* shows the underlying truth of their condition. I was asked by students, in one communist country, to lecture on Orwell, and I did so willingly, against some official disapproval, because I wanted to follow the whole argument through: not just what could be mocked or hated but what could still, genuinely, be believed. Beyond the obvious pyrotechnics of the projection there is, however qualified, a steady insistence on the value of thinking for oneself and of refusing the official simplifications which all ruling groups employ. The more there is to be mocked or hated, in any system, the more it is necessary to resist these feelings being used by others, for their own governing purposes. One scene in the novel sticks in my mind, in this later period, when the figurehead of the Opposition, Goldstein, appears on the screen –

> demanding the immediate conclusion of peace with Eurasia [...] advocating freedom of speech, freedom of the Press, freedom of assembly, freedom of thought [...] And all the while, lest one should be in any doubt as to the reality which Goldstein's specious claptrap covered, behind his head on the telescreen marched the endless columns of the Eurasian army (14–15).

This trick is now being played so often: certainly in official denunciations of unofficial peace, civil rights and workers' movements in Eastern Europe as "Western-inspired"; but just as certainly in the West, as when the independent peace movements are directly accused of serving Russian interests, "the endless columns of the Eurasian army." Meanwhile anyone can see that the other side's Big Brother is a tyrant and a fraud, but the endlessly imposed ruling faces of one's own side are supposed indeed to be "loved."

It is interesting that what has really survived, from *Nineteen Eighty-Four*, is Orwell's understanding of propaganda and thought control. There have been changes of style and technology but certain basic methods of the oligarchy – endlessly repeated slogans, displacements of one kind of news by another, the regular institution of hate-figures – are still clearly recognizable. In 1946 Orwell wrote:

> in England the immediate enemies of truthfulness, and hence of freedom of thought, are the press lords, the film magnates, and the bureaucrats (*Collected Essays, Journalism and Letters* Vol. 4, 87).

That familiar case still holds. But there is another key element in Orwell's diagnosis:

> but [...] on a long view the weakening of the desire for liberty among the intellectuals themselves is the most serious symptom of all (87).

It was from this conviction that some of the most specific features of *Nineteen Eighty-Four* were composed. In a way what is most surprising about its tyrannical system is that it more or less neglects eighty-five per cent of the population and is concerned mainly with controlling the thoughts and the very memories of a minority.

It is difficult to follow this kind of anticipation through. There are no obvious objective events from which to assess it. But I have sometimes felt that almost the exact opposite has happened. I do not mean that there have not been time-serving and even lying "intellectuals", together with a much larger executive group with conveniently selective memories. I mean that there is a case for saying that in the capitalist democracies there has been intense and continuous attention to the state of mind of the eighty-five per cent (or whatever the precise figure for majority popular opinion might be) and a relative indifference to what "intellectuals" – already marked off as peculiar – believe or do. It is different, I know, in the "actually existing socialist" societies, where there has been intense pressure, and worse, on just these minority groups. It can be reasonably argued that because the capitalist societies are electoral democracies attention to majorities is inevitable, while minorities can be disregarded and even sneered at or, obscurely, shown to be "wrong" *because* they are minorities. Yet, beyond this difference of systems, and even after allowing for the fact that Orwell was parodying monolithic one-party societies, it is still the case that he thought that the state of mind of intellectuals would be decisive. And then there is indeed some basis for saying that we could wish that he had been right.

The point bears most closely on the notorious "memory hole." For if there is one thing that has not proved necessary, in manipulating majority opinion, it is systematically rewriting the past. On the contrary, the past in itself becomes a kind of memory hole, from which only a few scholars and researchers bother to uncover and recover the facts. Why were the first atom bombs dropped on Japan *after* its government had proposed the outline of a peace? What really happened in the Gulf of Tonkin? Which way and during what peace negotiations was the *General Belgrano* sailing? These are questions (none, in their whole context, with very simple answers) which with a thousand others, from the role of Trotsky in the Russian Revolution to the policy of Mao and the Red Guards in China, are still intensely inquired into by small minorities, while the dominant public stance, in one social order after another, is to go blithely on with the news of the day, leaving the past to the obsessive and to the dry-as-dust. General versions of the past, selected and packaged to show the present as inevitable and the ruling future as desirable, are of course deployed. But the detail, the two-and-two of the inquiry, can be there and not there: in the books and the monographs and the seminars but not in what is aggressively presented as "the real world." Orwell was right, of course, to attack the time-serving, submissive and lying intellectuals whom he had encountered and saw proliferating. But in *Nineteen Eighty-Four* there is another level, quite contrary to his own best practice, in which the scheming and the power-hungry are of this intellectual kind, and the only actual alternative to them are the stupid and ignorant, protected by stupidity and ignorance. And what then of the Party slogan, *Ignorance is Strength*?

It has not, on any reckoning, worked out like that. This is especially the case in what he saw as the worst danger: power-worship. There has been plenty of that, but not just from some intellectual habit. Militarism, chauvinism, tough policing, penal cruelty have been general epidemics. And the people in charge of them, in any social order, have not needed intellectuals to justify what they are doing, though in some systems they take care to employ hacks. The powerful and the fraudulent have been the powerful and the fraudulent. Their interests are their reasons; they do not need cogitators.

But this brings us to the hardest question in a reassessment of *Nineteen Eighty-Four*. Worried and fascinated by Burnham's arguments that power is the only political reality, whatever phrases may accompany it, Orwell observed:

> It is curious that in all his talk about the struggle for power, Burnham never stops to ask *why* people want power. He seems to assume that power hunger, although only dominant in comparatively few people, is a natural instinct that does not have to be explained (*Collected Essays, Journalism and Letters* Vol. 4, 211).

It is fascinating that when Winston Smith comes to the point in his reading of the Book when this motive to power is to be explained he realizes that Julia has been asleep for some time and puts the book away, still wondering what the secret could be. The question returns only during his torture by O'Brien, and O'Brien answers it:

> The object of persecution is persecution. The object of torture is torture. The object of power is power. Now do you begin to understand me? (276)

"A natural instinct that does not have to be explained"? This is the terrifying irrationalism of the climax of *Nineteen Eighty-Four*, and it is not easy, within the pity and the terror, to persist with the real and Orwell's own question. The point of Burnham's position is to discredit all actual political beliefs and aspirations, since these are invariably covers for naked power or the wish for it. But if this is so, there is not only a cancellation of history – as Orwell in his essay went on to observe. The real variations of what happened, as well as of what was said and believed, are flattened into a meaningless, degrading uniformity of human action. There is also a cancellation of inquiry and argument, and therefore of the possibility of truth, since whatever is said can be instantly translated into the base and cruel reality which it is known to cover. It is not necessary to deny the existence, even the frequent occurrence, of persecution and power and torture "for their own sake" (meaning, for the private gratification of their executors, rather than for any objective cause) to go on resisting the cancellation of all links between power and policy. And this cancellation *must* be resisted, if only because it would then be pointless to try to distinguish between social systems, or to inquire, discriminatingly, where this or that system went good or went bad.

There is plenty of room for disagreement about the social and political systems which make arbitrary power, persecution and torture more or less likely. In the world of the actual 1984 there is so vast an extent of these practices, in social systems otherwise dissimilar – from Chile to Kampuchea, from Turkey and El Salvador to Eastern Europe, and with instances from as close to home as Belfast – that it is tempting to override the discriminating questions, to recoil from man become brute. Yet it is the two-plus-two kind of reckoning – obstinately factual and truthful, however complex the sums may become – that is then most at risk. There *are* reasons, as outside the fiction Orwell well knew, why there are systems and phases of systems in which, as throughout recorded history, opponents and even inconvenients are imprisoned, tortured and killed; just as there are other systems and phases of systems – nearly all of them modern; nearly all of them achieved by prolonged political argument and struggle – when these brutal short-cuts are lessened or brought under control. Of course Orwell is warning against a modern totalitarian system, developed beyond even Stalin or Hitler. But there is a totalitarian way of warning against totalitarianism, by excluding just those discriminating historical analyses, those veridical political distinctions, those authentic as distinct from assumed beliefs and aspirations, which are a much better protection against it than the irrational projection inspiring either terror or hate. It is useful to remember what he said of Burnham:

> Burnham is trying to build up a picture of terrifying, irresistible power, and to turn a normal political manoeuvre like infiltration into Infiltration adds to the general portentousness (*Collected Essays, Journalism and Letters* Vol. 4, 203).

It can be the same with Ingsoc. As he again said in discussing Burnham's thesis:

> Power worship blurs political judgment because it leads, almost unavoidably, to the belief that present trends will continue (207).

Yet Orwell himself, always an opponent of privilege and power, committed himself, in the fiction, to just that submissive belief. The warning that the world could be going that way became, in the very absoluteness of the fiction, an imaginative submission to its inevitability. And then to rattle that chain again is to show little respect to those many men and women, including from the whole record Orwell himself, who have fought and are fighting the destructive and ignorant trends that are still so powerful, and who have kept the strength to imagine, as well as to work for, human dignity, freedom and peace.

PART FOUR
## The Future Novels

READING 15

# From *The Volunteers* (1978)

## Editor's Introduction

Williams's eventual reputation will no doubt depend on his academic and scholarly work, perhaps even his political involvements, more than on his novels or plays. This does not seem to have been his own view, however. He thought of the novels especially as an important part of his work. Williams described *The Volunteers* as a "political thriller," rather than as sf. And, in Reading 11, he claimed to have "no direct experience" of writing the latter. Yet his recollection of wanting "to write a political novel set in the 1980s" (*Politics and Letters* 296), that is, in the then near-future, marks it out as the kind of future story he closely associated with sf in *The Long Revolution*. By most conventional academic definitions – Suvin's for example – the book is indeed sf and, ironically enough, sf written in the dystopian mode. For it is organized around the sociopolitical novum of a complete ideological and organizational collapse of the British Labour Party into "X-Planning" and coalition government with the Conservatives. This is, of course, more or less exactly what New Labour eventually achieved in historical reality, but in 1978 it remained a dystopian fictional novum. This novum is set within a changed technological landscape: a jet from London to Cardiff, an air-taxi to St Fagans, coin-operated seat-screens in railway station waiting-rooms. As Tony Pinkney observes, *The Volunteers* is "packed with gadgetry" and sf is the genre "that in its heart of hearts it truly aspired to" (*Raymond Williams* 93). But, as with Orwell's telescreens or Huxley's feelies, these technological devices remain narratively subordinate to the hegemonic sociopolitical novum.

The novel begins *in media res* on 9 July 1987 – *Nineteen Eighty-Four* had begun on 4 April 1984 – with news of an attempted assassination of Edmund Buxton, Secretary of State for Wales, shot by the Volunteer, "Marcus." Lewis Redfern, the novel's narrator and central protagonist, Marcus and his comrades, Mark Evans, the onetime Labour junior minister turned NGO organizer, the secret "Volunteers" with whom he is involved: all share connections with 1970s utopian activism. But, by virtue of these very connections, Redfern has now become a consultant analyst for Insatel, a global satellite TV station, specializing in spectacle and news, "tin gods of the open sky," as a critic describes it (154). Geo-spatially, the novel is structured around this opposition between hi-tech, global capitalism and its ruined and impoverished localities, from Wales to East Africa. In Williams's 1987, Wales enjoys pseudo self-government through a Welsh Senate, but its finances are firmly controlled by the Financial Commission, represented by Buxton, also a former Labour minister, but now in the service of the coalition. "So it is not his inherited class," Redfern tells us at the end of this extract, "that has produced his undoubted authoritarian character. He is that now more dangerous kind of man, whose authority and whose ruthlessness derive from his absolute belief in his models." In short, he is an X-Planner. He is also widely suspected of having ordered in the strike-breaking troops who shot and killed Gareth Powell, a picketing loader, at Pontyrhiw Power Depot. Hence, the charge of murder levelled at him by the Volunteers.

Buxton's shooting is Redfern's assignment, but the investigation leads back to Powell, to Evans, and to the Volunteers. The cynical journalist as hardboiled detective, Redfern makes use of his own radical connections to unravel what is, at one level, a mystery story. But it is also at least as good an attempt at postmodern "cognitive mapping" as that which Fredric Jameson found in William Gibson's *Neuromancer* (*Postmodernism* 54, 38). Provided with proof that Buxton was indeed personally responsible for ordering in the Army, and that Evans is indeed a Volunteer, Redfern is forced to choose between his profession and his erstwhile political allegiances. He resigns, goes into hiding, and finally gives evidence against Buxton at the Pontyrhiw Inquiry. As Pinkney notes, there are interesting parallels between Williams's Redfern and Ridley Scott's Deckard in *Blade*

*Runner*: both are eventually turned into that which they hunt (*Raymond Williams* 104–105). Though Pinkney fails to notice this, both also provide their respective texts with the occasion for an ambiguously optimistic resolution. For, although Redfern testifies to the Inquiry, he neither joins the underground nor comes to identify with his ancestral Welshness, nor even accepts the lift to the station offered by Powell's brother-in-law, Bob James. "No thanks, Bob," Redfern replies in the novel's closing line, "I'll find my own way back" (208).

# From *The Volunteers* (1978)

I was in the air fifty minutes after Buxton was shot. The fax was terse:

> MINISTER BUXTON SHOT WOUNDED GROUNDS FAGANS POST CEREMONY SUB RIOT HOSPITALIZED CARDIFF ASSAILANT NIL.

In the upstairs office the literati were already translating:

> We are just receiving a report that Mr Edmund Buxton, Secretary of State (Wales) in the Financial Commission, has been shot and wounded in the grounds of the Welsh Folk Museum at St Fagans, near Cardiff. Mr Buxton was visiting St Fagans to open a new extension and a newly re-erected building in the Folk Museum, which has extensive open-air exhibits. Earlier today he had presided at a joint session of the Financial Commission and the Financial Board of the Welsh Senate. When he arrived at St Fagans there was a noisy demonstration against him, but this was kept under control by the police. The shooting occurred later, but as yet we have no precise details. There are no reports of the assailant or assailants being detained. Mr Buxton, who is fifty-seven, has been flown to hospital in Cardiff. We shall of course keep you up to date with any further news as it comes in.

As a trailer this would do. Political sensation comes through like that. It might even jerk a few people awake. But almost everything that mattered was still there to find. We can all make the moves to catch history on the wing. But story and history are hard masters, once you take time to stay with them. The literati could fill in. We, downstairs, had to get out and meet the world.

There were eight of us on standby, but there was never any doubt who Friedmann would send. In my three years with Insatel, working out of their London terminal, I have acquired this instant identity: what the ex-intellectuals who run Insatel insist on calling a field. I am what they call their consultant analyst, on the political underground. Insatel is a news and events service. "Wherever it's happening, with Insatel you're there." In fact not you, public you; me, public me. Our reporter, your reporter. Wherever it's happening, Mr X marks the spot. But at conferences and in promotions they don't call us all reporters; they call some of us consultant analysts. Reporters are steam people, pre-media people. But we, I, have still to get up and go. If anything happens that sounds political, but that isn't a speech or a party conference, there I am sent: young mole burrowing.

Of course I've accepted the field: the underground field. It is all that keeps me in work. Insatel cost a fortune even before oil and wheat got together to inflate the international economy. As an idea it had belonged to the fast smooth days of universal expansion. Where better to put other people's money than an international television satellite service? After the moonshot, friends, this is the globeshot, the space-time fusion. That is to say, relatively fast television coverage of relatively predictable and relatively accessible events. Most of the events, of course, Insatel arranges itself: all the big sporting contests, the festivals, the exhibitions; Insatel's sponsoring contracts are virtually the only means of finance, in the capitalist world. But somewhere in the margins, on a different principle, other things occasionally happen, and that's where we become relevant, we in News Division. The network already installed for spectacle has this subsidiary facility for unarranged events.

Yet we go up and down, financially, on heavy things like oil and wheat; on cars and trucks and washing machines; on fibres, on metals, on food packaging. To run at all we depend on these other things moving. Incidents can occur anywhere, but incidents are not news. News depends on a system, and the system depends on resources. Insatel gets its resources from advertising, from the big para-national companies, who push round the oil and the fibres and the metals. To run fast we depend on them booming, and lately they haven't been booming. Consultant analysts, by the score, have become, overnight, out-of-work reporters.

Only Insatel's internal ratings saved my own job. In News Division the political underground runs second only to sport. International terrorist movements, bombs, hijackings, kidnaps: there is no better news in the business. Thus even in a (relatively) quiet part of the world, I was a consultant analyst they needed. I can get near these people. I understand their mental processes. I speak their language. Or so Insatel believes.

Nothing is now more respectable, in my kind of world, than an underground past. Until the middle eighties, with new things happening all around them, the media still sent their seasoned old men: tough veterans of the lobbies, the press conferences, and the small-hour ministerial negotiations. They never got within shouting distance. For a start they'd forgotten how to shout. No one now knows what they really did. My private guess is the airport bar, drinking with Immigration and Customs and stolidly alert for a shipment of foreign arms or foreign gold.

Then a new generation took over, or, to be strictly accurate, was inserted. There were a good many of us, a few years out of the active movement, needing jobs and a new kind of action. A few of us made it, while most of the generation drifted, fairly happily, into teaching and publishing and the respectable agencies. We lost touch with them, easily. But we didn't lose touch with the few who were sticking it out: squatting, translating, organizing, splitting, regrouping, marching, researching, recruiting, being recruited. That is still our world, we still think in its ways, though the consequent distinction between observer and participant has become, to put it mildly, a bit of an issue.

The really hard groups never touch us; we have to dig for them. Even when they issue their distant, quasi-official communiqués, they don't give them to us, who would know what questions to ask. They give them straight to the establishment, who wrinkle their long noses but still take them at face value, like all the other official handouts they're used to reporting. But many groups that appear quite hard do accept us, circumspectly, for what they can get, and that, of course, is publicity, visibility, some minimal sign that all that sustained, dedicated, voluntary work is having a little registered effect: of course distorted by the media but present in the media; a bitter habituation; the best exposure you can get.

All the soft and mixed groups come out to greet us, of course. When we arrive, they've arrived. "Sure," they say, "Insatel defines the spectrum, but look right into it, look at the contradictions of the system. It picks us up and distorts us; it also picks us up and connects us. The hard Right understands this; it wants all this coverage banned. And that's correct, because the whole situation is so dynamic and contradictory that our paradoxical news value is a danger to it. Once we're seen as existing, we become a real possibility, outside the orthodox channels. Dialectically, in fact, the media use us and we use the media." Nice sensible people otherwise. Much too nice to contradict.

It wasn't a soft group that had shot Buxton. Friedmann half expected me to solve it right there in his office, but he was very jumpy because he knew he'd just lost. Two days earlier, I had put this up to him. I hadn't known what was coming, but I'd seen something coming. I'd said that to let Buxton go to Wales, within four months of the events at Pontyrhiw (where a worker had been killed and eight others wounded, as the army moved in to occupy a power depot; moved in, it was widely suspected, on direct orders from Buxton) was provocative in anybody's language: anybody, that is, except the people who arrange these affairs, who are so much inside their tight little world they think public life is a sort of timetable: official visits must be paid, normal civil service must continue. I'd shown Friedmann leaflets of the huge demonstration that had been called for St Fagans when Buxton was due to arrive. I'd said it might be anything, though the most I'd then imagined was some kind of riot. He'd pushed it back at me. "You tell me, Lewis, the difference between these heaving images you'd get and any Welsh rugby crowd, singing for dear heart before some match or other."

He was having to digest that dismissive rhythm now. It had been his judgment, as Senior Analyst, that a factory occupation in West Bromwich was much more significant.

"Tell me the difference," I'd echoed, "between that and any library footage of locked gates and pickets."

*From The Volunteers (1978)*

"No," he'd said, "this may be different, Lewis. I just have that feel it may be different."

His feel had been rough. West Bromwich was respectable, by now in effect constitutional. Everything visible and reportable even finished early. And St Fagans, meanwhile, had erupted; the first political shooting in Britain this century. Either I could solve it then and there or I could turn round and take his jet. The offer indicated the depths of his disgust and remorse. That plane is his ego; even to ask for it, normally, amounts to personal assault. But here he was telling me to take it. He had been wrong so badly that I could have chartered a flying carpet and six gilded flamingos, so long as I got there.

"The crew's already moving," he said, with what would have been reproach if he'd quite had the nerve.

I took a car to the field, and was driven right up to the waiting plane. I enjoyed this routine immensely. Now there was only the actual work.

*II*

I went straight from the airport by air-taxi to St Fagans. A police headquarters had been set up in the castle: that kind of instinctive move which is always reassuring; it lets you know where you are, and what kind of world is assumed. Down to quite small details, in fact. The police themselves were in the office and the hall: the press-room was in that old kitchen, with its museum collection of ancient spits and utensils; stone-cold, hollow, but with plenty of room for menials like us. We sat at the plain scrubbed tables, facing the collections of old ladles and carving knives, in a kitchen which had everything but food.

We got a first briefing, towards midnight, from Superintendent Walter Evans. It was superficially very clear; in fact very vague. There was a large map of the immediate area: the castle, the main museum building, the park with its open-air reconstructions. Alongside it was a timetable of the main events. The Superintendent took us through both, and from this, and from what I had got earlier from the local reporters, an outline of the story emerged.

After the day's meetings in Cardiff, Buxton was due to open, at seven o'clock, the new wing of the main museum building. He would then go on into the park to open the latest re-erected building: the eighteenth-century Customs House and Harbour Master's Office from Aberesk, which had been taken down and removed during the construction of the new marina. The new wing was easily guarded, and Buxton landed by helicopter, straight from the joint session, in a cleared area of the car park. Six hundred police formed a square around the landing area. In the wing itself there were only carefully selected and invited guests.

Most of the programme had been known in advance, and one of the largest demonstrations ever seen in South Wales had gathered around the car park, after a march from Llandaff. Even before Pontyrhiw, Buxton had been unpopular, but then it had been a more ordinary politics. Since the Welsh Senate was established, in the further devolution of powers under the second coalition government, the Financial Commission has been the political storm-centre. For what the devolution said, in effect, was this: you can govern yourselves, on this range of issues, within the limits of the money we are prepared to allocate to you. The important effect of the Senate was to make this process, which in different ways had been there all the time, very much more visible and contested. It became apparent, above all, in the figure of the Financial Commission's Secretary of State (Wales). He was supposed to be an impartial figure, indeed not a figure but figures: a rational accounting procedure. But of course he was political, and through his office flowed all the fierce currents of political conflict between an impatient people and a constrained, fatigued and impoverished administration. Anyone holding Buxton's position was then a marked man in Wales: marked and resented if not actively hated.

The passage from resentment, however fierce, to what can properly be called hatred, depended, of course, on a single event. The army's attack at Pontyrhiw, which ended with the death of Gareth Powell, would have led, in any case, to a very deep bitterness. But when the public inquiry opened, and the army's evidence was given, it became more and more likely that what had been widely suspected was true: that Buxton was involved, not just as an adviser, or as the responsible minister visiting a trouble-spot, but in effect as a commander, as chief strategist. This was of course denied; there was no real evidence of it, of a kind you could prove. But still he was seen, throughout Wales, at the time of his visit, as the man primarily responsible for that bloody Thursday and indeed as the murderer of Gareth Powell.

It was then extraordinary, as I had told Friedmann, that within four months he was again appearing in public in Wales. Of course his work required him to go regularly to Cardiff, to the offices of the Senate and the Assembly. But that can be and usually is hermetic. Demonstrations, repeatedly, had tried to intercept him, but there was the smooth police passage from train to car, or, more often, the arrival by helicopter in the closed grounds. His visit on 9 July was primarily for a meeting of this kind: a joint session of the Financial Commission and the Financial Committee of the Senate. His visit to the Folk Museum had been arranged for many months, from before the confrontation at Pontyrhiw. I have no idea whether he was urged to cancel it. He was bound to have been aware of the feeling against him. As we all now know, he went on with it. He said in a statement, when he arrived in Cardiff, that he was in the habit of fulfilling his normal engagements. Whether this was courage or contempt for the feeling against him there is no easy way of knowing. I would still call it courage; a kind of courage: a kind characteristic of one sort of ruling-class man, in whom physical bravery can never quite be separated from the associated emotions of arrogance and contempt. Yet Buxton is not, by origins, a ruling-class man. He is an educational meritocrat, a career politician, who moved from the public bureaucracy, where he was a scientific officer, to parliament and the administration: an effective and successful move in his mid-thirties. So it is not his inherited class, or any kind of inherited property or position, that has produced his undoubted authoritarian character. He is that now more dangerous kind of man, whose authority and whose ruthlessness derive from his absolute belief in his models: rational models of what is and must be. It is never Buxton you challenge; it is fact and reason itself. Of course the version of fact and reason that the administration has selected: the Buxton version.

READING 16

# From *The Fight For Manod* (1979)

## Editor's Introduction

The most common description of Williams's novels is as "social realist." And it is a fair enough comment on the first two in his Welsh trilogy, *Border Country* (1960) and *Second Generation* (1964). The third volume, *The Fight for Manod*, is a very different matter, however. For, like *The Volunteers*, its subject matter is the future, rather than the past and the present. As Williams himself observed of *Manod* in "The Tenses of Imagination," it is set ahead of its time of writing, but as "a plan" rather than "an action." The novel brings together the protagonists of the two earlier volumes, Matthew Price from *Border Country* and Peter Owen from *Second Generation*, to explore "the relation between necessary and desirable plans for the future and [...] the ways in which they get distorted and frustrated." *Manod* was begun in 1965 and completed in 1978, so that its composition overlapped entirely with that of *The Volunteers*, begun in 1970 and completed in 1976. The lectures that became "Tenses of Imagination" were delivered in 1978, so must have been drafted more or less immediately thereafter. Those reflections on future novels, Le Guin's *The Dispossessed* included, thus provide a framework for understanding *Manod* which points beyond the Welsh trilogy itself. As Pinkney observes, this is "a realist 'limit-text', a work where literary realism stumbles upon something which exceeds its grasp, falters badly, but is not altogether quelled [...] we are in a world that is both realistic and science-fictional" (*Raymond Williams* 71, 77). This opening encounter is between Price and Robert Lane, a one-time Oxford academic, now attached to the Department of Environment under a new Labour Government, who believes "the only way to defeat a bureaucracy is to get inside the bureaucracy." But it also allows Lane to introduce Price to the plans for Manod and to the idea of Owen as a co-consultant. The reader can't yet know it, but the book's central concern will become what Williams elsewhere describes as "a specific contemporary sadness: the relation between a wholly possible future and the contradictions and blockages of the present" (*Politics and Letters* 294).

## From *The Fight For Manod* (1979)

The telephone rang, with a conventional urgency. He lifted it abruptly, still looking at his work.
"Price."
He had learned the convention.
But then a girl's voice, light, uninquiring.
"Is that Dr Price?"
"Yes, speaking."
"Dr Matthew Price?"
"Yes."
"Hold on, please, I've a call for you."
He looked back to the desk, to his unfinished calculation. But he went on holding the receiver. There was the sound of a room at the other end of the line: a background of unknown voices, a typewriter, another phone ringing. He heard that phone being answered, somewhere within that unknown and continuing life.
"Yes?"
"Your call for Dr Price."
"Who was it called him?"
"It was from your extension. Dr Matthew Price."
"Hold on. I'll find out."
Footsteps away from that phone. Then a voice at some distance, moving away across the room.

## From The Fight For Manod (1979)

"There's a call for a Dr Price. Do you know who it is?"

"Dr Lane, I think."

"Well, ask him, Joan, will you?"

A longer pause, with other voices in the background. A distant door slammed. He looked again at his work. He would not be kept from it. He put back the receiver.

It was several minutes before it rang again.

"Dr Price?"

"Yes."

"We were cut off."

"No. I hung up."

"I see. Well, I'm sorry. But we have Dr Lane for you now."

A man's voice cut through.

"Lane here."

"Price."

After the exchange of identities, the next convention: an adjustment of the voice, a quick move up the register, an injection and projection of engaging human speech.

"Dr Price, this is Robert Lane. We've not met, I'm afraid, but ..."

"Robert Lane?"

"Yes, I used to be at Oxford."

"I know. I've read your books."

A sudden heavy breath, surprisingly loud on the line.

"You remind me, Dr Price, of my past. I've moved out of all that. Well temporarily, anyway. I'm at the Department of the Environment. Since our good government got in again."

"I didn't know that. I'm sorry."

"I'm not asking you to agree to the good government. There are several opinions on that. But I called you, particularly, because a problem's come up and I'd value your advice. Can I tell you about it? If I'm not interrupting you? And then we might meet, if you're at all interested."

"I don't know. Yes."

"Well, does the name of Manod mean anything to you?"

"Manod?"

"In the Afren valley. Welsh border country. Your part of the world, am I right?"

"Yes, I know that Manod, of course. It's about forty miles from where I grew up."

"I was sure you'd know it. Up here, of course, it's not primarily a place. It's a name, a codesign, perhaps even a symbol."

"I don't understand."

"You don't remember the Manod development?"

"The city, you mean? But that was …"

"Yes, I know. It's eleven years, now, since it was first announced. When there was a whole choice, you remember, of new worlds. On paper."

"It seemed a very serious idea."

"You think so? I'm glad. Because it's been in and out of every department, council, committee, pigeonhole, until for all of us here it's not a city but a chaos."

"Yes."

"Well either way. I meant administratively. Like most other new worlds it's just a debris of yellowing paper."

"I assumed that had happened. I read the opposition."

"Did they convince you at all?"

"They made some real points. Though mainly about the past. But in any case …"

"I know. It could never have been easy. It reached a kind of deadlock, just from its own difficulties. Then for years it simply got lost: a change of Minister and then a change of Government. Like you, I expect, we all supposed it was forgotten. Just another new world indefinitely postponed."

"Due to lack of interest, tomorrow has been cancelled."

"Exactly. It's what they will say of us eventually. But now here's the strange thing. It would take too long to explain on the phone, but the point is that Manod's come up again, actively, by a rather unusual route. And since I have to give some advice, well – may I put it frankly? – I feel the need for a different mind. Somebody who's not been in on it yet who would know what it's about. I mean really about."

"I see."

"It seems very arbitrary, but the more I looked at it, the more I pencilled in your name. There are problems of course, and we'd have to discuss them. But if you were interested enough to come and have a talk about it. Or if only to tell me why you are not interested."

"I see. Yes. But you don't have to ask me if I'm interested in Manod. It isn't a matter of choice."

*II*

He stood on the island, looking along the street of the Ministries.

Buildings opaque from the street that are blind to the street. In the centre of the street stone men, cast men, metal horses. Stone helmeted features running with grime. An upraised stone arm, leading an empty charge. Power in stone.

A girl was waiting in the lobby for the visitor to arrive. A man of fifty-eight: you can only ask.

"Dr Price?"

"Yes."

"I'm Joan Reynolds. Dr Lane asked me to look out for you. I'll take you along to his office."

A man of fifty-eight. Tall, heavy-boned, with thinning dark hair. An old rough dark coat, like a porter's. A deep, broken voice, perhaps Welsh. A hard, set face, almost carved. Then the sudden break to mobility.

"It must be difficult for you. Recognizing people."

"I suppose so. We get used to it. It's in the new block. We go up and over the bridge."

"This is only the public face then? This opaque stone front?"

Beyond the wide staircase and the long narrow corridor a bridge spanned the yard to the new building: a lighted glass tower, glittering and dazzling.

"The new block is much more convenient. And warmer. But people lose their way to it. We have to come across."

"Do you mind that?"

"No, not really."

"When I was first rung up I heard someone speaking to you. In this office I didn't know there was a succession of voices and then I heard someone say: 'Well ask him, Joan, will you?'"

"It's the switchboard. They're always ..."

But then suddenly she laughed.

## III

Robert Lane got up and shook hands. He said friend, friendliness, all over his short stocky body. You weren't bound to believe all he said.

Very thick greying hair. Soft pink clear skin. But fatigue in the eyes: grey and shrinking. Intelligent features seeming to come and go in a face blurred with overweight.

"We should have met before, Dr Price. I don't know why we haven't."

Matthew took the hand and sat where he was put, in the leather chair by the window, with the wide view out over the miles of the city. Robert Lane stood over him, his voice like a hand on his shoulder.

"Your book impressed me very much, Dr Price. I believe I wrote and told you."

"Yes, I remember. Thank you."

"You didn't reply."

"No. I'm sorry. I was nervous of patronage."

Lane moved and sat at his desk.

"It took a long time, I expect?"

"Yes, very long. I keep being reminded it's the only thing I've done."

"It took a long time because it had to be lived."

Beyond the window there was a railway terminus: sidings, engine sheds, glass roofs over the platforms. Matthew looked at the signal-boxes: long rectangular brick buildings: each ten times bigger than the little box in Glynmawr. Beyond the terminus the land rose to what had once been a hill. The grey streets climbed, brick and slate. There was a haze over them, under the wide sky. Lights were coming on, in irregular patterns. In the

*From The Fight For Manod (1979)*

fading daylight a tower block was slowly losing its mass and becoming a column of light.

"Just because it was a book on population movement it wasn't only," Lane said, "the statistics. You had the statistics but you turned them back into people."

"I tried to."

"We should have met before, at the beginning of this scheme. It's not the same, of course, but it's the kind of thing you described. A human movement. The flow of actual men and their families into the mining valleys. And now in Manod another movement, a planned movement, into valleys as empty as those valleys were before the coalrush started."

"The planning now making the difference?"

"Making some of the difference. And the rest of it, Matthew, we have to get clear."

He stopped and lit his pipe. He looked intently at Matthew through the thin screen of smoke.

"In a job like this …"

The pipe had gone out. He laid it impatiently aside.

"One doesn't get cynical, Matthew. It may look like that from outside. But there's still a kind of numbness: a hard rut of hopes deferred. A project begins with some clear human content. If we had real power we would simply order it. But we can only negotiate, through the long overlapping meetings. It becomes more actual than any general social vision. But past a certain point only the plan is real. Nothing directly human attaches to it."

Matthew shifted.

"You said, on the phone, you'd consulted almost everyone. But that can't be true. In all the councils and committees, what, two or three hundred people?"

"Representing," Lane began, and then broke off and smiled.

"You're making what you think is a point against me."

"Yes, that in that valley alone there are several thousand people."

"I took the point. But then that was just the reasoning that led me to you."

"To add one to three hundred?"

Lane smiled and re-lit his pipe.

"Yes, I wanted this stubbornness. But let me go over it. Manod started, I suppose, in the early sixties. The idea of new towns, and of regional development. These came together in several places and among them mid-Wales. The people there need it, they have to leave their homes to get jobs and even so there is chronically high unemployment. At the same time, in what used to be cities, now great sprawling and jammed conurbations, life is simply breaking down, will break down altogether in a measurable period, unless there is relief, moving work and homes to a better environment. So it seemed to fit, as an initial idea. It was the human need of many thousands of people, but they couldn't solve it individually. It could only be solved by some social decision, indeed by a planned and conscious development."

On the hill beyond the terminus there was now only the network of lights. Far away, to the horizon, only the lines of the streets were visible, past the high lighted towers. Lane turned and looked where Matthew was looking.

"You're seeing Manod, perhaps?"

"I was wondering, yes."

"No, whatever it may be it won't be like this. This is just layer after layer of muddle, money and dirt."

"It looks very conscious to me."

"But if so a past consciousness. Not of our own life and time. Anyway, as I was saying, Manod emerged. By the middle sixties it seemed easy to plan. A general idea got a local name. Along that valley, from Nantlais to Pontafren, we would build a new city. No smaller development would really stand up. Nantlais and Pontafren had asked for development, but just limited expansion, for their local needs. What could be done in either or both would be simply marginal. No significant body of work would be brought there, and without the work there is no real point. So a planning unit went down there. It was their report that was published. May I show you? I've got the map."

They got up and went across to the facing wall. Lane lighted the map on the high glass screen.

"Begin at each end of the valley. Nantlais and Pontafren would expand to their limits: say twenty thousand in each. Then along the Afren, in a

*From The Fight For Manod (1979)*

linked development, would be seven other centres. Manod's in the middle, that's how it gave its name. And because the Afren floods, and because in any case we don't want a ribbon along the banks of the river, the centres are set back on the higher ground: hill-towns really, except St Dyfrog, which has a different role. Each of the centres would go up to ten thousand. Between each, as you see, at least four or five miles of quite open country, which would go on being farmed. So what you get, as a whole, is a city of a hundred, a hundred-and-twenty thousand people, but a city of small towns, a city of villages almost. A city settling into its country."

"The descriptions are difficult."

"Yes, of course, because it's so new. There isn't, anywhere, a city like this. But there could be, that's clear. All the detailed work has been done and costed, and there's no real doubt that it's viable."

"Work, communications, roads, schools?"

Lane moved away from the map.

"If you go on with this, Matthew, you'll have more than enough of the details. It's about ten feet thick, just the technical studies. But they'll impress you, I guarantee that. Some very able people came in to work on it. The transport and communication technology is right at the frontier. The work-housing relation is also very advanced. If it ever gets built, and who knows about that, it will be one of the first human settlements, anywhere in the world, to have been conceived, from the beginning, in post-industrial terms and with a post-electronic technology. And then just think of it Matthew: a working city, an advanced working city, in that kind of country. With the river, the mountains, it would be a marvellous place."

"But then the politics start."

"You're right. The politics start."

They moved back to their chairs by the window. Matthew was silent for some time.

"You say if I go on with it. Go on with what exactly?"

"Well, let me be frank. A year ago, when I came back here, I'd have said it was dead, stone-dead. The general situation, the shortage of money and so on, but also a kind of deadlock in the idea itself. A political deadlock, of course. What the local people still want is nothing so grand. They want small local developments, improving but not altering the kinds of place they've got used to. But then even for that they need money, and to get the money, frankly, means having to fit in with what other people want, which is planned dispersal on a big enough scale to make the investment economic. At the two extremes that's the basic problem: two quite different views of what needs to be done."

"Yes."

"The political papers are twenty feet thick. If you go on you can read them, though it's a lot to ask."

"Go on with what? You still haven't explained."

"I said I thought it was dead. And I had, God knows, enough other things to do. But now most unexpectedly Manod has come up again, and come up in what are called around here very powerful quarters. I'm not really at liberty to give you all the details, and I may not myself know them all. But I can assure you of this. It has come really alive again: suddenly, urgently alive. This happens all the time, in what they call the political process."

"And you have to give an opinion?"

"Well, somebody has to. And the real trouble is, everything's happening at once. So that however alive and urgent it may be, nobody at all wants that formal process again. It would be another twenty feet thick and it would reach the same deadlock. And in the end, it's quite right, the government will have to decide. The information is all there; that isn't what's wanted."

"It could be published perhaps? Get a general response?"

"Thirty feet thick?"

"The essential issues."

"That will be done, of course. But not quite yet. My advice so far has been much more simple. That we should turn it back, from paper, to the human issue it began as."

Matthew stayed silent.

"I wasn't flattering you, Matthew, when I described your book. I was trying to define just what you had done: to make a history human and yet still a history. And what I want with Manod, what I'm asking you to do, is to come to this fresh, to make it human again, to help us see it again as it is."

"Going through the files?"

"Yes, you'd have, I'm afraid, to do that. But what I'm suggesting is a different inquiry: a lived inquiry. That you should go to Manod. That you should live there as long as you need – it could be anything up to a year. That you would go informed; you'd have every access. But that you would go as yourself. To the place, to the people. That you would live the problem. And then that you'd come back and tell us."

"The three hundred and first."

"Yes, perhaps, but having made the journey. Having come out of that country and now going back to it. Taking with you, in yourself, the two worlds you belong in. The two Manods."

## IV

"Did you get through the files?"

"I had a first look through."

"You have my sympathy. Still at least you came back."

"Yes."

It was the middle of the morning, a week later. Matthew found Lane more harassed, less mannered, than at their first meeting. He had made his offer, and as part of that had encouraged discussion. But now, clearly, he wanted a simple reply.

"And have you made up your mind?"

"It's as you said. It's complicated. Very deeply complicated."

Lane nodded understandingly. At the same time he looked at his watch.

"I'll be straight with you, Matthew. I could have chosen, couldn't I, a much easier man?"

"I don't know."

"I do. They come in great numbers. They depend on us for work."

"Perhaps a mutual dependence."

"I was given authority to appoint two consultants. I've asked you and Peter Owen. Do you know Peter Owen?"

"He wrote *Industrial Estate*."

"That's enough in itself. It's a marvellous book. And it's this problem exactly, from the other way of seeing it, in the existing cities and factories. So I've asked him, though the people I have to deal with, the permanent people, didn't like the idea at all."

"The idea of consultants?"

"Oh no, that's quite normal. And they have, by the way, no objection whatever to you. It was a popular nomination. But Peter, well – his book was very open and angry. And then of course he got six months in prison, after a Vietnam riot. He has no job, no real status."

"But he used to be your pupil."

"He left that. He went to work on an assembly line."

He looked again at his watch.

"So I don't have to stress it, Matthew. I'm not asking yesmen."

"You're still doing the asking. Someone said yes to that."

Lane got up and stood by the window. The outside light was reflected in the clear pink skin of his face.

"All right, you see me here in a government office. At some cost to yourself you've avoided the usual rackets. But when you look at me you say that's where rackets start."

Matthew didn't reply. Lane raised his hand and pointed.

"I could tell you what made me come here. The work's much harder than Oxford. And I'm a democrat, a radical. I hate the guts of this system. But I learned one thing, that the only way to defeat a bureaucracy is to get inside the bureaucracy. To fight officials in offices. Committee men in committees. Not avoiding where they're entrenched, but going directly in on them. It's the only way if we're to get anything done."

"Look, I'm not examining you. I'm not your inquisitor."

"You have that effect. No, I'm sorry, I didn't mean that. I mean you tend to dominate, without doing or saying very much."

"An idea, that's all."

Lane sat again at his desk. He pulled his papers towards him but did not look down at them.

"With you, Matthew, I'm thinking about Manod. I'm asking you to think about it. You may see me as managing men and opinions. But it isn't that. I'm just pushing at inertia. You must know what we're up against. The old drift, the old dirt, of the industrial revolution. The new drift, the new indifference, brittleness, of this stage of capitalism. This frantic southeast, the London-Birmingham axis. And beyond it, its counterpart, the emptying country, the men without work, the communities dying."

"Of course."

"Somebody will make decisions, you can be sure of that. And it's to help towards good decisions that I'm inviting you to go."

"Yes. And I must give you an answer. But first, if I may, a few practical questions."

"That's what I'm here for."

He bustled his papers. The movement brought his watch into view again.

"Well, first, I'd be allowed to say why I'd come there. I mean the people there, if they wanted, would know who I was and what I was doing."

"Of course. No problem. That's entirely up to you."

"I could only go if it was perfectly open."

"Perfectly open. With the one limitation, of course, that some of the documents have to be kept confidential."

"Which documents?"

"They're already classified. Minutes of some of the meetings. Some of the technical studies. But mainly, of course, the detailed land requirement studies. We have to sit on those to prevent speculation: people buying up the land."

"The particular areas, you mean?"

"Yes."

"But you've got them marked on the map."

"Not on the public map. The outline of the centres has been published, but no usable details of just where they'd be."

Matthew looked across at the high glass screen. The map was not lighted and he could see only a vague blur.

"Right. Then my own situation. I'd need leave of absence. I don't know if I could get it."

Lane smiled.

"You're too modest, Matthew. Anyway let me tell you. After our first talk I rang your Principal. I explained, of course, that it was all still provisional, but he was very reasonable. If you want to go, you have a year's consultancy secondment. Even if you don't stay the full year."

"I see."

The phone rang and Lane answered it. Matthew hardly noticed. He had caught the familiar smell of a world of arrangements beyond him; of things happening, planned, brought about, without people even being told. He stared through the window at the railway yard, the office tower, the streets climbing the hill. By narrowing his eyes he could see the window and the city beyond it as a framed picture. It reminded him of the map on the opposite wall. Lane put down the phone. He was now especially abrupt.

"Is there anything else then? I mean anything immediate?"

"Well yes. Two things. But they're difficult."

"Shall we try?"

"You said the scheme had come up again by an unusual route. You said there were details – presumably details inside the government, inside your department – you weren't able to tell me."

"Yes, and I'm sorry, but it's how these things happen. I didn't invent the system."

"Of course. But you're asking me to give a year of my life. Its general importance is obvious: a year for that is nothing. But I want one assurance: that it isn't merely some political manoeuvre, with no serious intentions. That it isn't a political kite, on some other wind."

Lane looked at him sharply, and hesitated.

"An assurance, that is," Matthew said, "that I shan't from the beginning be simply wasting people's time."

Lane was still watching him. The grey eyes were very tired.

"Matthew, no. How can I possibly give you an assurance like that? It's not a thing that can be said, in any real world."

"You mean it *is* a manoeuvre."

"It may be. I don't know. So far as I'm concerned I can assure you that it's not."

"But then ..."

"No, Matthew. This is where I stick. You can take my word, an honest word but no more than my own, in a system so shifting, so complex, that to ask for more is a moral fantasy. A moralist's fantasy."

Matthew got up, slowly. Lane's voice seemed to follow him.

"In any real activity there are so many motives. To abstain because of that would mean doing nothing at all."

Matthew remained very still. He was standing awkwardly: the stiff heavy figure struggling to cancel movement. His eyes were very dark and withdrawn.

Lane spoke quietly.

"Your Principal said that you had not been well."

Matthew didn't answer.

"I was very sorry to hear it. It was heart trouble, wasn't it?"

"Yes."

"Well a year in the country, a year of a different kind of life."

Matthew seemed not to be listening. When he spoke he went back to Lane's earlier point.

"I accept what you say about the assurance I asked for. And in the way you put it I'll take your personal word."

"Good. That's settled, then."

Lane got up as he spoke. He picked up a file.

"There was the second question."

"Yes?" Lane said quickly.

He now openly looked at his watch.

"The difficulty, you say, is the two ideas of development: what mid-Wales needs but then what others need and will pay for."

"Of course."

"Then why ask me to go to Manod? To go only there? Shouldn't I go, also, where there's this other need?"

"But Matthew, you can go where you like. It's entirely up to you."

"Maybe, but the dangers are obvious. The most likely outcome is not a city at all, but just the old overspill. An industrial estate dumped down in mid-Wales. And then we would be looking at Manod just to see on what terms it could happen."

"We've been through this, Matthew. And again I'd remind you of the people I've asked to advise us: you and Peter Owen. Overspill, dumping, an industrial estate: none of these, surely, would get past either of you."

"Maybe, but we'd not be deciding."

"Well you must accept that, surely. You'd be the first to say you have no right to decide. But advice, clarification, at a critical moment ..."

"I've accepted that. All I'm saying, really, is that the problem, the need, has to be looked at both ways round: from both kinds of place."

"Of course. Absolutely. And now you really must excuse me. I have a meeting I'm late for."

Matthew stood aside. Lane walked towards the door.

"Peter's in Sweden, did I tell you, until early November? But he's said that then he'll get straight on to it. He'll come and see you first."

"All right, I'll expect him."

Lane touched Matthew's arm.

"What I wanted, from the start, was you both working on it. Different generations, different experiences, but wouldn't you say the same interests, the same values?"

"So far as I know, yes."

Lane opened the door. The file he was carrying was prominent.

"The same language anyway, Matthew. Just as you and I have been able to talk."

# Bibliography

## Works by Raymond Williams

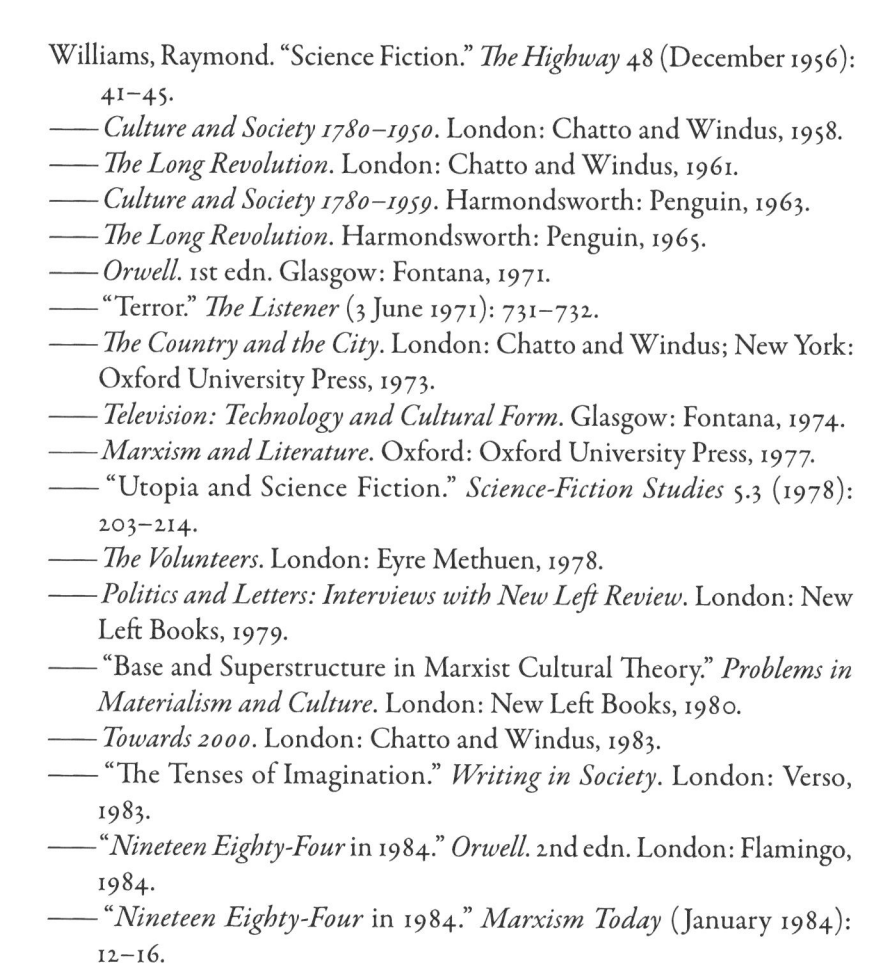

Williams, Raymond. "Science Fiction." *The Highway* 48 (December 1956): 41–45.
—— *Culture and Society 1780–1950*. London: Chatto and Windus, 1958.
—— *The Long Revolution*. London: Chatto and Windus, 1961.
—— *Culture and Society 1780–1959*. Harmondsworth: Penguin, 1963.
—— *The Long Revolution*. Harmondsworth: Penguin, 1965.
—— *Orwell*. 1st edn. Glasgow: Fontana, 1971.
—— "Terror." *The Listener* (3 June 1971): 731–732.
—— *The Country and the City*. London: Chatto and Windus; New York: Oxford University Press, 1973.
—— *Television: Technology and Cultural Form*. Glasgow: Fontana, 1974.
—— *Marxism and Literature*. Oxford: Oxford University Press, 1977.
—— "Utopia and Science Fiction." *Science-Fiction Studies* 5.3 (1978): 203–214.
—— *The Volunteers*. London: Eyre Methuen, 1978.
—— *Politics and Letters: Interviews with New Left Review*. London: New Left Books, 1979.
—— "Base and Superstructure in Marxist Cultural Theory." *Problems in Materialism and Culture*. London: New Left Books, 1980.
—— *Towards 2000*. London: Chatto and Windus, 1983.
—— "The Tenses of Imagination." *Writing in Society*. London: Verso, 1983.
—— "*Nineteen Eighty-Four* in 1984." *Orwell*. 2nd edn. London: Flamingo, 1984.
—— "*Nineteen Eighty-Four* in 1984." *Marxism Today* (January 1984): 12–16.

—— "A Defence of Realism." *What I Came to Say*. Ed. Neil Belton, Francis Mulhern, and Jenny Taylor. London: Hutchinson Radius, 1989.

Williams, Raymond and Edward W. Said. "Appendix: Media, Margins and Modernity." *The Politics of Modernism: Against the New Conformists*. Ed. Tony Pinkney. London: Verso, 1989.

## Other Works

Abensour, Miguel. "Les Formes de l'utopie socialistes-communiste." Paris: thèse pour le Doctorat d'État en science politique, 1973.

Abernethy, Robert. "Single Combat." Knight. 1–10.

Aldiss, Brian. "The Underprivileged." Knight. 195–209.

Atwood, Margaret. "George Orwell: Some Personal Connections." *Curious Pursuits: Occasional Writing 1970–2005*. London: Virago, 2005.

——*The Handmaid's Tale*. London: Virago, 1987.

Baccolini, Raffaella. "Gender and Genre in the Feminist Critical Dystopias of Katherine Burdekin, Margaret Atwood, and Octavia Butler." *Future Females, the Next Generation: New Voices and Velocities in Feminist Science Fiction*. Ed. Marleen S. Barr. Boston: Rowman and Littlefield, 2000. 13–34.

Bacon, Francis. *The New Atlantis in The Advancement of Learning and The New Atlantis* [1627]. Ed. A. Johnston. Oxford: Clarendon Press, 1974.

Bahro, Rudolf. *Die Alternative. Zur Kritik des real existierenden Sozialismus*. Köln: Europäische Verlagsanstalt, 1977.

—— *The Alternative in Eastern Europe*. Trans. David Fernbach. London: New Left Books, 1978.

Ballard, J.G. "Billennium." Knight. 87–101.

Bellamy, Edward. *Looking Backward, 2000–1887* [1888]. Harmondsworth: Penguin, 1982.

Blish, James. "A Case of Conscience." *If: Worlds of Science Fiction* 2.4 (September 1953): 4–51, 116–117.
—— *A Case of Conscience*. New York: Ballantine, 1958.
—— *Earthman, Come Home*. New York: Avon, 1955.
Boyd, Edward. "The Sons and Daughters of Tomorrow." *Out of the Unknown*. Dir. Gerald Blake. London: BBC Television, 19 May 1971.
Bradbury, Ray. *Fahrenheit 451*. London: Rupert Hart-Davis, 1954.
—— "The Fire Balloons." Crispin. 148–167.
Bulwer-Lytton, Edward. *The Coming Race*. London: William Blackwood, 1871.
Cevasco, Maria Elisa. "Whatever Happened to Cultural Studies: Notes from the Periphery." *Textual Practice* 14.3 (2000): 433–438.
Christopher, John. "The New Wine." Crispin. 168–182.
Clarke, Arthur C. *The City and the Stars*. London: Frederick Muller, 1956.
Crispin, Edmund (ed.). *Best SF: Science Fiction Stories*. London: Faber, 1955.
Delany, Samuel R. *The Jewel-Hinged Jaw: Notes on the Language of Science Fiction*. Elizabethtown: Dragon Press, 1977.
*Doctor Who*. London: BBC Television, 1963–89, 1996; Cardiff: BBC Cymru, 2005–9.
*Doomwatch*. London: BBC Television, 1970–72.
Eagleton, Terry. *Criticism and Ideology: A Study in Marxist Literary Theory*. London: New Left Books, 1976.
—— "Introduction." *Raymond Williams: Critical Perspectives*. Ed. Terry Eagleton. Cambridge: Polity Press, 1989. 1–12.
Engels, Friedrich. *Socialism, Utopian and Scientific* [1880]. Trans. Edward Aveling. London: Allen & Unwin, 1918.
Farhi, Moris. "Welcome Home." *Out of the Unknown*. Dir. Eric Hills. London: BBC Television, 26 May 1971.
Ferrara, Fernando. "Raymond Williams and the Italian Left." *Raymond Williams: Critical Perspectives*. Ed. Terry Eagleton. Cambridge: Polity Press, 1989. 95–107.
Forster, E. M. "The Machine Stops" [1909]. Knight. 163–192.
Golding, William. *The Inheritors*. London: Faber, 1955.

——*Lord of the Flies: A Novel*. London: Faber, 1954.
Greenblatt, Stephen. *Learning to Curse: Essays in Early Modern Culture*. London: Routledge, 1990.
Hall, Stuart. "Culture, Community, Nation." *Cultural Studies* 7.3 (1993): 349–363.
Hollinger, Veronica. "Contemporary Trends in Science Fiction Criticism, 1980–1999." *Science Fiction Studies* 26.2 (1999): 232–262.
Huxley, Aldous. *Brave New World* [1932]. London: Flamingo, 1994.
Inglis, Fred. *Raymond Williams*. London: Routledge, 1995.
Jameson, Fredric. *Archaeologies of the Future: The Desire Called Utopia and Other Science Fictions*. London: Verso, 2005.
——*Postmodernism, or, the Cultural Logic of Late Capitalism*. London: Verso, 1991.
Kaplan, E. Ann. "Introduction." *Postmodernism and Its Discontents: Theories, Practices*. Ed. E. Ann Kaplan. London: Verso, 1988. 1–9.
Knight, Damon (ed.). *Cities of Wonder*. New York: Doubleday, 1966.
Kuttner, Henry. "Jesting Pilot." Knight. 51–63.
——"Or Else." Crispin. 85–94.
Latham, Philip, "The Xi Effect." Crispin. 276–298.
Lawson, Sylvia. "How Raymond Williams Died in Australia." *How Simone de Beauvoir Died in Australia*. Sydney: University of New South Wales Press, 2002. 33–66.
Le Guin, Ursula K. *The Dispossessed* [1974]. London: Millennium, 1999.
MacLean, Katherine, "Pictures Don't Lie." Crispin. 35–55.
Mercier, Louis Sébastien. *L'An 2440, rêve s'il en fut jamais* [1771]. Paris: La Découverte, 1999.
*Metropolis*. Dir. Fritz Lang. 1926).
Miller, Walter M., "Dumb Waiter." Knight. 13–48.
Milner, Andrew. *Re-Imagining Cultural Studies: the Promise of Cultural Materialism*. London: Sage Publications, 2002.
Moore, C.L., "No Woman Born." Crispin. 95–147.
More, Thomas. *Utopia* [1516]. Trans. Raphe Robynson. Amsterdam: Theatrum Orbis Terrarum, 1551.
Morris, William. *The Collected Works of William Morris*. Vol. XXII. New York: Russell and Russell, 1966.

—— *The Collected Works of William Morris*. Vol. XXIII. New York: Russell and Russell, 1966.
—— *The Letters of William Morris to his Family and Friends*. Ed. Philip Henderson. London: Longmans Green, 1950.
—— *News from Nowhere* [1891]. *Three Works by William Morris*. Ed. A.L. Morton. London: Lawrence and Wishart, 1977.
—— *Political Writings of William Morris*. Ed. A.L. Morton. London: Lawrence and Wishart, 1984.
Moylan, Tom. *Demand the Impossible: Science Fiction and the Utopian Imagination*. New York: Methuen, 1986.
—— *Scraps of the Untainted Sky: Science Fiction, Utopia, Dystopia*. Boulder: Westview Press, 2000.
Mulhern, Francis. *The Present Lasts a Long Time: Essays in Cultural Politics*. Cork: Cork University Press, 1998.
Nearing, Homer Jr. "The Cerebrative Psittacoid." Crispin. 214–232.
Orwell, George. *Collected Essays, Journalism and Letters of George Orwell, Vol. 1: An Age Like This*. Ed. Sonia Orwell and Ian Angus. Harmondsworth: Penguin, 1970.
—— *Collected Essays, Journalism and Letters of George Orwell, Vol. 2: My Country Right or Left*. Ed. Sonia Orwell and Ian Angus. Harmondsworth: Penguin, 1970.
—— *Collected Essays, Journalism and Letters of George Orwell. Vol. 4: In Front of Your Nose 1945–1950*. Ed. Sonia Orwell and Ian Angus. Harmondsworth: Penguin, 1970.
—— *Coming Up for Air* [1939]. Harmondsworth: Penguin, 1962.
—— *Keep the Aspidistra Flying* [1936]. Harmondsworth: Penguin, 1962.
—— *Nineteen Eighty-Four: A Novel*. London: Secker and Warburg, 1949.
—— *Nineteen Eighty-Four*. Harmondsworth, Penguin, 1989.
—— *The Road to Wigan Pier* [1937]. Harmondsworth: Penguin, 1962.
*Out of the Unknown*. BBC Television, 1965–71.
Parrinder, Patrick. "Introduction: Learning from Other Worlds." *Learning from Other Worlds: Estrangement, Cognition and the Politics of Science Fiction and Utopia*. Ed. Patrick Parrinder. Liverpool: Liverpool University Press, 2000. 1–18.

Pinkney, Tony. *Raymond Williams*. Bridgend: Seren Books, 1991.
—— "Williams and the 'Two Faces of Modernism.'" *Raymond Williams: Critical Perspectives*. Ed. Terry Eagleton. Cambridge: Polity Press, 1989. 12–33.
Poe, Edgar Allan. "Thousand-and-Second Tale of Scheherazade" [1845]. *Edgar Allan Poe: Complete Tales and Poems*. Edison, NJ: Castle Books, 1985.
—— "The Unparalleled Adventure of one Hans Pfaal" [1835]. *Edgar Allan Poe: Complete Tales and Poems*. Edison, NJ: Castle Books, 1985.
Porges, Arthur. "The Ruum." Crispin. 262–275.
Russell, E.F. "A Present from Joe." Crispin. 199–213.
Sargent, Lyman Tower "The Three Faces of Utopianism Revisited." *Utopian Studies* 5.1 (1994): 1–37.
Sedgwick, Peter. "The Two New Lefts." *The Left in Britain 1956–1968*. Ed. David Widgery. Harmondsworth: Penguin, 1976.
Shelley, Mary. *Frankenstein, or The Modern Prometheus* [1818]. Ed. M.K. Joseph. Oxford: Oxford University Press, 1980.
Shiach, Morag. "A Gendered History of Cultural Categories." *Cultural Materialism: On Raymond Williams*. Ed. Christopher Prendergast. Minneapolis: University of Minnesota Press, 1995. 51–70.
Sinfield, Alan. *Faultlines: Cultural Materialism and the Politics of Dissident Reading*. Berkeley: University of California Press, 1992.
Stuart, Don A. "Forgetfulness." Knight. 227–252.
Suvin, Darko. *Metamorphoses of Science Fiction: on the Poetics and History of a Literary Genre*. New Haven: Yale University Press, 1979.
—— "Novum Is as Novum Does." *Science Fiction, Critical Frontiers*. Ed. Karen Sayer and John Moore. Basingstoke: Macmillan, 2000. 3–22.
Thompson, E.P. "Romanticism, Moralism and Utopianism: the Case of William Morris." *New Left Review* 99 (September–October 1976): 83–111.
——*William Morris: Romantic to Revolutionary*. London: Lawrence and Wishart, 1955.
Thomson, James. *The City of Dreadful Night and Other Poems*. London: Reeves and Turner, 1880.

—— "The Doom of a City: A Fantasia." *The Poetical Works of James Thomson.* Vol. II. Ed. Bertram Dobell. London: Reeves and Turner, 1895.

van Vogt, A.E. "Dormant." Crispin. 17–34.

Walsh, James. "George Orwell." *Marxist Quarterly* 3.1 (January 1956): 25–39.

Wells, H.G. *Experiment in Autobiography: Discoveries and Conclusions of a Very Ordinary Brain (since 1866).* Vol. II. London, Gollancz, 1934.

—— *In the Days of the Comet* [1906]. London: Collins, 1966.

—— *The Sleeper Awakes.* Ed. Patrick Parrinder. London: Penguin, 2005. [first published 1899, revised]

—— "A Story of the Days to Come" [1897]. *The Complete Short Stories of H.G. Wells.* Ed. John Hammond. London: Dent, 1998.

—— *The Time Machine* [1895]. Ed. Patrick Parrinder. London: Penguin, 2005.

—— *The War of the Worlds* [1898]. London: Penguin, 2005.

West, Cornel. "In Memoriam: the Legacy of Raymond Williams." *Cultural Materialism: On Raymond Williams.* Ed. Christopher Prendergast. Minneapolis: University of Minnesota Press, 1995. ix–xii.

Wordsworth, William. "French Revolution, As it Appeared to Enthusiasts at its Commencement" [1809]. *Poetical Works.* Ed. T. Hutchinson. Oxford: Oxford University Press, 1969.

Wyndham, John. *Day of the Triffids.* London: Michael Joseph, 1951.

—— "Dumb Martian." Crispin. 56–84.

Zamiatine, Eugène. *Nous autres.* Trad. B. Cauvet-Duhamel. Paris: Gallimard, 1929.

Zamyatin, Yevgeny. *We.* Trans. B.G. Guerney. London: Cape, 1970.

# Index

ABC TV, 51
Abensour, Miguel, 94
   *Les Formes de l'utopie socialistes-communiste*, 94
Abertheney, Robert, 73
   "Single Combat", 73
Aldiss, Brian, 73, 79
   "The Underprivileged", 81, 87
anarchism, 102, 111
Anderson, Perry, 3, 83
anthropology, 3, 5, 13, 44, 51, 109, 113
Arnold, Matthew, 100
   *Culture and Anarchy*, 100
Asimov, Isaac, 51
Atwood, Margaret, 6
   *The Handmaid's Tale*, 6
Auden, W.H., 68
authoritarianism, 35, 57, 58, 60, 65, 70–71, 181, 192–194, 206, 213

Bacon, Francis, 98–99
   *The Advancement of Learning and The New Atlantis*, 106
Bahro, Rudolf, 125–130, 132–146, 148
   *The Alternative in Eastern Europe*, 127
   *Die Alternative*, 4, 125
Ballard, J.G., 51, 73, 80
   "Billennium", 80
Barnett, Anthony, 83
BBC, 51–52, 54
Bellamy, Edward, 76, 94, 100
   *Looking Backward*, 94, 100, 101

Blish, James, 13, 19, 44, 73, 81
   *A Case of Conscience*, 13, 19
   *Earthman, Come Home*, 14, 73, 81
Bolshevism, 138
bourgeois, 2, 40, 86, 107
Boyd, Edward, 54
   "The Sons and Daughters of Tomorrow", 54
Bradbury, Ray, 12, 15, 18, 51
   *Fahrenheit 451*, 12, 16, 45
   "The Fire Balloons", 18
Bulwer-Lytton, Edward, 100
   *The Coming Race*, 100–101
Bunyan, John, 21
   *The Pilgrim's Progress*, 14
Burnham, James, 178–179, 186–189, 192–193, 200–202
   *The Struggle for the World*, 186

capitalism, 2, 4, 28, 60, 70–71, 84, 100–101, 105–106, 129, 133–134, 137, 149, 152, 161, 166, 168, 171, 177–179, 183, 192–195, 206, 227
capitalist democracy, 69–70, 71
capitalist system, 28
Carlyle, Thomas, 22–23, 101
Christopher, John, 12, 18
   "The New Wine", 12, 18
Clarke, Arthur C., 73, 79
   *The City and the Stars*, 79
Cobbett, William, 24, 29
Cold War, 11, 84
commercialism, 5, 25, 29, 30

Communism, 2, 36, 58, 59, 125–126, 184
Cronenberg, David, 179
culturalism, 2, 9, 11
cultural revolution, 129–135, 139–148
Cultural Studies, 1, 3
culture, 2, 3, 11, 16, 21, 24–25, 30, 33, 49, 51–52, 54, 65, 70, 74, 89, 111, 123, 129–130, 149, 153, 157, 175
  minority culture, 2, 12, 21, 26, 107

Darwin, Charles, 115, 116
democracy, 33
democratic socialism, 84, 178, 194
Dickens, Charles, 23, 33, 66
*Doctor Who*, 51, 54
documentary, 43–46
*Doomwatch*, 51, 53
Dostoevsky, Fyodor, 46
  *Crime and Punishment*, 46
dystopia, 1, 2, 5–7, 11, 13, 21, 43, 87, 93–95, 106–108, 112–113, 177, 179
dystopian, 2, 4, 5, 7, 11–12, 73, 93, 95, 97–98, 106, 109, 111–112, 205

Eagleton, Terry 1, 85
  *Criticism and Ideology*, 1
  *Exiles and Emigrés*, 85
ecology, 77
Eliot, George, 55
  *Middlemarch*, 47
Eliot, T.S., 2, 12
  *The Cocktail Party*, 18

Fabianism, 101, 138
fascism, 58, 69–71, 193
fatalism, 95, 166
Faust, 18
feminism, 114, 156–157, 159, 170, 173
Forster, E.M., 46, 51, 73, 80
  *A Passage to India*, 46
  "The Machine Stops", 81

Gaitskell, Hugh, 85
Galileo, Galilei, 127
  *Discorsi*, 127
Gibson, William, 206
  *Neuromancer*, 206
Gissing, George, 66, 76, 78
globalization, 2, 4
Golding, William, 43
  *Lord of the Flies*, 43, 45
  *The Inheritors*, 43, 45
Gothic, 14, 28
Greenblatt, Stephen, 1
  *Learning to Curse: Essays in Early Modern Culture*, 1
Greene, Graham, 46, 68, 85
Guevarism, 2

Hall, Stuart, 1
hegemony, 3
*Highway, The*, 11, 87
Hitler, Adolf, 70, 184, 201
humanism, 98, 99–100
Hungarian Revolution, 65
Huxley, Aldous, 12, 68
  *Brave New World*, 12, 16, 45, 77, 101, 106, 179

ideology, 3, 12, 59, 60, 61, 85, 99, 127, 134, 135, 141, 157, 166, 168, 172, 194–196, 205
imperialism, 64, 69, 71, 134
industrialism, 26, 34, 35, 75, 132–133
Isherwood, Christopher, 68

Jameson, Fredric, 206
  *Postmodernism, or, The Cultural Logic of Late Capitalism*, 206
Joyce, James, 66

Kafka, Franz, 46
Kaplan, Ann, 5

*Index*

Keats, John, 68
Knight, Damon, 79
   *Cities of Wonder*, 79
Kornbluth, C.M., 51
Kuttner, Henry, 14, 73, 80
   "Jesting Pilot", 80
   "Or Else", 14

Labour Party (British), 2, 35–36, 59, 64, 158, 184, 205
*Land of Cokaygne*, 97
Lang, Fritz, 73
   *Metropolis*, 73, 76
Latham, Philip, 12, 17
   "The Xi Effect", 12, 17
Lawrence, D.H., 37
Le Guin, Ursula K., 5, 51, 94, 109
   *The Dispossessed*, 5, 94, 109, 111, 113, 114, 122, 215
   *The Left Hand of Darkness*, 113–114
   *The Telling*, 113
   *The Word for World is Forest*, 113
Leavis, F.R., 1, 2
   Leavisite ideas, 3, 11
*Listener, The*, 51
literary humanism, 1
Lithians, 13, 18, 44
London, 73–75, 78, 110, 167, 205, 208, 227

MacLean, Katherine, 14
   "Pictures Don't Lie", 14
Maoism, 2
Marxism, 1, 3, 4, 11, 12, 101, 128, 130, 132, 135, 171, 177
   Western Marxism, 2, 3
Maugham, Somerset, 66
medievalism, 28, 103
Mercier, Louis-Sébastien, 74
   *L'An 2440*, 74
   *Tableau de Paris*, 74

middle class, 25, 35
Miller, Walter M., 73, 80
   "Dumb Waiter", 80
Milner, Andrew 1
   *Re-Imagining Cultural Studies*, 1
Moore, C.L., 14–15
   "No Woman Born", 14
More, Thomas, 3, 18, 78, 98, 99, 100, 178, 187
   *Utopia*, 5, 9, 11, 81, 93, 95, 98, 99, 107, 136, 181, 192
Morris, William, 4, 7, 11–13, 15, 21–31, 43, 73–77, 87–89, 94, 100, 101, 104–105, 107–108, 110–111, 113
   *The Dream of John Ball*, 28, 88
   *News from Nowhere*, 5, 11, 15, 21, 28, 73, 75, 88, 94, 100, 101, 103, 104, 113, 114
Mulhern, Francis, 83, 149
Moylan, Tom, 114
   *Scraps of the Untainted Sky*, 114

Nation, Terry, 51
Nearing, H., Jr., 14
   "The Cerebrative Psittacoid", 14
*New Left Review*, 3, 4, 83, 87, 102, 125

"Oligarchical Collectivism", 194
Orwell, George, 4–7, 11, 12, 13, 16, 21, 33, 34, 36–43, 57–71, 73, 77–78, 83–87, 94, 103, 108, 122, 177–202, 205
   *Animal Farm*, 41, 84–85
   "The Art of Donald McGill", 34, 66
   *Coming Up for Air*, 36, 38, 66, 78
   *Down and Out in Paris and London*, 38
   *Homage to Catalonia*, 38, 67
   "How the Poor Die", 66
   "Inside the Whale", 64

*Keep the Aspidistra Flying*, 36, 62
"The Last Man in Europe", 71
*Nineteen Eighty-Four*, 4–6, 11–12, 16, 21, 33, 35, 40, 41, 45, 57, 58, 61, 63, 64, 71, 73, 77–78, 83–85, 94, 177–180, 182, 185–186, 188, 190–191, 193, 194, 196–200, 206
    Big Brother, 6, 59, 198
    "The Principles of Newspeak", 58, 182
    doublethink, 59–60, 185, 196
    thoughtcrime, 59, 60
"Raffles and Miss Blandish", 66
*The Road to Wigan Pier*, 34, 35, 36, 38, 61, 65
"Writers and Leviathan", 39
*Out of the Unknown*, 51, 52, 54, 59–60, 62
*Out of this World*, 51
Oxford, 24, 25, 118, 215, 217, 226

Pinkney, Tony, 1, 213–215, 223
Poe, Edgar Allan, 14
    "Thousand-and-Second Tale of Scheherazade", 14
    "The Unparalleled Adventure of one Hans Pfaal", 14
Pohl, Frederick, 51
political imperialism, 69
postmodernism, 2, 4, 91, 206
    (anti-)postmodernism, 2
    Postmodern New Left, 2
Priestley, J.B., 51
Putropia, 2, 9, 12, 15, 17

radicalism, 2, 4
realism, 5, 6, 16, 46, 48, 49, 50, 54, 93, 94, 97, 113, 215
Robinson, Kim Stanley, 179
Ruskin, John, 22, 23, 24, 27, 28, 87, 89
Russell, E.F, 14
    "A Present from Joe", 14

Said, Edward, 1
science fiction (sf), 1, 2, 3, 4, 5, 11, 12, 13, 14, 15, 16, 17, 18, 19, 21, 43, 44, 45, 51, 52, 54, 73, 79, 87, 88, 93, 95, 96, 97, 106, 108, 109, 114, 121, 149, 179, 205
Scott, Ridley, 206
    *Alien*, 179
    *Blade Runner*, 179, 206–7
Second World War, 78, 177
Sedgwick, Peter, 2
Shakespeare, William, 123
    *A Midsummer Night's Dream*, 115
    *The Tempest*, 14
Shelley, Mary, 14
    *Frankenstein*, 14, 15
Sinfield, Alan 1
    *Faultlines: Cultural Materialism and the Politics of Dissident Reading*, 1
socialism, 4, 22, 23, 24, 25, 29, 30, 35, 36, 59, 69, 125, 126, 184, 187, 188, 193, 195
Soviet Union, 69, 84
"Space Anthropology", 3, 9, 12, 15, 18
Spain, 62, 69, 70
Stalin, Josef, 59, 70, 184, 201
    Stalinism, 2, 11, 105
*Star Trek*, 51
Stuart, Don A. 73, 79
subalternity, 132
Suvin, Darko, 13, 205
    *Metamorphoses of Science Fiction*, 13
Swift, Jonathan, 14
    *Gulliver's Travels*, 14

technical intelligentsia, 145–146
technological transformation, 93, 95, 97, 98, 99, 100, 102
Thompson, Edward Palmer, 88

Thomson, James, 76
 *City of Dreadful Night*, 76–79
 *Doom of a City*, 76
Tolstoy, Leo, 46
 *War and Peace*, 46
totalitarian, 39, 77, 141, 169, 170, 177, 178, 179, 181, 183, 201
totalitarianism, 4, 57, 178, 179, 181, 184, 201
*Tribune*, 66, 185
Trotskyism, 2

University of Wales, Aberystwyth, 5, 113
utopia, 1, 2, 5, 6, 13, 43, 87, 93, 94, 95, 98, 99, 100, 101, 103, 104, 105, 106, 107, 110, 111, 112, 113, 114, 144, 149
utopian, 2, 5, 6, 11, 13, 21, 73, 87, 88, 93, 94, 95, 97, 98, 100, 101, 102, 103, 104, 106, 107, 108, 109, 110, 111, 112, 113, 114, 125, 126, 127, 132, 136, 206

Van Vogt, A.E., 12, 17
 "Dormant", 12, 17
Vietnam, 1, 59, 71, 226
Vietnamese National Liberation Front, 2

Wells, H.G., 14, 63, 66, 73, 74, 76, 77, 78, 79, 80, 87, 88, 94, 98, 105
 *In the Days of the Comet*, 98
 "A Story of the Days to Come", 73, 76, 114
 *The Time Machine*, 76
 *War of the Worlds*, 14
 *When the Sleeper Awakes*, 76

West, Cornel, 1
Williams, Raymond, 1, 2, 3, 4, 5, 6, 7, 11, 12, 13, 21, 43, 44, 51, 57, 58, 73, 83, 87, 93, 94, 113, 114, 125, 126, 149, 177, 178, 179, 205, 206, 215, 216
 *Border Country*, 117, 120, 215
 *The Country and the City*, 3, 4, 73, 93, 177
 *Culture and Society 1780–1950*, 2, 4, 11, 21, 43, 57, 87, 94
 "A Defence of Realism", 3
 *The Fight for Manod*, 5, 117, 121, 122, 215, 216
 *The Long Revolution*, 2, 12, 43, 44, 126, 136, 205
 *Marxism and Literature*, 4
 *Politics and Letters*, 5, 39, 114, 205, 216
 *Second Generation*, 117, 119, 215
 *Television: Technology and Cultural Form*, 51
 *Towards 2000*, 4, 5, 114, 126, 149, 178, 179
 *The Volunteers*, 5, 121, 122, 179, 205, 207, 215
working class, 40, 84, 138, 141, 145, 146, 151, 192, 193
Wyndham, John, 12, 14, 17, 51
 *The Day of the Triffids*, 12

*Yesterday's Witness*, 54

Zamyatin, Yevgeny, 6, 12
 *Nous autres (We)*, 61

# Ralahine Utopian Studies

*Ralahine Utopian Studies* is the publishing project of the Ralahine Centre for Utopian Studies, University of Limerick, and the Department of Intercultural Studies in Translation, Languages and Culture, University of Bologna at Forlì.

The series editors aim to publish scholarship that addresses the theory and practice of utopianism (including Anglophone, continental European, and indigenous and postcolonial traditions, and contemporary and historical periods). Publications (in English and other European languages) will include original monographs and essay collections (including theoretical, textual, and ethnographic/institutional research), English language translations of utopian scholarship in other national languages, reprints of classic scholarly works that are out of print, and annotated editions of original utopian literary and other texts (including translations).

While the editors seek work that engages with the current scholarship and debates in the field of utopian studies, they will not privilege any particular critical or theoretical orientation. They welcome submissions by established or emerging scholars working within or outside the academy. Given the multi-lingual and inter-disciplinary remit of the University of Limerick and the University of Bologna at Forlì, they especially welcome comparative studies in any disciplinary or trans-disciplinary framework.

Those interested in contributing to the series are invited to submit a detailed project outline to Professor Raffaella Baccolini at Department of Intercultural Studies in Translation, Languages and Culture, University of Bologna at Forlì, Forlì, Italy or to Professor Tom Moylan or Dr Joachim Fischer at the Department of Languages and Cultural Studies, University of Limerick, Republic of Ireland.

E-mail queries can be sent to h.godfrey@peterlang.com.

Series editors:
Raffaella Baccolini (University of Bologna, at Forlì)
Joachim Fischer (University of Limerick)
Tom Moylan (University of Limerick)
Managing editor:
Michael J. Griffin (University of Limerick)

Ralahine Centre for Utopian Studies, University of Limerick
http://www.ul.ie/ralahinecentre/

| | |
|---|---|
| Volume 1 | Tom Moylan and Raffaella Baccolini (eds): Utopia Method Vision. The Use Value of Social Dreaming. 343 pages. 2007. ISBN 978-3-03910-912-8 |

| Volume 2 | Michael J. Griffin and Tom Moylan (eds): Exploring the Utopian Impulse. Essays on Utopian Thought and Practice. 434 pages. 2007. ISBN 978-3-03910-913-5 |
| --- | --- |
| Volume 3 | Ruth Levitas: The Concept of Utopia. (Ralahine Classic) 280 pages. 2010. ISBN 978-3-03911-366-8 |
| Volume 4 | Vincent Geoghegan: Utopianism and Marxism. (Ralahine Classic) 189 pages. 2008. ISBN 978-3-03910-137-5 |
| Volume 5 | Barbara Goodwin and Keith Taylor: The Politics of Utopia. A Study in Theory and Practice. (Ralahine Classic) 341 pages. 2009. ISBN 978-3-03911-080-3 |
| Volume 6 | Darko Suvin: Utopian Horizons and Hollows. Essays on Utopia, Science Fiction, and Political Epistemology. (Ralahine Reader) Forthcoming. |
| Volume 7 | Andrew Milner (ed.): Tenses of Imagination: Raymond Williams on Science Fiction, Utopia and Dystopia. (Ralahine Reader) 253 pages. 2010. ISBN 978-3-03911-826-7 |